REBELS IN REPOSE

CONFEDERATE COMMANDERS AFTER THE WAR

Allie Stuart Povall

THE History PRESS

Published by The History Press
Charleston, SC
www.historypress.com

First published 2019

Manufactured in the United States

ISBN 9781467144001

Library of Congress Control Number: 2019950041

Notice: The information in this book is true and complete to the best of our knowledge. It is offered without guarantee on the part of the author or The History Press. The author and The History Press disclaim all liability in connection with the use of this book.

I dedicate this book to Janet, my rock and the love of my life.

And to the officers and men of the USS Princeton *(LPH-5), who served with me from July 1964 to June 1966, and to my shipmates and lifetime friends Lieutenants Junior Grade Peter S. Werle, Francis E. Neir and Eldon L. Thompson.*

Officer's Club, Subic Bay, Philippines, June 1966. *From left to right*: Neir, Povall, Werle and Thompson. *Courtesy of the author.*

And also to our beloved den mother, Jannie Werle, who saw us through thick and thin.

And, finally, in loving memory of our comrades in arms and veterans, with us, of many Western Pacific and California adventures and misadventures: Lieutenants Junior Grade Bruce "the Duper" Byle and Gordon Campbell.

Resquiescat in pace, fratres.

Requiem

The tumult and the shouting dies;
The Captains and the Kings depart;
Still stands Thine ancient sacrifice,
An humble and contrite heart.
Lord God of Hosts, be with us yet,
Lest we forget, lest we forget!

—"Recessional," Rudyard Kipling

CONTENTS

PREFACE

From Baltimore to Los Angeles, from Montreal to St. Petersburg, from Austin to Indianapolis, the monuments and the plaques are coming down. These memorials honor men who fought long ago for the South during the American Civil War. They have become anathema, especially to African Americans—and rightfully so—since the attack by Dylann Roof, a twenty-one-year-old avowed white supremacist who killed nine African Americans in the Emanuel AME Church on June 17, 2015, in Charleston, South Carolina. In the aftermath of this horrific event, social media showed Roof with a Confederate battle flag.

Many of the monuments commemorate not specific generals but a generic "Our Confederate Dead," while others *are* dedicated to specific men, usually Confederate president Jefferson Davis or general officers in the Confederate States Army such as Robert E. Lee, Nathan Bedford Forrest and Thomas Jonathan "Stonewall" Jackson. Some are plaques, such as the one in Brooklyn denoting a tree that Robert E. Lee planted when he was stationed there during the 1840s, and the one at Yale University that honors its sons who died on both sides of the conflict.

The monuments have come down in New Orleans (Lee, Jefferson Davis and P.G.T. Beauregard), Memphis (Nathan Bedford Forrest), Austin (Lee, Albert Sidney Johnston and Davis), the Bronx (Lee and Jackson), San Diego (Jefferson Davis) and, of all places, Franklin, Ohio (Lee). At the U.S. Capitol, there are at least twelve monuments to Confederate commanders that were, for the most part, placed there by their states. They include, among others,

Jefferson Davis, Robert E. Lee, Edmund Kirby Smith, Joseph Wheeler and Wade Hampton. There is a move afoot to remove them, as might be expected, because together, among other problems, all of these monuments and plaques constitute tangible pillars of the "Lost Cause" movement that arose out of the ashes of the South's defeat, destruction and reconstruction, a movement that still exists today.

So who were these men? Where did they come from, and what did they do to further the aims of the Confederacy during the war? More importantly for our purposes, what did they do with their lives *after* the war? It is the latter question that is the subject of this book, and I hope that, armed with the perspective derived from this book, perhaps the reader can better understand not only the commanders' roles before, during and after the war but also how these men were viewed in both the North and the South during those times, as well as how they viewed one another.

But let us not fool ourselves: these men—these generals (and one admiral who became a general)—whatever their stated reasons for joining the Confederate States Army or Navy, fought for slavery, even though a number of them did not own slaves. As General Ulysses Simpson Grant would later say when he reflected on the surrender of the Army of Northern Virginia at Appomattox, "I felt sad and depressed at the downfall of a foe who had fought so long and valiantly, and had suffered so much for a cause, though that cause was, I believe, *one of the worst for which a people ever fought*" (emphasis added). Twenty years later, he would say that "the [Southern] men had fought so bravely, so gallantly and so long for the cause which they believed in—and as earnestly, I take it, as our men believed in the cause for which they were fighting." Grant would also speak of "that enemy, whose manhood, however mistaken the cause, drew forth such herculean deeds of valor."

Most of the major Confederate generals—Beauregard, Lee, Jackson, Johnston, Bragg, Longstreet and Early—were U.S. Army officers before the war, and they made friendships during their "Old Army" service that survived the Civil War. James Longstreet and Grant, for example, not only were friends but also were related by marriage, as Grant was married to Julia Dent, a cousin of Longstreet. Many fought together in that prerequisite course—the Mexican-American War—to the Civil War's final exam. Some—for example Philip Sheridan, Joe Wheeler, Stephen Dill Lee, John Bell Hood and Jeb Stuart—attended West Point when Robert E. Lee was superintendent. Set forth as their stories are, side by side, the reader will be able to examine the symbiotic relationships that formed between them, as well as the cracks that appeared in those relationships both during and after the war. The reader should be able to see the formation of the fault lines that irreparably broke those relationships apart as the Confederate generals began to attack one another verbally and in print: *Somebody caused us to lose the war, but it wasn't me. It was him.* Why did these generals turn on one another and engage in the internecine warfare that was later to become known as the "Battle of the Books?" Why did they feel it necessary to blame someone else for the South's defeat? Why did they throw their old relationships into the emotional ditch? The answers to these questions lie on the pages within. I hope that you, the reader, will enjoy finding them.

Finally, I should note that this is the first of two books about Civil War generals, with the next to be about Union generals. Without a doubt, those men fought for a better cause, and like their Confederate counterparts, their postwar lives were filled with triumph and heartbreak, success and failure, in the autumn years of their lives.

I thank my project editor, Ryan Finn, and the rest of the History Press editorial staff, for their keen insights and unerring judgment in preparing this book for publication. They are, simply put, the best.

Chapter 1
P.G.T. BEAUREGARD

"Little Creole," "Bory," "Little Frenchman," "Felix," "Little Napoleon"

PREWAR

One of the most controversial Confederate generals of the Civil War—as the reader will subsequently see, there are not many Confederate generals who are *not* controversial—Pierre Gustave Toutant Beauregard was born in St. Bernard Parish, Louisiana, at Contreras, his father's plantation below New Orleans, on May 28, 1818. At the time, two of his names, Toutant and Beauregard, were hyphenated, but later, at West Point, he removed the hyphen and dropped his first name, Pierre, becoming G.T. Beauregard. He was born into a prominent Creole family and spoke only French until he was twelve, when he entered a school in New York run by two French army officers who had served under Napoleon. This experience would lead him as a Confederate general to try to emulate Napoleon in his tactics and strategy.

Beauregard entered West Point at age sixteen and graduated second in his class in 1838. At West Point, he was known as "Little Creole," "Bory," "Little Frenchman," "Felix" and "Little Napoleon." He received his commission as a second lieutenant in 1838 and served first in the artillery. He then switched to the engineers.

The Little Creole served in the Mexican-American War as a first lieutenant but received brevet promotions to captain and then major. In a

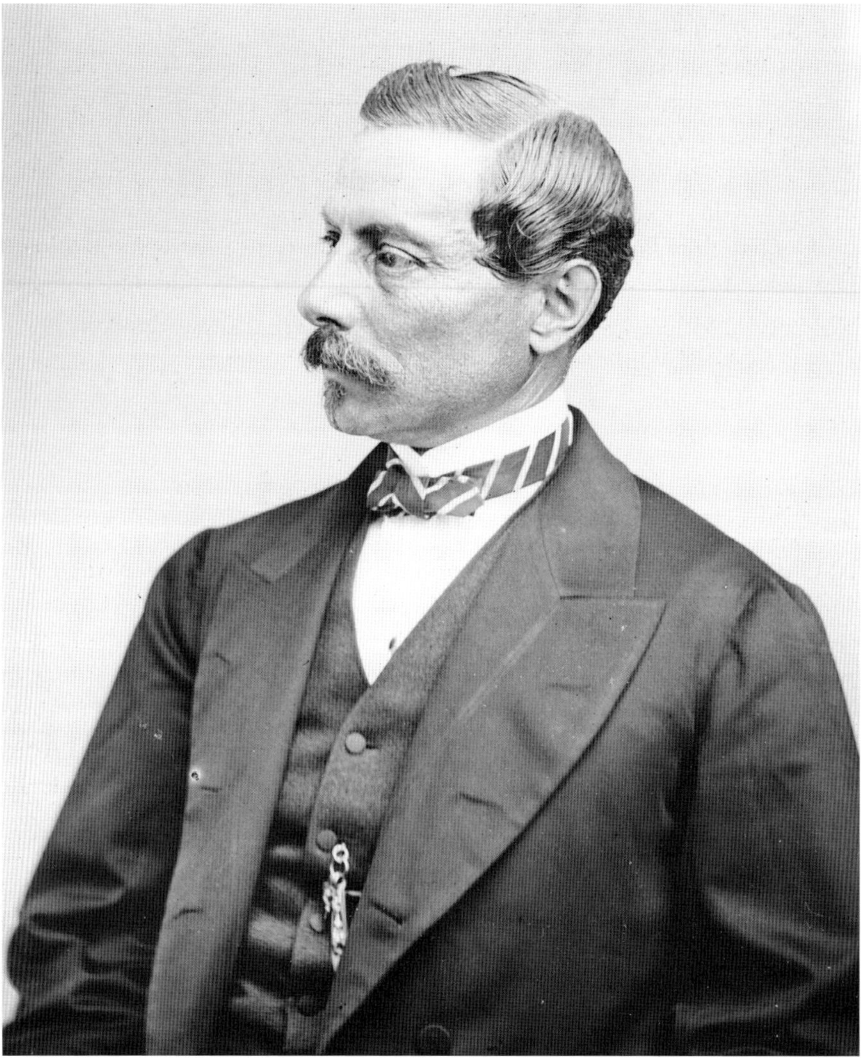

Pierre G.T. Beauregard. *Library of Congress.*

sign of his nascent personality traits, he was extremely jealous of Robert E. Lee, whom he thought had received superior accolades for service inferior to that rendered by Beauregard. After the Mexican-American War, Beauregard served twelve years as the officer in charge of the Engineering Department in New Orleans, working on defenses along the Gulf coast. In a somewhat curious turn of events, he ran for mayor of New Orleans while he was in the army but, not surprisingly, was defeated.[1]

Beauregard's brother-in-law, U.S. Senator John Slidell, secured his appointment as superintendent of West Point in January 1861, but after serving only two days, his appointment was revoked when Louisiana seceded from the Union. Subsequently, Beauregard resigned from the U.S. Army and received an appointment as the first general officer—a brigadier—in the Provisional Army of the Confederate States in command of Confederate forces in, and the defenses around, Charleston, South Carolina. At this point in his life, he was five feet, seven inches tall, weighed about 150 pounds and had dark hair and eyes and a faint French accent. People described him as "very courteous."[2]

CIVIL WAR SERVICE

At Charleston, his batteries thundered the beginning of the war when they shelled Fort Sumter for thirty-four hours. Beauregard then accepted the surrender of his former professor at West Point, Major Robert Anderson. As a result of his actions at Charleston, Beauregard became the South's first great hero. He was then called to Richmond and given command of what would become the Army of the Potomac, the precursor to the fabled Army of Northern Virginia. Beauregard, who was one of the few Confederate leaders to foresee a long and bitter war, traveled to Richmond by train and was "lionized" along the way. He then faced off against a West Point classmate, Union general Irwin McDowell, at Manassas. Beauregard, however, was actually under the command of General Joseph Johnston, who arrived just in time for the battle. Because of Beauregard's knowledge of the terrain around Manassas, Johnston allowed him to command Confederate troops during the clash. At the First Battle of Manassas, Beauregard gets credit for preventing Union forces from turning the Confederate left, and although Beauregard received credit for the decisions that turned the tide of battle toward the Confederates, there is still some dispute about who ordered the counterattack that led to victory: Beauregard or Johnston. Indeed, a number of historians say that Joseph E. Johnston's composure and Irvin McDowell's incompetence saved the day for Beauregard and the South.

From Manassas to the end of the war, Beauregard complained constantly of "incompetence and malice" on the part of the Confederate government. In addition, he fought with other Confederate generals over his "grandiose plans" that—when he didn't get support for them—led him to publish articles in newspapers pushing his plans and condemning those who didn't agree with him. This behavior on Beauregard's part did not engender goodwill among his fellow generals and his civilian superiors.

Following First Manassas, Beauregard and Johnston designed the Confederate battle flag, and Beauregard received a promotion to major general. Davis then shipped him west to serve under Albert Sidney Johnston. When Johnston was killed at Shiloh near the end of the first day—a smashing Confederate victory—Beauregard called off the attack and declared the battle won. He then sent Davis a telegram claiming a great victory.

Grant thought otherwise and, reinforced during the night by Don Carlos Buell's troops, launched a savage counterattack the next day that drove Beauregard's army from the field and down to Corinth, which he then abandoned in the face of Grant's approach. The decision to abandon the attack on the first day at Shiloh was one of the most controversial of the entire war, and the decision to abandon Corinth without a fight was not far behind.

Continuing his streak of controversial decisions, Beauregard then took medical leave without permission. Davis promptly sent Braxton Bragg to relieve him of field command. Davis then transferred Beauregard to Charleston to take command of coastal defenses in South Carolina and Georgia. Beauregard improved the coastal defenses in his eighteen months in Charleston and successfully defended the city against several Union attacks. He continued, however, to hatch wild plans for ending the war.

In April 1864, Beauregard transferred to North Carolina to defend Lee's rear. Grant then dispatched Major General Benjamin Butler to launch a surprise attack in what became known as the Bermuda Hundred Campaign, with landings on the James River. Beauregard, however, bottled Butler up and held him there in one of his greatest victories of the war; then he correctly predicted that Grant would cross the James River to try to capture the major railhead at Petersburg. Beauregard moved troops from Bermuda Hundred to meet him, and with roughly fourteen thousand men, he successfully defended Petersburg against a Union force of some forty to sixty thousand at the end of the day—until Lee could shift the Army of Northern Virginia southward to take up the defense of Petersburg and Richmond. This was the acme of Beauregard's career. He then sought command of the Army of the Shenandoah, but that command went to Jubal A. Early instead. Not surprisingly, Beauregard publicly questioned why he was not selected and expressed his resentment that he was not.

At that point, Beauregard's command of field forces ended. He assumed command of the Department of the West and, with little command authority, watched as John Bell Hood destroyed his army at the Battles of Franklin and Nashville. General Joseph Johnston relieved him of command of that department, and Beauregard became Johnston's subordinate. After Lee's surrender at Appomattox, Johnston and Beauregard told Davis that "further resistance would be futile and surrendered to General Sherman in Durham, North Carolina."[3] Beauregard was paroled at Greensboro, North Carolina, on May 2, 1865.

The criticism of Beauregard is extensive, almost as much as Beauregard's criticism of fellow military commanders Jefferson Davis, Lee, Albert Sidney Johnston, Joseph Johnston and John Bell Hood, among many others. It was said that Beauregard always wanted more troops, was always formulating elaborate Napoleonic plans for *others* to execute and was constantly hatching schemes for ending the war. His penchant for Napoleonic tactics—massing large armies and moving rapidly over large areas—assumed forces and logistics that the Confederacy simply did not have. Moreover, to be successful, his ideas required opposing forces to do nothing, to stay put or to do exactly what Beauregard wanted them to do *when* he wanted them to do it.

One observer perhaps best summed up Beauregard's Civil War career: "He was a talented Civil War general but often an unrealistic one, whose pride and pettiness prevented him from enjoying a cordial relationship with any of his superiors."[4] That last observation constitutes an understatement of biblical proportions.

POSTWAR

While Johnston was negotiating surrender of the Army of Tennessee's remnants with Sherman, word came that John Wilkes Booth had assassinated President Lincoln. Confederate soldiers gathered in front of Beauregard's tent and began celebrating. Beauregard ordered them to stop the celebration under threat of arrest. Subsequently, on May 2, 1865, Beauregard started for home accompanied by members of his staff, who gradually peeled away as the group headed south. Beauregard went to Mobile and caught a United States naval vessel headed for New Orleans. On May 21, he arrived home for the first time in four years.

Beauregard went to his mother's home in Algiers, across the river from New Orleans. "A man stopped him and asked, 'Are you Beauregard?' Beauregard said that he was. The man screamed, 'I believe you are a damn nigger. Tell me if you are a nigger or not.' Followed by a stream of abuse, the hero of Manassas proceeded hurriedly on his way." As biographer T. Harry Williams noted, "Confederate generals were not immune to insults and ridicule in the first days after the war, even in their own communities."[5]

A few days later, Beauregard bought his first set of civilian clothes since before the war from his tailor, Lewis Falk, who cried when he saw Beauregard. At that point, it was not clear whether Confederate generals would be prosecuted, and Beauregard debated whether to take the oath of loyalty and apply for a pardon. He wrote to Lee and Johnston, both of whom encouraged him to seek amnesty. So, on September 16, 1865, he "swore fealty to the United States in New Orleans" and then applied for a pardon from President Andrew Johnson. Johnson took no action on his application, but subsequently, he was included in a mass pardon issued by President Johnson in 1868. Beauregard then sought full reinstatement as a citizen, which was also granted the same year.

Beauregard considered leaving the United States to work with a foreign army. Thus, in 1865, he applied for a post in the Brazilian army. The Brazilians made him an offer, but he declined. The following year, while in Europe, Beauregard received an offer to head the Romanian army. The offer included a "huge cash payment and the title of prince." Beauregard considered taking the position and bringing a number of Confederate officers with him, but in the end, he decided to return to Louisiana.

The khedive of Egypt then offered him command of the Egyptian army. Beauregard subsequently entered into serious negotiations that came close to fruition. The khedive offered $12,000 a year plus rations. While Beauregard claimed that he declined the khedive's offer, Union general Benjamin Butler's son, George H. Butler, who was serving as U.S. consul there, later said that he, Butler, scuttled the negotiations by telling the khedive that Beauregard was "treacherous."[6]

Beauregard next applied for a position in the French army, which was locked in a desperate struggle with the Prussians, but that effort led to naught. Subsequently, bridling under Congressional Reconstruction, he applied once more to head the Egyptian army, but again, nothing came of it. He seemed willing to take anything that would get him out of the country. Finally, Argentina offered him command of its army, but Beauregard's demands for a salary of $20,000 and a bonus of $40,000 engendered only dismay on the Argentinean side; it thus withdrew the offer. Beauregard considered joining the Japanese army in its war with China, but by 1876, Congressional Reconstruction had ended and Beauregard had reconciled himself to staying in New Orleans. About this time, he wrote, "Negroes were naturally inferior, ignorant and indolent." He predicted that "in 75 years the colored race would have disappeared from America along with the Indians and the buffalo." In the meantime, he posited that whites could nevertheless "manage" free blacks politically just as well as they had when they had been slaves.[7]

Beauregard was the only Confederate general to become wealthy. An engineer by virtue of his West Point training, he first joined the New Orleans, Jackson and Great Northern Railroad as chief engineer and general superintendent at a salary of $3,500 annually, which later increased to $5,000 annually. The railroad had been built before the war, and it was in poor repair at the war's end. Beauregard undertook repairs and, with the trains operating, made the railroad profitable. Debt, however, was a major problem for the company. Therefore, in 1866, Beauregard undertook negotiations with creditors, traveling to New York, London and Paris to reorganize the railroad's debt. He "succeeded brilliantly." The State of Louisiana owned half of the stock, however, and Republicans controlled the state government. In 1870, they took control of the company and sold their stock, as did the City of New Orleans, another major stockholder, to Henry McComb, a northern industrialist, who then forced Beauregard out of the corporation.

Next, Beauregard took over management of the New Orleans and Carrolton streetcar company. New Orleans had one of the first streetcar systems in the country. Six companies served different parts of the city, and Beauregard's company was the only one to use locomotives to power its trains. The other companies used horses or mules. Beauregard's passenger cars had fare boxes, eight seats per side, and ceiling straps down the middle, advanced accommodations for that era.

The New Orleans and Carrolton had not made money for years and had paid no dividends in ten years. In 1866, the shareholders offered Beauregard a lease for twenty-five years pursuant to which he would pay the shareholders a guaranteed amount each year. Beauregard replaced the locomotives with horse-drawn cars and, in spite of financial setbacks, secured partners to help finance the enterprise. By 1873, the company had 59 cars with 249 horses and mules. The annual passenger count was almost 5 million, and the stock price increased from $7.50 to $115.00.

Nevertheless, the shareholders thought that they could make the company more profitable than Beauregard had, so they took over management of the company and, like the Republican railroad owners, forced Beauregard out. Beauregard next applied to be chief engineer of the New Orleans, Mobile and Texas Railroad but didn't get the job. Subsequently, he held several positions in entities ranging from a mining company to head of the Municipal Gas Company, which was to supply gas to homes. The company lacked capital, however, and therefore failed.[8]

Beauregard's next venture arose out of the Mississippi River's continuous silting of the passes leading to the Gulf of Mexico. Beauregard submitted to a federal commission appointed to study the matter a recommendation to build a canal and thus obviate the silting problem. James Buchanan Eads, however, recommended that the commission build jetties to narrow the passes, which would, therefore, increase the water flow so that it would scour the bottoms of silt. Moreover, Eads argued, the jetty solution that he proffered would be cheaper, faster and more effective than Beauregard's canal. To remove the socially and politically prominent Beauregard from the opposition, Eads hired Beauregard to lobby for him. The commission accepted Eads's recommendation and built the jetties, which "succeeded magnificently" in opening the passes. Not surprisingly, given his personality, Beauregard acted as though he had always supported the scouring method.[9]

THE LOUISIANA LOTTERY

Louisiana had no lottery, but a New York company learned that New Orleans residents "had a mania for gambling" and were buying tickets to the New York lottery "as fast as they went on sale."[10] The New York group decided to obtain a charter from the Louisiana legislature and employed a lobbyist named Charles T. Howard to obtain the charter. Howard gave away—or paid—$300,000 to get the bill granting a charter passed. Under terms of the charter, the Louisiana lottery company would be tax-exempt and was to pay the state $40,000 annually. Thus the Louisiana legislature created the largest gambling operation anywhere in the United States before the twentieth century, with gross annual revenue of $29 million.

The lottery operators were smooth: they contributed to various charities, from the New Orleans Opera House to flood victims. Then, when the Democrats took over the Louisiana legislature, the lottery executives bought them too. Their legislative power became "absolute."[11] About 90 percent of the lottery's business came from outside Louisiana, and the value of its stock rose from $35 a share to $1,200. The lottery had profits of from $8.5 million to $13 million each year.

Critics, however, cried fraud and contended that the lottery was a deck stacked to steer winnings to itself or to its cronies by buying tickets itself. Lottery executives then decided to hire two Confederate generals to oversee the drawings. They offered one of the positions to Beauregard, who was skeptical of the lottery but was without a job at the time. Beauregard did not initially accept, fearing that the position would damage his reputation. His family, however, convinced him to accept the offer. Beauregard was to select the second general.

He offered that position to General Wade Hampton of South Carolina, but Hampton became governor and declined. Next Beauregard asked the unreconstructed rebel General Jubal A. Early to serve, but Early would not accept Beauregard's offer until he received assurances that Republicans did not control the lottery. Thus assured by Beauregard, Early accepted.

Their pay was munificent. In 1881, Beauregard made $15,000 to $20,000, and Early made about $10,000. By the time the lottery became extinct in Louisiana, Beauregard had made close to $30,000 per year and Early a bit less.

Beauregard wore black suits, and with his "handsome face, snow-white hair and dignified form…was undeniably a figure of distinction.…Even in civilian clothes he looked military in the Gallic manner."[12] Early, however, wore only suits of Confederate gray and was likely a drab contrast to the handsome Beauregard.

In spite of the lottery's best efforts to maintain its charter through control of the Louisiana legislature, frequent political attacks there steadily weakened its position. Finally, in 1892, the United States Post Office decided that the lottery could no longer sell tickets through the mail; mortally wounded, the lottery ceased operations in 1893 and moved to Honduras.

Literary Achievements

Confederate general Daniel Harvey Hill started a magazine titled *The Land We Love*. Devoted to Confederate history, Hill solicited submissions from other Confederate leaders. Beauregard wrote an article in which he said of the Southern apotheosis of Robert E. Lee: "I don't think he has much military foresight or pre-science [*sic*] or great powers of deduction."[13]

There was a significant market for Civil War literature, and in the South, Southern military leaders "wanted to consecrate the Lost Cause and to show that it would not have been lost if their advice had been followed."[14] Thus, in the war's aftermath, they wrote articles attacking one another and blaming one another for losing the war.

General Joseph Johnston wrote his *Narrative of Military Operations*, in which his description of the First Battle of Manassas suggested that he had led the South to victory.[15] Beauregard was outraged and said that after reading Johnston's account, "[H]e had doubts he [Beauregard] was present at the battle."[16] Beauregard, in turn, savaged Johnston in the press, thus destroying one of the great friendships of the war.

William Preston Johnston, son of Albert Sidney Johnston, published a biography of his father in which he wrote of Shiloh that Beauregard had snatched defeat from the jaws of certain victory by not continuing the attack at the end of the first day. Jefferson Davis, who hated Beauregard almost as much as Beauregard hated him, repeated Johnston's philippic in a speech. Again Beauregard was outraged, and his anger engendered a strong desire to write his own memoir.

Beauregard hired a man named Alfred Roman to help with his memoir. He insisted that Roman be identified as the author of the book, however. By naming Roman as the author, the book—which would thus seem to have been written by an objective second party—could praise Beauregard more and more savagely attack his enemies. The real author, however, was Beauregard, and Roman's role was "technical and minor."[17]

Unfortunately for Beauregard, Davis was writing his own memoirs at the same time, and in the end, he would beat the publication of Beauregard's book by three years. His treatise, *The Rise and Fall of the Confederate Government*, came out in 1881. It was "intended for his work to be a justification of [his] leadership and an absolute demolition of his enemies, who were legion."[18] He intended to devote special attention to Beauregard—and he did.

The treatise fairly "bristled with attacks on, and criticisms of, Beauregard." Once again, Beauregard was outraged, and once again, he went on the attack. He finished his memoir at the end of 1881 but could not get a publisher. Finally, in May 1884, after Beauregard removed his criticisms of the North and of the Republican Party, Harpers published *The Military Operations of General Beauregard*. He went after Davis and all of his advisors but also criticized Joseph Johnston, Albert Sidney Johnston and Lee.

Beauregard then wrote a magazine article on Manassas. In it he criticized Davis for refusing to allow a concentration of Confederate forces before the battle, Joe Johnston for saying that he (Johnston) had been in actual—as opposed to titular—command at Manassas and Richard Ewell for not obeying an order to cross Bull Run. Davis and Johnston, as well as Ewell's family, were predictably outraged.

The Creole wrote three books in all on the Civil War. Besides his memoir, he wrote *Principles and Maxims of War* and *A Commentary on the Campaign and Battle of Manassas*. Roman wrote articles for him on Shiloh, Charleston and Petersburg, again assaulting Beauregard's critics, as well as Robert E. Lee. Finally, Beauregard refused to participate in Davis's funeral in 1889. "We have always been enemies," he declared. "I cannot pretend I am sorry he is gone."[19]

Beauregard had two marriages, the first to Marie Antoinette Laurie, by whom he had three children: Henri Rene, who was a judge and died in 1910; Henri Toutant, who lived until 1916; and Laurie, who died in 1884. Marie, however, died giving birth to Laurie in 1850. Ten years later, Beauregard married Marguerite Caroline Deslonnde, who died in 1864 in New Orleans, while it was under occupation. They had no children.

OTHER POSITIONS

In 1879, Beauregard, who was sixty-one at the time, was appointed adjutant general of the Louisiana State Militia, which he promptly—in the Napoleonic tradition—renamed the National Guard. Once again, his military creativity flourished. Beauregard posited that since modern weapons made daylight fighting too dangerous, fighting should take place at night, with his troops wearing phosphorescent uniform backs so that their comrades could see their rears.

In 1888, he became commissioner of public works for New Orleans. Thinking that the purpose of his job was to clean up the department, he began firing inept incumbents and appointing competent people to replace them. Cleaning up the department, as it turned out, was not why he had been appointed. Indeed, the Public Works Department was a bastion of patronage and a sinecure for the incompetent but well connected. The city council refused repeatedly to confirm his appointments and instead nominated and approved its own slate of incompetents and bunglers. Beauregard, not unexpectedly, resigned.

Beauregard's living arrangements during all of this time in postwar New Orleans were many. Indeed, he lived at ten different addresses between 1865 and 1893. His final home was a house at 355 Esplanade that he bought in 1889.

Beauregard spent many summers in White Sulphur Springs, West Virginia. There he "could loll the weeks away, talk about the war with old comrades, and utter gallantries to thrilled young ladies."[20] He also spent time in Asheville, North Carolina; on the Maine coast; and in northern Wisconsin.

Beauregard was a wealthy man. He owned a hotel in St. Louis and property in Chicago, Los Angeles, San Diego, Corona Beach and Santa Barbara, California. He was also "one of major sights of New Orleans. On the streets, parents pointed him out to children, and natives whispered to awed tourists that 'le general' was passing. The erect, compact body, the handsome face crowned by luxuriant white hair, and the soldierly bearing would have attracted attention in any assemblage. In looks he was the 'ideal soldier'—a Creole incarnation of Napoleon."

Beauregard was active in social affairs, attending horse races at Fairgrounds Park and acting as a shareholder in the French Opera House and a director of a theatrical association. In 1869, he was a founder of the Southern Historical Society, which grew into a regional organization and subsequently moved its headquarters to Richmond.

John Bell Hood died destitute in 1879. Beauregard took Hood's memoirs, got them published and gave the proceeds to Hood's ten children. Beauregard would outlive Hood by fourteen years.

General P.G.T. Beauregard, the fourth-ranking general in the Confederate army, died of cardiovascular disease on February 21, 1893, almost thirty years after his second wife and ten years after his daughter, Laurie. His remains lay in state at the New Orleans City Hall. They then buried Little Napoleon at the Tomb of the Army of Tennessee at Metairie Cemetery.

Chapter 2
BRAXTON BRAGG

BEGINNINGS

Braxton Bragg was born on March 22, 1817, in Warrenton, North Carolina, the third of twelve children. One of his older brothers, Thomas Jr., would serve as governor of North Carolina and adjutant general of the Confederacy, and another—John, a University of North Carolina graduate—would be a judge in Alabama. Legend holds that Bragg was born in jail, where his mother was imprisoned for killing a black freedman who had been "impertinent." A jury acquitted her, however. Bragg's ancestors had settled in Jamestown with the first colonists. His father, Thomas Bragg, was a carpenter who ultimately became a building contractor. He owned nearly twenty slaves and became a member of Warrenton's middle class in spite of his somewhat plebian trade.

Braxton Bragg's early education consisted of nine years at the Warrenton Male Academy. Thomas Bragg chose Braxton's career path when his son was ten: West Point and, upon graduation, an army engineer. Thomas's theory was that if Braxton did not like the army, he could always make a living as an engineer. At the time of his entry into West Point, Bragg stood five feet, ten inches tall and weighed 130 pounds. He finished fifth in his class out of fifty graduates in the class of 1837 and received his commission as a second lieutenant in the Third Artillery on July 1, 1837. The army promoted him to first lieutenant the following July.[21]

PREWAR SERVICE

Bragg served in the Second Seminole War and saw combat in that nasty little affair. As a result of service in and around the fetid swamps of south Florida, he developed health problems that would plague him the rest of his life, and many believe that his health issues—malaria for one—engendered what would become an increasingly combative personality that would alienate both subordinates and superiors.

As a result of his various health issues, Bragg took sick leave in Philadelphia and then became an army recruiter in New York. Subsequently, in October 1840, for some reason the army strangely—and perversely—reassigned him to Florida, where he remained for three years. The posting to Florida gave rise to the Bragg proclivity for griping and carping that would characterize his abrasive personality for the rest of his life. First, he complained about the assignment and then about the disrepair of the fort to which the army assigned him. He argued long and hard with the paymaster, and one colleague even accused him of arguing with himself, an allegation that appears in several of his biographies but is denied by one authority. A colleague wrote that "he was of saturnine disposition and morbid temperament."[22] Nevertheless, Bragg somehow made friends, one of whom, William Tecumseh Sherman, would remain a friend for life. His friends also included future Union generals George H. Thomas and John F. Reynolds, but "Cump" Sherman was, and would remain, the best. Sherman would write of Bragg in 1888 that Bragg's "heart was never in the Rebel cause."[23]

During this period, 1844–45, and consistent with his increasingly contentious personality, Bragg wrote a series of articles for a magazine entitled "Notes on Our Army." Writing anonymously, he posited in the articles a series of reforms needed to modernize the army, and he also criticized a number of army officers by name. Caught, he was court-martialed for disrespect of a superior officer. That offense brought him a two-month suspension at half pay and a reprimand, but it seemed to have little effect on his future deportment.

Then came the Mexican-American War, in which Bragg and many of his future colleagues and adversaries would serve in preparation for the greater conflict to come. General Zachary Taylor selected Bragg and his artillery battery to help with the defense of Texas in 1845. It was here where he met his future adversaries George Thomas and Joseph Reynolds—his lieutenants in the battery—as well as his fellow Confederate general D.H. Hill, who joined the battery, and another prominent Civil War opponent in

Braxton Bragg. *Library of Congress.*

George Meade, who was posted nearby. Bragg foresaw the need for mobile artillery, and it was in this manner that he prepared his battery for combat. An acquaintance at this time described Bragg at this time as "a tall thin man with large black eyes and heavy Brows."[24]

First, Bragg participated in the defense of Fort Brown, Texas, engaging the enemy in several artillery duels that earned him a brevet promotion to captain. A permanent promotion to that rank followed quickly. Next, Bragg fought at Monterrey and received a brevet promotion to major only three months after his promotion to captain. Then came his day in the sun: Buena Vista. There Bragg took his "flying artillery"—Battery C of the Third Artillery—and moved it rapidly from one gap in the American lines to another, successfully filling those holes with shot and canister to prevent a Mexican breakthrough. Bragg's innovative approach was perhaps the first use of artillery in this manner and led Maxwell Taylor to say that Bragg "had saved the day."[25] Years later, Union general Joseph "Fighting Joe" Hooker would say that Taylor's statement was "the highest praise…ever awarded an officer of [Bragg's] rank…on the battlefield."[26] Hooker would also say that Bragg, George Thomas and Don Carlos Buell were "the three young officers…who were foremost in…the Army at the close of the Mexican War."[27]

Bragg then received another brevet promotion, this time to lieutenant colonel. In spite of his success, however, others continued to be put off by his personality. As a result, Bragg had differences with almost every superior or junior officer with whom he worked. U.S. Grant described him as a "remarkably intelligent and well-informed" with "an irascible temper…[a man who was] naturally disputatious."[28] Grady McWhiney, one of his biographers, called him "the most cantankerous man in the Army."[29] Erasmus Keyes said that Bragg's "ambition was of the vitriolic kind." Keyes thought he was intelligent, however, but noted that Bragg was "a fierce defender of his native region." As a result, Bragg's friend Cump Sherman had to break up a duel between Bragg and a newspaper correspondent who had insulted the state of North Carolina.[30]

Not surprisingly, given his other personality traits, Bragg was a strict disciplinarian and somewhat a martinet; equally unsurprisingly—in a precursor to the "fragging" of the Vietnam War—one of his artillerymen tried to kill him twice by planting explosives outside his tent. Both attempts on Bragg's life failed.

Following the Mexican-American War, Bragg returned to the United States a hero for his work with the "flying artillery" at Buena Vista. In recognition of his valor, the army named a Fort Bragg in California for him. Then, in 1849, Bragg married a wealthy woman from Louisiana, Eliza (she went by "Elise") Brooks Ellis, and together they moved from one frontier location to another. Elise, their contemporaries said, was a beauty and was also "intelligent, poised…witty…and rich." Bragg continued to criticize the army in his letters during this period until finally, in 1856, he resigned his commission when he didn't get his way with respect to the efficacy of horse-drawn artillery and because of a general dissatisfaction with his duty stations.

CIVILIAN INTERLUDE

The Braggs moved to Elise's plantation, Evergreen, near Thibodaux, Louisiana, and used her inheritance to buy a sugar plantation, which they named Bivouac, for $152,000. Bivouac consisted of about 1,600 acres, and more than one hundred slaves came with the property. Farming would make Bragg a wealthy man, but it was at Bivouac that Bragg developed a physical malady that would plague him the rest of his life: boils on his hands.[31]

Bragg served as commissioner of public works for his district and was a member of the State Board of Public Works. He was, therefore, involved in designing the state's drainage and levee system. Seeing a need for engineers to take on this kind of work, Bragg was also instrumental in the founding of the Louisiana Military School in 1860, which later would become Louisiana State University. He pushed successfully for the hiring of his old friend Cump Sherman to serve as superintendent of the school. But his real love was the plantation culture, in which he became immersed. In May 1856, the caning of U.S. Senator Charles Sumner by South Carolina Representative Preston Brooks for insulting the South delighted Bragg. In spite of what Sherman would say of him thirty years later, Bragg had become a rabid secessionist.[32]

CIVIL WAR SERVICE

In December 1860, with war clouds gathering, Governor Thomas Moore appointed Bragg to the State Military Board to organize a five-thousand-man army. The governor then appointed him to command the army with a rank of major general. This galled P.G.T. Beauregard, who thought he should have been appointed, and he "smoldered." Subsequently, on September 12, 1861, Bragg received an appointment as a brigadier general in the Confederate army. As the Confederacy began seizing Union armories all over the South, Bragg took five hundred volunteers and secured without a fight the surrender of the U.S. Armory at Baton Rouge.

After his appointment in the Confederate army, Bragg posted to Pensacola, where one of only two forts still in the possession of the United States, Fort Pickens, was located on Santa Rosa Island, about a mile and a half offshore. Bragg's friend Beauregard went to Charleston to capture Fort Sumter, the other fort. Bragg, once again in Florida, had numerous health issues: "dyspepsia, nervousness and severe migraine headaches." Nevertheless, Bragg soldiered on, establishing his headquarters at Fort Barrancas, nine miles west of Pensacola. From Fort Barrancas, he could see Fort Pickens, which, like Sumter, Lincoln was determined to hold and the Confederacy wanted to capture. Fort Pickens, however, was across Pensacola Bay from Barrancas, and there was thus no way for Bragg to capture the fort, as he lacked transport, guns and money to buy supplies. Bragg was further troubled by his army, which he characterized as little more than a "drunken mob." He declared martial law in Pensacola and closed the saloons to his men. He also cashiered incompetent officers, of whom there were many.

A de facto truce between Bragg and the Union garrison at Fort Pickens emerged, and it would hold from April 1861 to March 1862. Bragg couldn't attack the fort, and the Union troops couldn't attack him because neither had transports to carry them across Pensacola Bay. Beauregard, meanwhile, became a Confederate hero with the capture of Fort Sumter. The disparity was a function of the luck of the draw. An acquaintance, William Russell, described Bragg at this time as being "of a spare and powerful frame; his face is dark, and marked with deep lines, his mouth large and squarely set in determined jaws, and his eyes, sagacious, penetrating and not by any means unkindly. He looks out from under beetle brows, which run straight across and spring into a thick tuft of black hair, which is thickest over the nose."[33]

Bragg, ever the military strategist and putative strategic advisor, advocated to Jefferson Davis that the South abandon the defense of the entire Confederacy and instead concentrate its armies in the most vital areas. Bragg would have had the Confederacy abandon the defense of Texas, Missouri and Florida, thus eschewing its penchant for the protection of *geography* and instead seeking *destruction of the enemy's army*. He thus urged upon Davis the "Napoleonic strategy of rapid concentration and attack."[34] With the benefit of hindsight, his proffered strategy does not seem unreasonable, but his advice fell on plugged ears in Richmond, much as it had for his colleague Beauregard.

Then, on April 6, 1862, came Shiloh, which would be the bloodiest battle of the war up to that point. Albert Sidney Johnston commanded the Confederate forces, which came up from Corinth, Mississippi, to confront a Union force at Pittsburg Landing, Tennessee, commanded by U.S. Grant. Once again, Bragg's path crossed that of Beauregard, who was Johnston's second in command. Johnston went to the front to command his army, while Beauregard stayed in the rear. The difference in their approaches to the battle would prove significant. It would also cost Johnston his life. Bragg was Johnston's chief of staff and also commanded the Second Corps on the Confederate right.

The battle took place over two days. On the first day, Johnston's Confederate army drove Grant back against the bluffs of the Tennessee River. The Confederate approach and attack, however, were hampered by the terrain, which divided and then confused the attacking Confederate units, and there was a general lack of command and control, all punctuated by the inexperience of Johnston's army. Bragg did not arrive on the field until noon, and by that time, the Confederates had been held up at a place that would forever after be known as the Hornet's Nest. Several head-on but piecemeal Confederate attacks had failed, and upon arriving, Bragg ordered another. It, too, failed. Undaunted, he continued to throw his troops into battle in piecemeal attacks that ultimately cleared, at great cost, the Union position.

Late that afternoon, Bragg—and the right side of the Confederate line that he commanded—stood prepared to mount the final assault on the Union left and drive the Union army into the river. Unfortunately for the South, General Johnston was dead—shot in the leg—and Beauregard had taken command. To Bragg's chagrin, Beauregard, thinking that he had won a signal victory, called off the attack. It was one of the great blunders of the war. Beauregard thought that he could complete the destruction of Grant's army the next morning. He could have, but for one significant development: the arrival of Don Carlos Buell. In spite of Bragg's reported chagrin when Beauregard called off the attack, there is a split of authority with respect to Bragg's reaction to Beauregard's order. Some think that he supported it, and others think he did not. The weight of authority is with the latter, although perhaps his chief biographer posited that he was in accord with Beauregard.

That night, a little-known cavalry commander named Nathan Bedford Forrest tried to warn his superiors that forces under Union general Don Carlos were reinforcing Grant and that unless Beauregard attacked that night, they would be "whipped like hell" the next day.[35]

The next morning—the second day at Shiloh—Grant counterattacked and drove the Confederates from the field. They were indeed "whipped like hell." Beauregard then ordered a general retreat to Corinth. Beauregard and Bragg, however, unfortunately missed the lessons of Shiloh, which would haunt them and their troops in the years to come. First, piecemeal bayonet attacks by infantry against fortified positions manned by protected riflemen backed by artillery do not work. Second, when you have your foot on the enemy's throat, go for the kill. And third, if you are going to stop an attack on the first day, you had better have a plan for the second day. Bragg failed on the first count, and Beauregard failed on the other two.

As the Confederates moved south on the morning of April 8, Cump Sherman led about fifteen thousand troops in pursuit. At about noon, his troops came up on the Confederate rear, and Sherman ordered a charge. Unbeknownst to Sherman, the same colonel in the Confederate cavalry who had made the "whipped like hell" statement was in charge. With only eight hundred men, Forrest lay in wait for Sherman on a ridge parallel to and right of the road down which Sherman's troops marched. Undaunted by the size of his opponent, Forrest ordered a charge, and out of the trees and down the ridge came his screaming eight hundred cavalrymen. Sherman's men panicked, threw down their rifles and ran away. The bloody Battle of Shiloh was over.

Bragg, however, his errors overlooked, received acclaim for his role at Shiloh. Facing what he characterized as "overwhelming numbers," Beauregard retreated from Corinth without so much as a skirmish and headed south for Tupelo. At this point, feeling ill and without permission from President Davis, Beauregard took leave and went to Bladen Springs, Alabama, to take the cure. Davis, incensed with Beauregard's performance at Shiloh, his ignominious retreat from Corinth to Tupelo and his failure to apply for a furlough before abandoning his army, notified the Creole in mid-June that he was relieving him of command and that Bragg would take over. Davis promoted Bragg to full general and then instructed him to move his army to meet a threat from Don Carlos Buell. Bragg recognized that a disaster would ensue if Buell captured Chattanooga, as it would open North Georgia to a Union invasion.

It was during the retreat to Tupelo that Bragg was saddled with an accusation that would follow him for the rest of his life. Ever the disciplinarian, Bragg was accused by no less than Mary Chesnut—the erstwhile Southern diarist—of executing a soldier for shooting a chicken. There are many versions of the story, one of which holds that Bragg had issued an order not to fire weapons during the retreat and that the shooter killed another soldier while shooting at a chicken. Another version is that the man shot and killed a "Negro child" while shooting at the chicken. In the end, all that mattered at the time was that Bragg had executed a Confederate soldier.

Bragg moved his army by rail, making a long end run around Union forces by taking trains south through Mobile and then north to Chattanooga. Buell, at that point, had roughly fifty thousand men, while Bragg had twenty-seven thousand. Avoiding a head-on battle, Bragg instead flanked Buell and headed for Kentucky, forcing Buell to abandon his base at Nashville.

A Bragg observer noted at this time that Bragg "stands so straight he leans backward" and is "an altogether fine looking man."[36] Notwithstanding Bragg's posture, there was a problem with the Confederate invasion plans, and it was a problem that would plague the Confederate army until the end of war: a split command. This time, it was Kirby Smith and Bragg. Smith's command was independent of Bragg's, both in a command sense and physically. That split would engender serious problems for the invasion, which gradually disintegrated. Bragg became preoccupied with installing a Confederate governor in Frankfurt and wasted time meeting with Kirby Smith. Bragg then turned over command of his army to Leonidas Polk and told him to fall back if he were confronted by a large force, which was like telling a fish to swim or a bird to fly. Moreover, Kirby Smith did nothing to assist Bragg with the invasion, and it was Smith's behavior that finally doomed it to an ignominious end. One of the purposes of the invasion—to rally Kentuckians to the cause—failed because Kentuckians were not interested in serving in the Confederate army. Bragg then made a move to capture Louisville, but Buell beat him there. Bragg chose not to attack Buell at Louisville and headed back to Tennessee with Buell in pursuit.

At Perryville, Buell caught up with Bragg, who was outnumbered three to one. Bragg attacked Buell's disorganized, thirsty army and rolled up the Union left in sharp fighting; then he withdrew during the night and moved back into Tennessee. The campaign released a torrent of Bragg criticism by his corps commanders and the Confederate press, which assailed him as a "tyrant, assassin, [and] murderer," as well as "utterly incompetent."[37] The Kentucky Campaign ruined Bragg's reputation as a field commander, and the press called his a "failed command." Jefferson Davis ordered him to Richmond but backed him in retaining his command, as did the Confederate Congress. There were, however, other critics with whom he had to deal, not the least of whom was Leonidas Polk, the recalcitrant subordinate who had disobeyed Bragg's direct orders multiple times, costing Bragg potential success in several battles during the Kentucky Campaign and possibly a successful invasion, at least from a military standpoint. It is doubtful, however, whether those victories would have translated into political success in that neutral state. The Kentucky Campaign thus came to its sorry conclusion, and Bragg took his army back into Tennessee.

Jefferson Davis assigned overall command of the region between the Blue Ridge Mountains and the Mississippi River to Joseph Johnston in the aftermath of Bragg's fizzled Kentucky Campaign and the criticism that followed. On December 28, 1862, Bragg's army of thirty-eight thousand settled in at Murfreesboro, Tennessee. William S. Rosecrans, who had replaced Buell, came after him with an army of forty-two thousand. Then Jefferson Davis ordered Bragg to transfer nine thousand of his men to John C. Pemberton in Mississippi, once again violating the principle of warfare favoring concentration of armies. Bragg's force, now down to twenty-nine thousand, faced an army almost one and a half his army's size.

On December 31, at Murfreesboro, Rosecrans planned to attack Bragg's right, but before he could mount his attack, Bragg attacked Rosecrans's right flank, catching it by complete surprise, and pushed the Union troops back about a mile. In the meantime, General Joseph Wheeler's cavalry circled behind Rosecrans and destroyed much of his wagon train. The Federals finally stopped Bragg's attack in what was known as the "Round Forest." Bragg, claiming victory, called off the attack, which by this point had unraveled. At the end of the day, only the left of the Union line remained intact. There was only skirmishing on the second day, but Rosecrans used the time for his men to dig in. On the third day, January 3, Bragg ordered Breckenridge, against the latter's wishes and advice, to attack the Union left, an ill-conceived plan in keeping with the highest traditions of Bragg's proclivity for frontal bayonet charges. The attack failed, with horrific losses. Bragg, then thinking that Rosecrans had seventy thousand men, withdrew on the fourth, claiming a victory at Murfreesboro. The Union called that battle Stone's River and also claimed a victory.

Most historians agree that if Kentucky did not completely destroy Bragg's reputation, Murfreesboro did. He lost the respect and confidence of his subordinates, and the press pilloried him for bungling the battle. As a field commander, Bragg was done. Nevertheless, when Jefferson Davis ordered Joseph Johnston to evaluate Bragg's fitness for command, Johnston inexplicably recommended that Bragg keep his command. Davis, equally inexplicably, accepted Johnston's recommendation.

Bragg took his army to Tullahoma, Tennessee, where he remained for six months. During that period, consistent with his reputation as a martinet, Bragg had three soldiers executed for desertion. Other than those executions, Bragg did nothing. In the early summer, Rosecrans advanced on Tullahoma with ninety thousand men. The Union army flanked Bragg and threatened to cut him off from Chattanooga, his supply source, so Bragg retreated on July 1, 1863. The press, outraged once again, assaulted him viciously, and Bragg, in poor health, retired to Cherokee Springs, Georgia, where Elise, also in poor health, awaited him. There he remained for ten days, while his army continued to maneuver and retreat to Chattanooga. The Federals then caught up with Bragg's army and maneuvered it into North Georgia, where he received much-needed reinforcements from Virginia.

The reinforcements were troops commanded by James Longstreet, John Bell Hood and D.H. Hill from the now-famous Army of Northern Virginia, and on September 19, 1863, Bragg took on Rosecrans's army in a three-day battle at Chickamauga. It would turn out to be Bragg's only major victory, but once again, Bragg's performance even in a victory would release a flood of criticism, this time for his failure to follow up his army's success of the second day, when Longstreet and Hood found and then exploited a major gap in the Union lines, collapsing the Union defense in the Confederate center and on the Confederate right. And once again, Polk failed to follow Bragg's orders when he and D.H. Hill did not attack on the Confederate right when ordered. Also, Bragg maintained his headquarters in Thedford Ford, far to the rear of the front, like Beauregard at Shiloh. He thus had little idea of what was happening and no idea of what he should be doing to take advantage of the Longstreet-Hood breach. Longstreet begged for reinforcements to continue the attack. Bragg refused and then refused to follow Rosecrans to Chattanooga and attack before he had time to set up his defenses. D.H. Hill would classify that failure as a major blunder on Bragg's part. Chickamauga was, therefore, a tactical, but not a strategic victory.

In the battle's aftermath, the irrepressible Mary Chesnut wrote:

> *Bragg—thanks to Longstreet and Hood, he won Chickamauga. So we looked* [for] *results that would pay for our losses in battles, at least. Certainly they would capture Rosecrans. No! There sits Bragg—a good dog howling on his hind legs before Chattanooga, a fortified town—and some Yankee Holdfast grinning at him from his impregnable heights. Waste of time.*
>
> *How?*
>
> *He always stops to argue with his generals.*[38]

Then followed what would be recalled as the "Revolt of the Generals." First, Bragg ordered Forrest, who had urged Bragg to launch an immediate attack on Chattanooga, to attack the Union supply line. Forrest did not, and Bragg then ordered him to transfer his troops to Wheeler. Forrest did, but what followed was one of the more famous diatribes of the war. Forrest's philippic—it would become known as the "Damned Scoundrel" speech[39]—verbally assaulted Bragg, who, at Forrest's request, recommended him for an independent command. Bragg, following criticism from Polk and Hindman, suspended both from command. He relieved D.H. Hill, of whom Bragg was especially critical, with Breckenridge and demoted Buckner.

But there were other rebellious generals. Longstreet, for example, wrote to Secretary of War James L. Seddon concerning Bragg's ineptitude in the aftermath of Chickamauga. He asked that Seddon send Lee south to take charge of Bragg's army. That request went nowhere. Jefferson Davis and Joseph Johnston then traveled to Chattanooga to see firsthand the purled waters. There, Longstreet, Buckner, Cleburne and Cheatham all urged Bragg's relief. Bragg, however, blamed Polk and Hill for all of his troubles. He termed Forrest "a good raider" but a poor cavalryman because he did not work well with the army he was supposed to support. Somewhat amazingly, Davis and Johnston backed Bragg, and by early November, the revolt had been quashed.

Bragg besieged Rosecrans in Chattanooga, but the Union resupplied and reinforced that army as Longstreet failed to stop Union troops from crossing the Tennessee River at Brown's Ferry. Meanwhile, Bragg's army shrank as the result of desertions and the transfers of his troops to other commands. Finally, after losses at Chattanooga and Lookout Mountain and a rout at Missionary Ridge, where the Confederate line broke, Bragg retreated into North Georgia. The loss at Missionary Ridge was also

Bragg's fault: he trusted too much in the topography to defeat a Federal assault, and he did nothing to defend the ridge with earthworks or other defensive measures.

At this point, Bragg had lost eighteen thousand men and now had only twenty-eight thousand men to face Grant's ninety thousand. Bragg then asked to be relieved, and Davis did so with Joseph Johnston on February 5, 1864. Bragg's career as a field commander, which had teetered on the thin line between success and failure for so long, was over. Mary Chesnut commented, "Bragg begs to be released from his command. The army will be relieved to get rid of him. He has a winning way of earning everybody's detestation. Heavens, how they hate him."[40]

A reporter wrote of Bragg, "It is better to have an army of asses led by a lion than an army of lions led by an ass."[41] On that note, Bragg—the reviled ass—headed for Richmond, where he would gain the title of "commander in chief" but in reality would be only a military advisor to Davis with little authority. Not unexpectedly, Bragg's appointment generated negative reactions among the public. One lady wrote, "Pray God that Bragg may have nothing to do with the campaign against [Grant]. He has been beaten too often by him already."[42] That sentiment was typical.

Davis's intent was to use Bragg as his "eyes and ears" in the field in both Virginia and Georgia. In the former, Benjamin Butler was making his way toward Richmond from the southeast. Beauregard, true to his traditions, proposed a complicated plan that Bragg and then Jefferson Davis rejected. Bragg instead ordered Beauregard to attack immediately; the result was a great victory at Bermuda Hundred that enabled Beauregard to bottle up Butler there, Beauregard's finest hour. Beauregard and Davis dispatched Early and a corps to the Valley to confront David Hunter, who threatened Lynchburg. It was Bragg who devised the idea for Early to march on Washington, and it was only the eleventh-hour arrival of the Union Sixth Corps that saved the capital.

In early May, Sherman approached Johnston near Dalton, and the latter retreated once again. Johnston, however, had only 60,000 men, while Sherman had 110,000. Bragg then sent a report to Davis positing that the only solution to the situation in Georgia was to take the offensive. He did not recommend Johnston's removal, but he said that if Johnston had to go, Hood was the man to replace him. Davis next asked Lee his opinion on Hood. Lee's reaction was lukewarm at best. Nevertheless, Davis ordered Hood to relieve Johnston, a move that would turn out to be one of the most disastrous personnel changes of the war.

Johnston would forever after blame his old friend Bragg for Johnston's relief by Hood, who immediately launched an attack at Peachtree Creek, followed by one at Bald Hill, followed by another at Jonesborough. Hood's "offensive" was a disaster. His army strength was down to 23,000 men, and he had lost Atlanta. Bragg, however, argued that Peachtree Creek and Bald Hill had been successes. He inexplicably based that opinion on relative losses: Hood had lost 6,900 and Sherman 5,600. Equally absurd, he called the campaign up until the abandonment of Atlanta a "brilliant affair."[43]

Davis then dispatched Bragg to Wilmington to take charge of that port's defenses. The *Richmond Enquirer* noted, "We [hear] that General Bragg is going to Wilmington. Good-bye Wilmington."[44] And goodbye it was. After successfully repulsing an attack on Fort Fisher—"the most formidable bastion in the Confederacy"—by a Union fleet commanded by David Dixon Porter, a second attack succeeded, and Bragg was driven from Wilmington. He then joined Johnston in time for an attack at Kinston, which, on the first day, was a success for the Confederates. On the second day, however, as so often happened, Union forces drove the Confederates from the field, and Johnston's army retreated to Goldsboro. Not unexpectedly, Bragg blamed Johnston for the defeats, and Johnston naturally blamed Bragg. It was a prelude to what would follow among Confederate generals in the postwar years, as they battled it out in print. Mary Chesnut's final note on Braxton Bragg was: "Bragg is our evil genius. We had the best of it at Kinston. Bragg came and spoiled it all."[45] Another lady wrote in her diary as the end loomed, "Bragg looked like an old porcupine." He was not a popular man.

Johnston and Bragg met with the fleeing Davis after the fall of Richmond on April 26, 1865. Davis wanted to fight on, but his generals still in the field urged surrender. Johnston then surrendered to Sherman, but Bragg accompanied Davis south into Georgia, where they were subsequently captured. Union forces paroled Bragg on May 9, 1865, to return to Mobile. For the old porcupine, the war was over.

POSTWAR

Bragg would find his economic situation difficult in the war's aftermath. That difficulty would manifest itself again and again in his life, generally affecting his ability to find work and, concomitantly, dramatically reducing his financial circumstances. Initially, he and Elise lived in an overseer's house on his brother John's plantation out from Mobile, but he was unable to make a living farming. In January 1867, he became president of the New Orleans, Opelousas and Great Western Railroad. Then, in an effort to reclaim his prewar plantation, Bivouac, but still in his railroad capacity, he moved to New Orleans, while Elise lived at her mother's plantation, Evergreen. Trying to enlist assistance in the recovery effort, Bragg wrote to his old friend Cump Sherman, but Sherman would not get involved. Bragg did, however, renew his friendship with Sherman, who invited Bragg to attend his daughter's wedding. Bragg, however, could not reconcile with his fellow Confederate generals. Randall L. Gibson, for example, said that Bragg was "an imbecile, coward, tyrant," as well as "a crazy man."[46]

In August 1867, Bragg became superintendent of the New Orleans Water Works, but a year later, the new Republican administration fired him. In May 1869, Bragg became vice-president of the Southern Historical Society, "a new organization of Confederate Veterans" headed, as already stated, by P.G.T. Beauregard. Bragg never wrote for that organization—indeed, he never wrote his memoirs.

Bragg tried to help his old colleague John Bell Hood in New Orleans, who was suffering financially, but James Longstreet, who also lived in New Orleans, was another case. Bragg, among many others, hated Longstreet because he "had gone over to the Republicans" and because Longstreet was critical of Robert E. Lee as well as Bragg. President Grant appointed Longstreet "surveyor of customs" for the Port of New Orleans, for which Longstreet was paid handsomely: $6,000 per year. Bragg, however, thought that Longstreet was *underpaid* in light of Longstreet's "service" to the Union during the Civil War. In addition, Bragg said Longstreet lacked courage, integrity and "moral or mental capacity."

Beauregard, although for different reasons, came into Bragg's crosshairs when he claimed credit for the Confederate successes on the first day at Shiloh. Bragg was incensed, but unlike many other Confederate generals, who spent their postwar years attacking one another, Bragg did not respond.

In March 1870, Jefferson Davis, who was president of the Carolina Life Insurance Company, appointed Bragg its New Orleans agent, a position in which he found it difficult to make a living, and less than a year later, he considered a position in the Egyptian army, as several other Confederate generals had before him. That did not pan out, however, and he next became chairman of the Board of Improvements of the River, Harbor, and Bay of Mobile for the next four years.[47] Subsequently fired from this position—a recurring theme in his postwar life—he went to Galveston, Texas, and became chief engineer of the Gulf, Colorado and Santa Fe Railroad. True to his tradition and consistent with his abrasive personality, Bragg got cross with management and resigned in June 1875. Next he worked to find a cure for yellow fever, but that project went nowhere, and in July 1876, he became inspector of railway roadbeds being constructed on land subject to Texas land grants. During this entire postwar period, Bragg continued to mourn the end of slavery, which he said was the "best and most humane labor system ever known."[48]

On Wednesday, September 27, 1876, at about 9:00 a.m., Bragg was walking to the Galveston Post Office and chatting with Captain L.E. Trevevant, a former member of the Twenty-Sixth Texas Cavalry and Bragg's messenger at Shiloh, when he suffered a massive heart attack. A physician, Dr. J.F. Kerr, was nearby and tried unsuccessfully to save him. They carried Bragg to a drugstore owned by J.G. Goodall, but he died ten minutes later—never saying a word—at the age of fifty-nine.

The Lone Star Rifles and a platoon of the Galveston Artillery escorted Bragg's body to the Armory of the Galveston Artillery, and a detachment of Washington Guards received it there. The body lay in state on Thursday morning "under guard" of the Lone Star Rifles, and at 11:30 a.m., heavily escorted, the body was placed aboard a ship bound for New Orleans and then on to Mobile.

Bragg's funeral took place at Mobile's Christ Episcopal Church on October 6, and the First Alabama Regiment attended the funeral, as did survivors of the Twenty-Fourth Alabama and the state artillery, both of which had served under Bragg, the latter unit from Pensacola to Missionary Ridge.

Elise moved from Mobile to New Orleans, where she lived with her brother, William Towson Ellis, and spent her summers in the mountains of Virginia. She died on September 27, 1908, the thirty-second anniversary of her husband's death. The couple had no children. In 1917, somewhat surprisingly, the federal government named Fort Bragg for him in recognition of his Mexican-American War service.[49]

The debate with respect to Bragg's military ability continues to this day:

> *In Bragg, the Confederacy found its strictest disciplinarian and at least* [in] *the western theater, its best organizer. Long the most detested of Confederate generals, Bragg is enjoying somewhat more favorable treatment by Civil War historians and some of the tarnish is receding from Bragg's star. However he is regarded, Bragg's association with the American military will continue as long as Fort Bragg, the enormous military base in North Carolina…continues to operate.*[50]

Chapter 3

JUBAL A. EARLY

CHILDHOOD

Jubal Anderson Early was born the third of ten children to Joab and Ruth Hairston Early on November 3, 1816, in Rocky Mount, Franklin County, Virginia. His family was wealthy and occupied a high social position in the town and county. Joab Early, his father, was of Irish descent, and his mother's ancestors were Scots, strains that would combine to produce a highly combustible son. Joab served in the Virginia legislature, and his brother Sam graduated from William and Mary.[51]

WEST POINT

In June 1837, Early entered the United States Military Academy. As he would later say, correctly, "there was nothing worthy of particular note in my career at West Point."[52] While he managed to graduate eighteenth out of fifty, the military side of his career at West Point was anything but exemplary. At that time, 200 demerits in a year warranted dismissal, and Early racked up 142 his first year, 189 his second, 196 his third and 189 as a first classman. Thus, he received no appointment as either a commissioned or noncommissioned officer in the Corps of Cadets, which he attributed to

Jubal A. Early. *Library of Congress.*

the fact that he "had very little taste for scrubbing brass."[53] It was at West Point that his reputation for irascibility arose. In one incident, Early debated Joseph Hooker about slavery and then waited outside and kicked Hooker as he left the building. His saturnine disposition made him an unpopular student, which he later acknowledged.

Early's classmates included Lieutenant Generals Braxton Bragg and John C. Pemberton and Major Generals Arnold Elzey and William Walker, all of whom would serve in the armies of the Confederacy. Classmates who would later serve in the Union army included Generals John Sedgwick and the aforementioned Joseph "Fighting Joe" Hooker. Some of Early's contemporaries, though not classmates, were Confederate generals Richard Ewell, P.G.T. Beauregard and Lewis Armistead, the latter of whom broke a mess hall plate over Early's head in a dispute, was discharged from the academy and would later die in Pickett's Charge. Union generals Irvin McDowell, William Tecumseh Sherman, Henry W. Halleck and George Meade were also contemporaries.[54]

POST WEST POINT

Upon graduation, Early was commissioned a second lieutenant and chose artillery as his branch. After a brief stint training new enlistees at Fortress Monroe, Virginia, he went to Florida, where he served in the Seminole Indian War and first heard the whine of bullets. Early subsequently traveled to Chattanooga, Tennessee, and under the command of General Winfield Scott participated in removing the Cherokees from their ancestral lands to Oklahoma. He then resigned from the army.

His rejection at this point by a "Philadelphia socialite" may have laid the emotional foundation for lifelong bachelorhood. Early returned to Rocky Mount in 1838 and began the study and practice of law under an experienced attorney, N.M. Taliaferro. He was admitted to the bar in 1840 and practiced law in Rocky Mount until the outbreak of the Mexican-American War in 1846, at which time he returned to the army. Prior to the Mexican-American War, however, he was elected to the Virginia legislature and served as a Whig from 1841 to 1843 and as the legislature's youngest member. Ironically, he was defeated in his bid for reelection by his former law partner, Taliaferro.[55]

MEXICAN-AMERICAN WAR

Early served in the north of Mexico after the Battle of Buena Vista had already been fought—and won—by Zachary Taylor, and he thus engaged mostly in garrison duty, serving at one point as the "Governor of Monterrey." Early did persuade Taylor at one point to allow him to take fifty men on an expedition involving some degree of risk. The adjutant who prepared the orders told him, "Jubal, I can testify that you are an Early who is never late, but I fear that you will soon be known as the late Early."[56] He survived, however, and the highlight of Early's Mexican-American War service was meeting Jefferson Davis, who commanded the First Mississippi Rifles, initiating a lifelong friendship.

Between the Wars

Upon his return from the Mexican-American War, he began a long affair with seventeen-year-old Julia McNealey. Early was thirty-two at the time, and she bore him four children for whom he provided support, even naming one of them Jubal Early. As Charles Osborne pointed out, Early didn't care what people thought of him then, and he would not care later.

Throughout the 1850s, Early practiced law in Rocky Mount. A unionist, he was strongly opposed to secession and represented Franklin County in the Virginia Convention of Secession in 1861. That convention eventually voted for secession, but Early, to the end, voted against leaving the Union. He said that secession would "occasion such a war as this country has never seen."[57] Early was, of course, correct.

Civil War

Nevertheless, Early was loyal to Virginia and accepted an appointment as a colonel in the Virginia State Militia. After organizing three regiments in Lynchburg, Early took command of the Twenty-Fourth Virginia Regiment and fought at Blackburn's Ford, a prelude to First Manassas. At First Manassas, Early rapidly moved his troops to Beauregard's left and from that position attacked McDowell's right at a critical point in the battle, turning McDowell's flank and initiating what became a rout of the Union army.[58] It was Early, then, who saved Beauregard from defeat, although others—Joseph Johnston in particular—would take credit for the South's victory.

Subsequent to the battle, Jefferson Davis visited Early's camp, and Beauregard recommended Early for promotion to brigadier general, which Davis granted. Early then took command of a brigade consisting of the Twenty-Fourth Virginia, the Fifth North Carolina and the Twenty-Third North Carolina.

After First Manassas, Union general George B. McClellan replaced General McDowell, and Confederate general Joseph Johnston replaced General Beauregard. McClellan then invaded Virginia, initiating what would become known as the Peninsula Campaign. At the Battle of Williamsburg, Early led his brigade in a wild charge—reminiscent of the Scots at Culloden—against entrenched Union artillery and took a Minié ball in his shoulder. McClellan skillfully drove Johnston back toward Richmond, and at the Battle of Seven

Pines, General Johnston was wounded. In perhaps the greatest personnel move of the war, Robert E. Lee then assumed command of the Confederate forces, which he renamed the Army of Northern Virginia. Thus ensued the "Seven Days," a series of sharp battles in which Lee's army drove McClellan away from Richmond and back down the Peninsula following a series of relentless Confederate attacks. Early returned from convalescence to take command of a brigade in General Stonewall Jackson's Corps in time for the Battle of Malvern Hill, but there he became separated from his brigade and missed the battle. Early blamed General Richard Ewell for this blunder, while others blamed Early.[59]

While on convalescence leave, a visitor of Early's described him with

> *shoulders as stooped as those of a man far older, piercing dark eyes; thin grizzled hair and beard. A handsome sculptured nose, pursed lips, and thickset jaws communicate determination and an appearance of profound self-confidence. He habitually wore a large white slouch hat, adorned with a black plume…* [and] *a long white overcoat that fell dramatically to his heels.*
>
> *His voice was high and piping and* [he] *expressed his opinions in terms that were often blunt, sarcastic, disrespectful and…interestingly lurid and picturesque.* [He] *was scathing and profane, spitting out oaths with streams of tobacco juice from a plug that was seldom absent from his jaw.*[60]
>
> [Early] *mistrusted anyone's popularity, including his own, scorning the multitude and its views. He nonetheless liked a convivial drink, and he loved to talk. He said things about his superiors…sufficient to have convicted him a hundred times over before a court martial.*[61]

Pugnacious and ill-tempered, Early had a hard time making friends. He "appeared older than his years because of painful arthritis and a pronounced stoop. The pain may have contributed to [his] surly disposition, which manifested itself in a quick wit accompanied by a biting satire."[62] He acknowledged that his attire was described as "that of a stage coach driver."[63] His men called him "Old Jube" or "Old Jubal."

At Second Manassas, Early again demonstrated an extraordinary penchant for exquisite battlefield timing. Late on the first day, Early moved his brigade to the left behind A.P. Hill, who was under heavy attack by Pope. At the moment that Union forces were about to overrun Gregg's regiment on the Confederate left, "a roar came from behind, and Early's Division arrived on the field" to prevent Pope from turning Gregg's and Hill's flanks with catastrophic results. Early counterattacked and drove the right of Pope's army from the field, thus setting the table for the stunning Confederate victory the next day.

Lee's invasion of Maryland followed, resulting ultimately in the Battle of Antietam, where Early assumed command of the wounded A.R. Lawton's division and, at a critical juncture in the battle, plugged a hole on Jackson's left that, if not filled, would have allowed Union forces under General Joseph Hooker, the recipient of Early's wrath at West Point, to turn Jackson's left and ultimately destroy Lee's entire army.

Following Antietam, Lee crossed the Potomac back into Virginia, and General Ambrose Burnside took command of Union forces. At Fredericksburg that December, Early's Brigade was stationed on the far right of Lee's lines, in reserve. A West Point classmate of Early's, General George G. Meade, attacked the Confederate right, under the command of Stonewall Jackson, and cut a hole in the Confederate lines. Union soldiers poured through the gap, again threatening to roll up Lee's entire army. At the last second, Early, now in temporary command of the wounded R.E. Ewell's division, and contrary to Jackson's order, came roaring out of the woods, slammed into Meade's forces and drove them back across their original lines. Fredericksburg, a disaster for the Union following Burnside's repeated attacks against the entrenched Confederates on Marye's Heights, gave rise to General Lee's famous statement, "It is good that war is so terrible, lest we should grow too fond of it."[64]

Subsequent to Fredericksburg, Early was promoted to major general and assumed permanent command of Ewell's Division, which consisted of four brigades. On the Union side, "Fighting Joe" Hooker replaced the hapless Burnside in command of the Army of the Potomac. At this point, Early was said "to wear the attire of a farmer" or, again, "a stagecoach driver." Some said that he wore rags. His voice was high, and he was "argumentative but persuasive, asserting his point with mingled ridicule and reason."[65]

Following the winter of 1862–63, Hooker skillfully maneuvered his troops so that the main part of his army moved up the Rappahannock River and crossed it to threaten Lee's left, while opposite Fredericksburg, a force of about sixty thousand confronted Lee's army there. Commanded by Early's West Point classmate General John Sedgwick, that force occupied the Stafford Heights, from which Burnside had launched the costly attacks against Marye's Heights the previous December. Lee split his army at Chancellorsville, Jackson flanked Hooker and Hooker was crushed.

Following Lee's greatest victory, he dispatched Early and his division to the Shenandoah Valley to clear it of Union forces prior to his second invasion of the North. Early complied and, with a decisive victory at Winchester, secured the Valley and Lee's rear prior to the Army of Northern Virginia's march into Pennsylvania.

Jackson's death at Chancellorsville forced Lee to reorganize his army. Instead of two corps under Longstreet and Jackson, Lee split his army into three corps—a fateful decision that would bear bitter fruit in the days and weeks to come. Longstreet had First Corps; Ewell, known as "Old Bald Head" to his troops, was assigned Second Corps; and A.P. Hill took Third Corps. Early's Division was part of Old Bald Head's Second Corps, which spearheaded Lee's army as it moved north into Pennsylvania.

After capturing Gettysburg, Early moved on to take York and was moving toward Lancaster when Lee ordered his army to consolidate around Gettysburg, where A.P. Hill had encountered a strong Union force under Lincoln's sixth commanding general of the Army of the Potomac, George C. Meade, another of Early's former classmates at West Point.

On July 1—forever after known as the "first day"—Early's Division, attacking from the west, once again filled a gaping hole in Hill's line just in the nick of time and then swept through Gettysburg, capturing four thousand enemy soldiers. Early saw an opportunity to continue the attack beyond the town and capture Cemetery Hill, which would have rendered Cemetery Ridge untenable for Meade's army. Early urged such an attack upon Ewell, who, in all fairness, had earlier been ordered by Lee not to engage in a fight if Union troops were around Gettysburg in force. Nevertheless, the criticism of Early is that he should have continued the initial attack and taken the lightly defended Cemetery Hill with or without Ewell's permission and support. That evening, Ewell, with Early's support, convinced Lee that they should not make an evening attack on the largely undefended hills. Early would later say that the failure to capture Cemetery Hill on the first day was critical: "Perhaps… victory might have been made decisive so far as Gettysburg was concerned by a prompt advance of all of the troops that had been engaged on our side against the hill upon which and behind the enemy had taken refuge, but a common superior did not happen to be present, and the opportunity was lost."[66] Authority at that point was split between A.P. Hill and Ewell. Longstreet had not yet arrived on the scene, and Jackson was, of course, dead. Nevertheless, Early characterized the first day as "a brilliant victory," which may explain why he did not continue his attack and take the hills on Meade's right: there had been enough glory for one day.

July 2, the "second day," dawned. Like the first day, it was day of missed opportunities for Lee's army, and also like the first day, there remains considerable controversy about the South's failure to carry the day. The evening before, Lee wanted Ewell and Early to attack on the left at dawn, but the two argued against an attack on the left and instead urged an attack by Longstreet's Corps on the Confederate right. Lee finally ordered Ewell and Early to "make a show" of attacking on the left and to be prepared to mount a real attack if they saw a chance of success. That was just the out that Ewell needed. He did not attack, Longstreet failed to attack on the right until too late in the day to carry the Round Tops, and Lee's army returned to Seminary Ridge to lick its wounds.

Early was not involved in any action on the "third day," the day of the fateful charge by Pickett's doomed legions. Lee then took his defeated army back into Virginia, and thus ended the Battle of Gettysburg and Lee's Pennsylvania Campaign. Amazingly, Early characterized the disastrous Pickett's Charge as "sanguinary" and the entire battle as a draw, arguing that Lee withdrew not because he had been defeated, but rather because his army was low on ammunition and food.

During the winter of 1863–64, Early left his division with Lee and, accompanied by other troops, deployed west to the Shenandoah Valley to assume command of Confederate troops there and meet a Union force commanded by General W. Averill that was threatening Staunton, Virginia. After arrival, Early drove Averill from the valley and into West Virginia. It was during this campaign that Early first, and openly, expressed his disdain for the Confederate cavalry supporting him. It was an opinion that he was to urge repeatedly in the months to come.

Early returned to the Army of Northern Virginia at Orange, Virginia, in March 1864, sporting a new uniform and a black, plumed beaver hat. What followed, sequentially, were three of the most brutal battles of the entire war in the "Overland Campaign." Lieutenant General U.S. Grant had taken command of all U.S. forces, including the Army of the Potomac, still under the direct command of Major General George Meade, who reported to Grant.

Grant intended to engage Lee in a war of attrition, reasoning that the North's superior resources in men and material would eventually wear Lee down. Thus began the penultimate Northern Virginia campaign of the Civil War.

At the Wilderness in early May 1864, Early's Division, which included among others General John Gordon's brigade, was deployed on Lee's left when Gordon discovered that the Union right was "in the air"—that is, unprotected and thus vulnerable to a flanking movement by the Confederate forces, specifically those of Gordon. Ewell and Early, as at Gettysburg, once again demurred and thus lost a golden opportunity to roll up Grant's right, even though Lee had stated his desire for just that kind of attack on the right. It was a missed opportunity to inflict a major defeat on Grant's army.

After the Wilderness, Grant moved east, to Lee's right, toward Spotsylvania Court House, but Lee won the race. Lee used Ewell's physical problems as a pretext for relieving him and assigning command of Ewell's Second Corps to Early. At Spotsylvania Court House, Early's Corps was in the middle of Lee's lines and successfully defended its position against a massive attack engineered by Ambrose Burnside.

Grant again moved east, and with Early now a corps commander, Lee stopped Grant at Cold Harbor with heavy casualties, including at one point six thousand in a half hour. In the three battles, Grant had lost fifty-four thousand men killed, wounded and missing, almost as many men as Lee had in his entire army.

After Cold Harbor, Lee dispatched Early and the Second Corps back to the Valley to meet yet another threat posed by Union general David Hunter. A long, fertile indentation, the Valley was Lee's breadbasket and furnished by rail most of the food for his army. Lee ordered Early to retake the northern part of the Valley—known strangely as "the lower valley," with the "upper valley" to its south—and then to "menace" Washington or return to the Army of Northern Virginia at his discretion.

Predictably, Early drove Hunter from the Valley, defeating him at Lynchburg. Not surprisingly, Early chose to take his corps and "menace" Washington. He encountered a Union force at Harper's Ferry Heights, which he drove across the river onto Maryland Heights, which he then bypassed. These skirmishes, however, cost him a precious day.

By this time, Early's little Army of the Valley comprised roughly 10,000 infantry and 4,000 cavalry. They moved on toward the capital virtually unopposed. Union general Lew Wallace, who would later write *Ben-Hur*, was in Baltimore with only a few troops. Scraping together an amalgam of roughly 5,800 militia and regular army troops, he, on his own initiative, moved to Monocracy Junction. Early attacked him there and eventually drove him away, but Early lost another precious day. This gift of time allowed Grant to send the Sixth Corps to Washington from Northern Virginia, and they, given the extra two days, arrived in time to defend the capital against the approaching Confederates. Early split his army into two divisions, one to come in on the Georgetown Pike and the main body to come down from Rockville and onto Seventh Street. Early and his group "arrived in sight of the dome of the Capitol and [had] given the Federal authorities a terrible fright."[67] President Lincoln watched the skirmishes. Early said, "Well, we haven't taken Washington, but we've scared Lincoln like hell."[68] But it wasn't enough.

Early's troops were worn down by the intense heat and the long march from Lynchburg, and *seeing* the Capitol was as close as they would get to capturing Washington. By now, the fortifications were manned, and a frontal attack would be difficult, if not impossible. Early gathered his little army and, under cover of darkness, pulled out and headed back to Virginia. The third Confederate invasion of the North was over.

Thus began Early's final campaigns. He returned to the Valley and once again took on a large Union force commanded by General George Crook, whom he faced and defeated at Kernstown, again driving a Union army from the Valley. However, the Union forces under Averill, Hunter and Crook had, pursuant to orders from Grant, destroyed everything in the Valley of any use to Lee's army. Early was, justifiably, outraged and determined to gain revenge, which he did by burning Chambersburg, Pennsylvania.

Grant had finally had enough of Early's success in the Valley and dispatched General Philip Sheridan with thirty-five thousand infantry and eight thousand cavalry to destroy Early's Army of the Valley, now consisting of thirteen thousand men. In another battle at Winchester—the third—Sheridan's army, not surprisingly, routed Early's smaller army and did it again at Fisher's Hill, where Early, now with only ten thousand men, took another severe whipping. Then at Cedar Creek took place one of the most controversial tactical decisions by a Southern general in the entire war, and there were many. Here, the decision in question was Early's.

Reinforced and now with twenty-one thousand men, Early orchestrated an early morning surprise attack and, with Sheridan ten miles away after attending a meeting, rolled up the Union left and routed the much larger Union force of thirty-eight thousand. Then, at 10:00 a.m., the attack stopped in what forever after became known in Southern lore as "the fatal delay" or "the fatal halt." There are various theories about why what was an overwhelmingly successful attack ended. One is that Early's troops broke off the attack to plunder the camps that the Union troops had just vacated, leaving their supplies behind, and the attack therefore fizzled out on its own.

Another theory is that Early himself called off the attack. Writing many years later, General John B. Gordon, whose division led the successful attack on the Union left, said that he had urged Early to continue the offensive and perhaps destroy the entire Union army but that Early declined, saying the victory was won, just as he had after the first day at Gettysburg and just as Beauregard said after the first day at Shiloh. From 10:00 a.m. to 1:00 p.m., little is known about Early's whereabouts at Cedar Creek. At 1:00 p.m., he appeared and authorized a "reconnaissance in force," which amounted to nothing.

It did not matter. Sheridan had returned to his army at noon, and the delay gave him time to rally and reorganize his army, more than three times the size of Early's. Around four o'clock, Sheridan attacked and routed the Confederate force. The Battle of Cedar Creek, so promising for the Confederates that morning, ended in disaster for the Army of the Valley.

After Cedar Creek, it was all downhill for Early. Most of his surviving army left to join Lee's army at Petersburg, reducing his force to about two thousand. At Waynesboro, Sheridan, with ten thousand men, again routed and virtually destroyed what was left of Early's small force. Thereafter, Lee relieved Early, and Early went home. Lee surrendered three days later.[69]

POSTWAR

Immediately after Lee's surrender, Federal troops came to Franklin County looking to arrest Early, but he "was saved by the devotion of a faithful Negro," who pointed the Federal troops in the wrong direction. Because he had not been present at any of the surrender ceremonies and because of his relief from command, Early did not think the terms of the surrender applied to him.[70]

On May 21, 1865, accompanied by three young men, one of whom was his nephew, Early headed southwest from Franklin County toward the Trans-Mississippi command of General Edmund Kirby Smith, whom he hoped to join and continue the fight. The three young men eventually left him, and he soon learned to his sorrow that Smith had surrendered.

A Federal grand jury in Norfolk, Virginia, indicted Early for treason in June 1865. That grand jury also indicted Robert E. Lee, Richard Ewell and many others, so Early, the unreconstructed and very angry rebel, decided to go on to Mexico. He went to Galveston, bought his first civilian suit—Confederate gray with Confederate army buttons—caught a ship and sailed via Nassau, Bahamas, and then Havana to Mexico. The Confederate gray suit of clothes was to be his standard attire for the rest of his life.

In Mexico City, Early sought employment with Maximilian—the puppet of French emperor Napoleon III—whom, he hoped, would start a war with the United States "to which Jubal could add his lance and continue to kill Yankees."[71] While in Mexico, he wrote his memoirs of the Shenandoah Campaign and, somewhat strangely, wrote a letter to the *New York News* stating that Mexico was unstable and all Americans should stay away.

Employment with Maximilian came to naught, so Early left Mexico City and moved on to Canada. Unlike Robert E. Lee, who applied to President Andrew Johnson for a pardon, Early had no intention of doing so; indeed, Lee's "act affronted many Confederates because it seemed to acknowledge that the South was guilty of wrongdoing in fighting the war." Early was among those affronted.[72]

In Canada, he settled in Niagara, just across Canada's border with the United States, and finished his narrative on the Shenandoah Campaign, which John C. Breckenridge, a fellow exile, read and criticized. The book was published in Canada. Nevertheless, Early had few financial resources. He could not practice law in Canada without a five-year waiting period to get licensed, so he lived on money sent to him by his brothers and friends.

Early thought little of the dead Lincoln; his successor, Andrew Johnson; and U.S. Grant, whom he predicted (presciently) would be no more than a "tool for others." In 1867, Early advocated that his former Confederate army associates "take up arms" against the Union and fight to the death. He wanted to arm the Indians and lead a band of twenty to thirty thousand Comanches and Apaches through the Midwest and across the Mississippi, "so that he could leave a trail behind that would not be erased in this century."[73] As Fitzhugh Lee observed "when Jubal Early had drawn his sword for war, he discarded the scabbard and was never able to find it."[74]

In that same year, Early began work on his "complete" memoirs. He still would not seek a pardon from Andrew Johnson, and because that was a requirement for returning home to Virginia, Early, almost destitute, remained in Canada. Bitter and angry toward the Union, he hoped for a series of political events in the United States—a split in the Republican Party and an alliance between southern whites and northern Democrats—that would lead to southern independence. He would, he said, return to the United States only under the flag of the Confederacy.

In December 1868, however, Johnson granted an "unconditional amnesty" that resulted in the dismissal of all indictments of former Confederates and full pardons granted. This event, combined with the end of his relationship with Julia McNealey and his meager means of support in Canada, finally led him to return to Virginia by way of Missouri, where his father had settled. After a few months visiting his father, General Jubal A. Early, the "Savior of Lynchburg," returned there in July 1869.

Early "took quarters" above a store on Main Street owned by an E. Crump. A visitor said that Early lived in a "grimy building" that reminded the visitor of a "New York tenement." His room was dirty and unkempt, filled with piles of papers, letters and books. "God a Mighty" was a favorite expression.

He joined the Democratic Party, his move a harbinger of what was to become the "one-party" South that would follow Congressional, as opposed to Presidential, Reconstruction. There is evidence that the Carolina Life Insurance Company offered him an agency, but there is no evidence that he accepted. Instead, he reestablished his law practice, which he would maintain until 1877, when another, more lucrative opportunity would come his way.

Early had been vehemently opposed to secession in 1861 but now became one of its most vocal defenders, analogizing it to the withdrawal of the American colonies that precipitated the American Revolution. States, he argued, were sovereign; thus, having created the federal government, they were free to abrogate that arrangement and to withdraw just as the colonies had from Great Britain some eighty-odd years before.

Then, with Early struggling with financial difficulties, an opportunity arose to undertake duties entirely removed from the practice of law in Lynchburg, from which he never made a good living. There were two problems with his law practice; one, he did not collect the amounts due him for his work, and two, there just was not much legal work in Lynchburg, even though his celebrity status attracted a good portion of what was there.

Early's old commander at First Manassas, General P.G.T. Beauregard, wrote to him in December 1876 about becoming a commissioner of the Louisiana State Lottery. Beauregard had previously offered the position to Wade Hampton, but as noted, Hampton had been elected governor of South Carolina and thus refused, so Beauregard's friend Early was next up. He began commuting to New Orleans by train. Early's salary to start was $5,000 per year, but by 1881, Early was drawing an annual salary of $10,000 per year, a princely sum then.

The lottery had been plagued with "venality and fraud" since its inception. Chartered by the state and granted a monopoly, the lottery drew participants from out of state and was highly profitable, raking in annual revenues as high as $28.8 million, with profits of $8.5 million to $13 million. For twenty years, the lottery was the most powerful political force in Louisiana, dominating state and local governments, which enjoyed the revenues that it produced.

Early's duties were to attend semiannual drawings and lobby in Baton Rouge—and Washington, if necessary—on behalf of the lottery. Early actually conducted the lottery drawings and announced the winning numbers. Beauregard then announced the amount of the prize.

Legislation calling for repeal of the lottery's charter was an annual event in Louisiana, and finally, the federal government refused to allow the lottery to send tickets through the mail and also refused even to send newspapers containing advertisements for the lottery through the mail. In addition, the lottery once again encountered charges of corruption, so it packed up and moved to Honduras. Beauregard and Early then resigned.

Early continued to have issues with the South's defeat and continued to wear only suits of Confederate gray to express his dissatisfaction with the Union. A Charlottesville haberdashery supplied some of these suits. When a movement undertook the building of a monument to Robert E. Lee, Early found the statue "revolting" and threatened to rally survivors of his Second Corps and "blow up the thing with dynamite." He opposed using granite from Maine or any other materials from northern states.[75]

At his point in time Early said of himself that

> *I was never blessed with popular or captivating manners and…I was often misjudged and thought to be haughty and disdainful in my temperament.…I was never what is called a popular man. I was quite erect and trim in stature. My average weight for many years was from 154 to 164 pounds. The stoop with which I am now afflicted is the result of rheumatism contracted in Mexico, and when casual observers have seen me bent up, it has been very often the result of actual pain to which I have been very much subjected for the last nineteen years. One writer…has described me as having a rough, curly head and shaggy eyebrows, whereas the fact is that my hair always has been and what is left, still is straight as an Indian's and my eyebrows are very moderate and smooth. Some writer…has described my dress during the war as being that of a stage-driver. All tailors who have worked with me up to the present time will testify for the fact that I have always been one of the most particular men about the cut and fit of my clothes among their customers.*[76]

Early was a popular speaker about the war, and in his speeches he denigrated Longstreet and Colonel John Mosby, whom he characterized as a mere "plunderer." He blamed Longstreet, of course, for his failure on the second day at Gettysburg to mount an attack on the Union left until too late in the day, thus ensuring defeat for the Southern forces and loss of the war. Early was responsible for developing the philosophical underpinnings of the "Lost Cause," which became the "civil religion" of the South. The principles underlying the Lost Cause were that, first, the men of the Army of Northern Virginia fought four years in defense of a principle that they believed was right and was, in fact, right: the legal and constitutional right to secede. Second, the Army of Northern Virginia was never defeated; it "just wore itself out whipping the enemy" and was "beat by overwhelming resources and numbers."[77] Third, Robert E. Lee was the apotheosis of Southern manhood—a "Christlike figure," the "Godhead of the Lost Cause," elevated to the status of a deity. Lee had been done in by his subordinates, mainly James Longstreet at Gettysburg.[78]

In a speech on June 6, 1869 (Confederate Memorial Day), in Winchester, Virginia, Early concluded:

> *If ever I repudiate, disown, or apologize for the cause for which Lee fought, and Jackson died, may the lightning of Heaven blast me, and the scorn of all good women and true men be my portion, and I reiterate now, what I have often said before, that the Confederate who has deserted since the war is infinitely worse than one who deserted during the war, for the former has gone over to the enemy at no personal risk to himself, and simply from motives of gain, while the latter took his life in his hands, knowing that he would be shot if captured, and in a number of cases he was tempted to leave the service and go to the assistance of his family, which he was induced to believe was starving at home.*[79]

Early used the Confederate speakers' platforms to blast Longstreet, Mosby and, later, John B. Gordon, William Mahone and Thomas L. Rosser, whom, like Longstreet, he blamed for various military blunders and shortcomings as commanders. By this time, he had a "stooped figure, his beard, his black piercing eyes and his gray clothing made him a conspicuous figure."[80] Early continued to defend the Lost Cause against all critics. His defense found its platform in the Southern Historical Society, which sought to prove that the Confederate soldier was superior to his Union counterpart, whom, Early said, was a member of a "mongrel race," an amalgam of "Yankees, negroes, Germans and Irish." The Union won only through superior numbers. The Confederate soldier was a better fighter and, thus, a superior man. The South, with its agrarian traditions, was simply unable to overcome the vast industrial power of the North and its "mongrel hordes."[81]

The organization, through speakers like Early, continued to blast Lee's subordinate commanders, who were, they maintained, his undoing. The primary target, of course, was James Longstreet, who disobeyed a nonexistent "dawn order." Longstreet's status as a Republican only served to intensify the attacks, and in defending himself, Longstreet criticized Lee, whose memory and wartime exploits were sacrosanct.

Union general George Crook met Early when Early was seventy-three years old. The two old adversaries sat up over drinks one night and talked of the war. Crook described him as "much stooped and enfeebled but as bitter and violent as an adder. He has no use for the government or the northern people. He boasts of his being unreconstructed and that he won't accept a pardon for his rebellious offenses. He…is living entirely in the past. He has fought his battles so many times that he has worked himself into the belief that many of the exaggerated and somewhat ridiculous stories are true. We sat up…until after midnight, taking a hot scotch with him."[82] He wore "a tall white hat…a long white beard, and had a habit of spitting through his teeth, in which he displayed a great deal of skill." Early continued to wear "a neat, gray suit. Jubal shot his cuffs to show his shirt-sleeve buttons, on which appeared a Confederate flag, gold with colors in enamel."[83]

Early continued to propagate the Lost Cause through speeches and articles. He predicted a "harsh punishment" for the victorious North for committing what he contended was a "harsh crime." The punishment would be a "civil rot" that would bring it down. It was the South that had vindicated the principles set forth by the founders of the Republic. "Unmarried, snarling and stooped, respected as a soldier but never widely popular as a man, 'Jube' lived on in Lynchburg."[84] At this point, "his face was like a full moon and [he had] a voice like a cracked Chinese fiddle, emitting a long drawl accompanied by an outpouring of oaths." He was "sarcastic and critical…a man of rough address, irascible temperament, and…wholly careless of whom he offended."[85]

Douglas Southall Freeman, author of two famous sets of books on Robert E. Lee, "glimpsed" Early on occasion. Freeman remembered him "dimly as a glowering old man, fiercely chewing tobacco," and "notorious, our nurses would have us remember, for eating a bad little boy every morning at breakfast." Freeman went on to say, "When he hobbled down to the Arlington Hotel in the morning, he might snarl and swear. Veterans would listen respectfully, and never would answer back. Had he not saved the city at the time of Hunter's Raid? Was he not the embodiment of the Confederacy…unreconstructed, a Lieutenant-General in the Army of Northern Virginia?"[86]

The beginning of the end came in 1890, when a building in Lynchburg collapsed, with Early in it. There had been a fire in the building, and Early—before the building collapsed—had gone upstairs to survey the damage to his papers. After the collapse, rescuers harbored little hope that he had survived, but after digging down through the rubble, Jubal was revealed, his white campaign hat (on his head) and his white beard blancoed to unnatural brilliance. He was quite unhurt sitting in his chair, where it had remained when the floor of his room dropped intact to the street level. When Early looked up and saw a friend in charge of the rescue efforts he bellowed, "Hey, Bob! Blast my hat to hell. I didn't know you were up there, boy. Damn it, you go get me a julep."[87]

Early said that he didn't know that there were that many bricks between him and hell. Four years later, he slipped, fell and went into shock. Jubal Anderson Early, the curmudgeonly warrior, Lee's "bad old man" and an unreconstructed rebel all the way, died on March 2, 1894. He was seventy-five years old. Early is buried in Lynchburg, the town that he once saved.[88]

Chapter 4

NATHAN BEDFORD FORREST

CHILDHOOD

Nathan Bedford Forrest was the oldest of fifteen children born to his mother, Mariam Beck, and her two husbands, William Forrest and Joseph Luxton. Forrest was named for his paternal grandfather, Nathan, and the county in which he was born on July 13, 1821, Bedford County, Tennessee. He would be called Bedford, never Nathan Bedford. His mother, Mariam Beck, was a formidable woman of Scots-Irish descent, almost six feet tall and weighing about 180 pounds. Only nine—all boys—of her fifteen children would survive the ravages of yellow fever and the rough frontier life of the old Southwest.

In 1842, Forrest, then twenty-one years old, joined his uncle Jonathon in the livery and livestock business in Hernando, Mississippi. In 1845, four men—three named Matlock and their overseer named Bean—ambushed Jonathan Forrest on the Hernando square and shot him dead. Bedford, armed with a two-shot pistol, then took them on. He shot two of the Matlocks, killing one, and then, armed with a Bowie knife that an onlooker tossed to him, stabbed the other two before they could kill him. One of them did manage to wound him, the first of several bullets that he would take during a fractious and violent life.

That same year, 1845, Forrest married Mary Ann Montgomery of Hernando, by whom he fathered two children: William, or Willie, in 1846

Nathan Bedford Forrest. *Library of Congress.*

and Fanny in 1847, named for Bedford's twin sister who had died of yellow fever. In 1852, the Forrest family moved to Memphis, where Bedford traded in cotton, real estate and slaves. Fanny, sadly and like her namesake, died of dysentery in 1854.

In Memphis, Forrest amassed a significant fortune, estimated at between $1 million and $1.5 million, a princely sum in those days. With Forrest rising in the Memphis social and political circles concomitantly with his growing economic success, Memphians elected him an alderman in 1858 and 1859, but that year he resigned as alderman and shut down his various Memphis trading businesses. Forrest then moved to Coahoma County in the Mississippi Delta, where he owned two plantations that would produce one thousand bales of cotton and about $30,000 net income per year for him, a huge sum for an already wealthy man.[89]

CIVIL WAR SERVICE

On June 14, 1861, six days after Tennessee's voters had ratified secession, Forrest went to Memphis and joined the army as a private in the Tennessee Mounted Rifles, his company commanded by Captain J.S. White. Forrest had been opposed to secession, but he would later say, "I went into the war because my vote had been unable to preserve the peace....I took a through ticket, and I fought and lost as much as anyone else; certainly as much as I could."[90] Private Forrest stood six feet, two inches tall; swarthy, lithe and powerful of frame, he had blue-gray eyes, iron-gray hair and a short black beard. He was described as "fierce and terrible," with a vile temper and with an extensive vocabulary of bad language. Forrest was said to be "violent and profane but never vulgar or obscene." He didn't drink or use tobacco.[91]

Forrest was not long to remain a private in what would soon become famous as the Seventh Tennessee Cavalry. Later that summer, Tennessee governor Isham G. Harris arranged Forrest's discharge and authorized him to recruit a battalion of mounted troopers for service in the Confederate cavalry. Forrest immediately placed an advertisement in the *Memphis Appeal* asking for men who could ride and provide their own weapons—"shotguns and pistols preferable."[92] By October, Forrest had raised and outfitted at his own expense an "eight-company battalion, of which he was elected lieutenant colonel."[93]

Forrest immediately took his unit to the field and joined Confederate forces headquartered at Hopkinsville, in southwestern Kentucky. Their first fight came at the end of December at a place called Sacramento, and it was a harbinger of what was to come from Forrest. There his men routed their Union opponents, and Forrest claimed the first of what would be many victories. It was said that while he had no formal military training, he "would soon prove to be a natural military genius with an intuitive grasp not only of tactics, but also of logistics."[94] His men were said to fear him more than they feared the enemy, but they also were willing to follow him anywhere.

Subsequently, Forrest came to the attention of his superiors at Fort Donelson when he refused to surrender to U.S. Grant with his fellow generals. He found a way out through freezing water that was saddle high and led his men to safety.

Next up was the Tennessee abattoir of Shiloh. Forrest's unit had been reorganized and reinforced to become the Third Tennessee Cavalry, with Forrest elected colonel. On the evening of the first day, after Confederate troops led first by Albert Sidney Johnston and then by P.G.T. Beauregard had almost pushed Grant's army into the Tennessee River, Beauregard stopped the attack, thinking that he had victory in the palms of his hands. It is unclear what happened next. One version has it that Forrest rode out in front of the Confederate lines. Another is that he sent men dressed in Union uniforms into Grant's camp. Either way, he became aware of Don Carlos Buell's men arriving in large numbers to reinforce Grant. Forrest went from Confederate general to general, saying that they either needed to attack that night or get off the field. As previously noted, he told them—he was unable to find Beauregard—we will be "whipped like hell."[95] They were indeed whipped like hell the next day, and Beauregard thus began a long and ignominious retreat south toward Corinth, with Forrest's cavalry ordered to cover his army's rear.

At a place that would become famously known as Fallen Timbers, Sherman's Brigade caught up with Forrest's regiment and poured after them into a ravine filled with fallen trees, on the attack. Forrest, however, saw something that Sherman had not foreseen: the line of the advancing troops had become unhinged while the Union troops struggled through the tree-strewn hollow. As Shelby Foote would write, Sherman's advance "was done in strict professional style, according to the book. But the man he was advancing against had never read the book, though he was presently to rewrite it by improvising tactics that would conform to his own notion of what war was all about: 'War means fighting. And fighting means killing.'"[96] It was "the fearsome Nathan Bedford Forrest" with an amalgam of about six hundred Tennessee, Kentucky, Mississippi and Texas cavalrymen, and they did what Forrest always did: the improbable and sometimes even the impossible. They attacked. With shotguns and revolvers, his men charged into the gap, and outnumbered heavily, "they blew the advance apart." The Union cavalry, posted behind the infantry, fired their weapons and then turned and galloped away. The rout was on.[97]

Then followed one of the most famous of Forrest's many famous exploits. Seeing the fleeing Union cavalry, Forrest, "brandishing his saber and crying, 'Charge! Charge!'...plowed in the solid ranks of the infantry brigade drawn up beyond." The trouble was that he was charging by himself—the others, seeing the steady brigade front, had turned back and were already busy gathering up their forty-three prisoners. Forrest was one gray uniform, high above the sea of blue. "Kill him! Kill the goddam rebel! Knock him off his horse!" It was no easy thing to do. The horse was kicking and plunging, and Forrest was hacking and slashing, but one of the soldiers did his best. Reaching far out, he shoved the muzzle of his rifle into the colonel's side and pulled the trigger. The force of the explosion lifted Forrest clear of the saddle, but he regained his seat and swung the horse around. As he came out of the mass of dark-blue uniforms and furious white faces, clearing a path with his saber, he reached down and grabbed one of the soldiers by the collar, swung him onto the crupper of the horse and galloped back to safety, using the hapless and helpless Union soldier as a shield against the bullets fired after him. Once he was out of range, he flung the fellow off and rode on up the ridge, where his men were waiting in open-mouthed astonishment. Sherman was astonished, too, but mostly he was just disgusted. He rounded up his troops and returned to Pittsburg Landing.[98]

Next, Forrest took command of a mounted brigade of roughly 1,400 men. Shelby Foote wrote, "In the gray dawn light, Bedford Forrest struck Murfreesboro with three regiments of cavalry, wrecking the railroad at that point and capturing the Federal commander…with all his men, guns and equipment."[99] The victory resulted from a bluff in which Forrest moved men and artillery around to create the impression of a much larger force when, in fact, he had only slightly more men than the Union forces inside the town. In a surrender demand to the Union commander, General Thomas Crittenden, Forrest threatened "to have every man put to the sword," and the Union commander surrendered 1,200 men and $250,000 in property. "When questioned later as to how he had managed this, he replied simply, 'I just took a short cut and got there first with the most men.' His famous success formula was thus born."[100]

Promotion to brigadier general followed Murfreesboro, as well as the newly won moniker "The Wizard of the Saddle."[101] Forrest next participated in Braxton Bragg's ill-fated Kentucky campaign. Bragg then relieved him of his command and sent him back to Tennessee to recruit and organize another brigade, which he did, whipping some 1,500 "raw levies" into what would become known as Forrest's "Old Brigade, a highly mobile force of mounted infantry and a new concept in this war that would reap immediate dividends for Forrest and the Confederacy," his "foot cavalry" that would ride to battle and then fight on foot, a precursor to the highly mobile units of World War II. Thus followed the first West Tennessee Campaign in which Forrest defeated several Union outfits, causing more than 1,500 casualties. He destroyed the Mobile and Ohio Railroad, causing it to close, and then outran and outfought all pursuers.

As Shelby Foote would write:

> *He was the only Confederate cavalryman of whom Grant stood in much dread, a friend of the Union general's once remarked. Then he told why. "Who's commanding?" Grant would ask on hearing that gray raiders were on the prowl. If it was some other rebel chieftain he would shrug off the threat with a light remark; but if Forrest was in command he at once became apprehensive, because the latter was amenable to no known rules of procedure, was a law unto himself for all military acts and was constantly doing the unexpected at all times and places.*[102]

Forrest next pursued a Union force of from 1,700 to 2,000 mule-mounted troops led by General Abel D. Streight with his own force of 600. Penning up Streight's force, Forrest picked up and placed on his horse a sixteen-year-old girl named Emma Sansom, who led him and his men to a ford across Black Creek that enabled them to flank Streight's position and defeat his force. That story would become part of the Forrest lore and a part of the Lost Cause catechism.

Although he would eventually be wounded in battle four times, Forrest came closest to death when one of his young officers, Lieutenant Willis Gould, incurred Forrest's wrath following the loss of some of his artillery. Forrest ordered Gould's transfer, and when Forrest refused to discuss the matter with him, Gould drew his pistol and shot Forrest in his left side. Seriously wounded, Forrest, who had been cleaning his teeth with a penknife that was now closed, used one hand to push Gould's pistol hand away from him and, after reopening the penknife with his teeth, used the other hand to drive the knife into Gould's gut. Gould lingered for two days and then died, but not before he and Forrest reconciled. Forrest, with the bullet in his side, drove himself and three doctors to a house where, after examination and the doctors' decision to extract the bullet, Forrest refused to have the "damn little pistol ball" removed and instead had them treat only the wound itself. Within twelve days, he was back in the saddle, in command of the now-deceased Earl Van Dorn's two mounted divisions.

Then came the Chickamauga slaughterhouse. Forrest posted his men on the right wing of Bragg's army as dismounted cavalry. "What infantry is that?" General D.H. Hill of Lee's army of Northern Virginia asked as Forrest's troops advanced rapidly toward the Union left. "Forrest's cavalry," he was told. When Forrest returned, Hill congratulated him on the "magnificent behavior" of his "brave men moving across that field like veteran infantry."[103]

Following the South's victory, Forrest confronted Bragg over his failure to exploit the victory, as well as the proposed transfer of Forrest's command to

Wheeler. His verbal assault on Bragg was vintage Forrest. It was the famous (or infamous) "damned scoundrel speech":

> *I have stood your meanness as long as I intend to. You have played the part of a damned scoundrel, and are a coward, and if you were any part of a man, I would slap your jowls and force you to resent it. You may as well not issue any more orders for me, for I will not obey them…and I say to you that if you ever again try to interfere with me or cross my path it will be at the peril of your life.*[104]

Bragg took Forrest's abuse because he valued too much his performance in combat. Following the diatribe, Forrest first submitted his resignation to Jefferson Davis—Davis refused it—and then requested a transfer away from Bragg, which Davis granted. His promotion to major general followed, and he shifted his forces to North Mississippi and West Tennessee. There, he successfully attacked Union troops headed from Memphis to Chattanooga. By this point, Forrest's exploits were legend throughout the South; his legendary status would remain not just for the duration of the war, as it would indeed grow exponentially after the war.

Then came some of Forrest's most famous battles. Sherman ordered General Sooy Smith to move south from Memphis with a force of from seven to ten thousand cavalrymen—this number varies with the source—whom Smith had described as the best-equipped cavalry outfit in the world. Simultaneous with Smith's move south, Sherman would march east from Vicksburg to Meridian, destroying railroads and other instrumentalities of war as he progressed eastward. Smith's mission was to destroy the north–south railroad as he moved south and destroy Forrest when he caught up with him. Then Smith was to link up with Sherman in Meridian, where they would move on east to Selma, Alabama.

Smith's large force of cavalrymen was armed with breech-loading rifles and twenty artillery pieces "double-teamed for speed."[105] To meet him, Forrest had a ragtag outfit of about 3,500 men, roughly 3,200 of whom he had recently recruited and trained. Forrest, would later say, however, that only 2,500 men rode with him. Smith was anxious to get at Forrest, and Forrest would soon afford him that opportunity. Indeed, Forrest would afford Smith multiple opportunities to "get at him."

In a series of lightning attacks beginning at West Point, Mississippi, up through, and culminating in, the Battle of Okolona, Forrest drove the feckless Smith back to Memphis in disarray. At one point in his pursuit of

Smith, Forrest came upon a position held by Union troops where his own troops had halted. "Where is the enemy's whole position?" he asked. "You see it, General....They are preparing to charge."

"Then we will charge them," Forrest said. And they did. The result was another blue rout.[106]

Sherman said that "Smith...permitted Forrest to head him off and defeat him with an inferior force."[107] It was an ignominious defeat for the best-equipped cavalry in the world.

Next came a raid that took Forrest's cavalry as far north as Paducah, Kentucky, on the Ohio River. Recruiting as he went, Forrest added about 2,000 men to his cavalry before heading for what would become one of the most controversial incidents of the entire war: the Fort Pillow assault on April 12, 1864. There, a Union force of roughly 550 men—about a half of them free blacks—held a fort that originally had been constructed by Confederates. By the time Forrest arrived at mid-morning on the twelfth, his subordinate Chalmers had already surrounded the fort and moved into position beneath the four-foot-thick earthen walls for the final assault.

Around 1:00 p.m., Forrest sent a surrender demand to the Union commanding officer, Major L.F. Booth. Forrest stated in his note that he could take the fort by assault and concluded, "[I]f compelled to do so you must take the consequences....Should my demand be refused, I cannot be responsible for the fate of your command."[108] Booth, however, had been killed, and his replacement, Major William F. Bradford, came back to Forrest with a request for an hour to deliberate. Forrest, however, fearing reinforcement from Union boats that he could see steaming toward them, rejected the request for an hour and instead offered twenty minutes, stating, "If in that time this demand is not complied with I will immediately proceed to assault your works, and you must take the consequences." Bradford, after consultation with his officers, refused.[109] Forrest then said, "We must take them," and the assault was underway. From their positions below the fort's walls, with the defenders pinned down by devastatingly accurate rifle fire from Confederate sharpshooters, Forrest's men attacked, firing as they went over the walls. The fight was over almost before it had begun. The Union troops who survived the assault ran from the fort to the river, hoping that an approaching gunboat would protect them with its cannon fire. It did not.

What followed has been a source of controversy and debate for 150 years. There is no question that killing followed the successful assault, although there was never a formal surrender by the Union forces, either in the fort or at the river, where some indeed continued to fight. On the other hand, survivors recalled the

Confederate cry of "No quarter." Forrest, the weight of authority holds, did not order the killing and indeed rode into the field ordering a stop to the fighting and killing. By the time the killing ended, 221 out of 557 Union troops were dead, and 63 percent had been either killed or wounded.

Shortly after the "Fort Pillow Massacre," as it was termed, a Congressional committee appeared at the fort to conduct an investigation. The committee interviewed survivors and subsequently concluded that a massacre had taken place. They found that Forrest's men had, among other acts, burned and buried prisoners alive and killed women and children during the massacre. They discovered, however, no bodies. Shelby Foote stated that those allegations were mostly lies. Foote also noted that after the Congressional committee promulgated the results of its investigation, Grant and Lincoln ordered Sherman to investigate and, if he found that the Confederates had killed Union troops as or after they were surrendering or afterward, to retaliate. Sherman, Foote pointed out, never ordered such retaliation.

After Forrest moved south, Union general Samuel Sturgis was the next commander with orders to destroy Forrest's command, and he thus headed south from Memphis in search of the elusive Forrest. There were two encounters: at the first, Forrest and his men successfully avoided Sturgis, and at the second, Forrest achieved his greatest victory at a little settlement called Brice's Crossroads. There, his men tore into Sturgis's force and, after ripping it apart, sent the survivors scampering back to Memphis in one of the North's most humiliating defeats of the war. Sherman, outraged by the defeat at Brice's Crossroads, said, "There will never be peace in Tennessee until Forrest is dead....I know I would have been willing to attempt the same task [as the one he had assigned to Sturgis] with that force; but Forrest is the devil and I think he has got some of our troops under cower."[110]

Forrest then raided as far north as Fort Heiman, Kentucky, and, amazingly, attacked Union shipping on the Tennessee River. In this encounter, Forrest's men captured and manned several Union gunboats (they became known as "Forrest's Marines") and so frightened Union forces that Forrest's men destroyed $2.2 million in supplies—Forrest said that they had destroyed $6.7 million in public property—and the Union forces abandoned their huge Johnsonville depot. "The campaign against Johnsonville would earn Forrest his second colorful nickname during the war. Sherman would never again refer to his old antagonist as the Wizard of the Saddle. His newest reference to Forrest was personal, because to Sherman, Forrest had become a demon that he could not seem to exorcize. As he said, 'That devil Forrest was down around Johnsonville making havoc among the gunboats and transports.'"[111]

Grant, in his memoirs, would say, "Forrest indeed performed the very remarkable feat of capturing, with cavalry, two gunboats and a number of transports, something the accomplishment of which is very hard to account for."[112] Indeed it remains "hard to account for" to this day.

But trouble lay on the horizon for Forrest and the Confederacy in Forrest's theater of operations. John Bell Hood, defeated repeatedly around Atlanta by Sherman, decided to attack Sherman's supply line coming into Nashville and then head north for the Ohio River. He hoped to recruit additional troops as he progressed and then move ultimately to Virginia, where he would join up with Lee's Army of Northern Virginia. Forrest now had command of all the cavalry in the Army of Tennessee and led that force into Tennessee. In his first encounter with a superior force of Union cavalry led by General James H. Wilson, Forrest outmaneuvered and then beat Wilson's force. But beginning at Franklin on November 30, the worm began to turn. Wilson's troopers first held their own against Forrest's troopers, and then, near Murfreesboro on December 7, Wilson's cavalry prevailed against Forrest in what would become known as the Battle of the Cedars, in which Confederate foot soldiers panicked, leaving Forrest's left flank exposed and leading to a rout of his force.

In the meantime, Hood's army had suffered disastrous defeats at Franklin and Nashville and had begun its long and disorganized retreat toward Corinth, Mississippi. Forrest's cavalry shielded Hood's rear echelon with, as a Union officer would later recount, "his audacious temper and enterprising cavalry."[113] The end loomed large on the near horizon, however, and Wilson's cavalry relentlessly pursued Forrest into Alabama as 1865 arrived. Ultimate defeat for Forrest and the Confederacy came inexorably on March 2, 1865. Forrest was promoted to lieutenant general, and with his outnumbered corps, he continued to oppose Wilson's mighty force of twenty-two thousand cavalrymen, fifteen thousand of whom carried seven-shot Spencer carbines. Finally, at Selma, on April 2, Wilson's cavalry overwhelmed Forrest's Corps, and on May 4, the Confederate forces in that region surrendered. On May 9, Forrest bade farewell to his troops, and his "critter cavalry" returned to their homes.

During the war, the rarely defeated Forrest was the only lieutenant general in either army to advance from private to that rank. He had twenty-nine horses shot from beneath him, and he had personally killed or seriously maimed at least thirty enemy soldiers in hand-to-hand combat. Forrest had also suffered four wounds. But he had survived, and it was now time for Bedford Forrest to go home.[114]

POSTWAR

On May 13, 1865, a northern writer named Bryan McAlister had a conversation with Forrest, to whom he referred as "the controversial Confederate." They met in a small cabin "dimly lit by small tallow candles." Forrest did not know that McAlister was a writer and spoke freely to him throughout the interview. McAlister described Forrest as "a man of fine appearance, about six feet in height, having dark piercing hazel eyes, a carefully trimmed moustache, and chin-whiskers, dark as night, finely cut features and iron-gray hair. [His] lithe figure connoted great physical power and activity. McAlister said he "would have marked him as a prominent man had I seen him on Broadway; and when I was told that he was the Forrest of Fort Pillow, I devoted my whole attention to him."[115] He continued:

> *But the heart sickens at the infamous conduct of this butcher. He is one of the few men that are general "blowers," and yet he will fight. Forrest is a thorough bravo—a desperate man in every respect. He was a Negro trader before the war and in "personal affairs," as he calls them, had killed several men. He has two brothers living, one of whom is spoken of as a greater butcher than the lieutenant general. He, the lieutenant general is a man without education or refinement, married, I believe, to a very pretty wife. Any one* [sic] *hearing him talk, would call him a braggadocio. As for myself, I believe one half* [of what] *he said, and only dispute with him with one finger on the trigger of my pistol.*[116]

Forrest went home by train from Gainesville, Alabama, heading for his plantation at Sunflower Landing in Coahoma County, Mississippi. He did not qualify for the mass pardon issued by President Andrew Johnson immediately after the war—it did not extend to Confederate generals, among other high-ranking Confederate officials—so Forrest went to Jackson, Mississippi, and applied to President Johnson for an individual pardon. It would take three long years for his pardon to come through.

Once home, Forrest began farming, using former slave labor to plant corn. He associated seven Union officers in his farming enterprises and worked with some of the officers on his two plantations. Forrest helped the others find their own plantations. Through the Freedmen's Bureau and with the help of his new Yankee friends, he hired 140 laborers, the largest use of black labor in that region. Unfortunately, however, Forrest still had promissory notes from the war—he had outfitted his cavalry at his own expense, and those notes were coming due—so on September 16, 1865, he sold 1,445 acres of his 3,400-acre enterprise to Henry Chambers, from whom he had originally purchased the land. Forrest then used the proceeds to open a sawmill, entering into a partnership with three Memphis businessmen about this time as commission merchants of everything from cotton to cigars, with wine and liquors in between. Their business was located at 278 Front Street in Memphis, but it failed, a portent of things to come.

Besides his economic problems, the miasma of vengeance was in the northern air, and Forrest, along with Jefferson Davis and Admiral Raphael Semmes, stood head and shoulders above most Confederate officers—Robert E. Lee was the other—as prime targets of Union revenge. Virulent articles began to appear in northern newspapers, and Forrest's friends became concerned that federal authorities would soon arrest and try him for treason, as well as for the Fort Pillow Massacre. They urged him to leave the country. Forrest, however, said, "I certainly do not intend to leave this country, for my destiny is now with the great American Union, and I shall contribute all of my influence toward strengthening the Government, sustaining its credits, and uniting the people once more in the indissoluble bonds of peace and affection."[117]

Union authorities arrested Raphael Semmes in Mobile, and the noose tightened around the neck of Jefferson Davis. Finally, the authorities indicted Forrest in federal district court in Memphis on a treason charge, and he appeared at the Clerk's Office on March 13, 1866, to post a $10,000 bond. Nothing came of this indictment, although another legal problem loomed.

On March 31, 1866, Forrest heard the screams of a woman in one of the cabins on his plantation and went into the cabin to find a free black man named Thomas Edwards beating his wife with a piece of firewood. Recognizing that the beating would soon result in the woman's death, Forrest ordered Edwards to stop. When he refused and cursed Forrest, the general hit him on the head with a broomstick. Edwards then lunged at Forrest with a hunting knife, wounding him in the hand. Forrest retreated, and as he reached for the door handle behind him, his hand found an axe in a kindling box. As Edwards charged, Forrest came up swinging and split Edwards's skull open, killing him instantly.

Slavery was dead, and with its death had passed the days when a white man could kill a black man with impunity. The next day, some two hundred black men, members of a self-styled "militia," marched on Forrest's home. Only he and his wife, Mary Ann, were there, and as the mob marched up to his house, Forrest went out onto the front porch. "Halt!" he ordered. The company halted. "Order arms!" he shouted at them. The men grounded their weapons. "Now get out of here and go back to work."[118] Another version has it that Forrest came out on the porch armed with two pistols and ordered the crowd to disperse or he would "shoot all their damn heads off." In either case, the mob turned and left. Forrest was indicted, and on October 1866, Forrest's trial was held before a black magistrate and a jury in Clarksdale. He was found not guilty.

The decline of Forrest's economic fortunes began to accelerate. He owed $30,000 to a Nashville group, and in February 1866, he entered into an agreement setting forth a schedule of payments that he was supposed to make for the remainder of the year. Pursuant to the agreement, if by January 1, 1867, he had not met the schedule of payments, he was to sell the remaining 1,900 acres of his plantation to satisfy the debt. In March 1866, he had to put up the $10,000 for the bond on his treason indictment, and when he could not make the scheduled payments on the Nashville debt, he sold off the rest of his land in early April 1866 and began sharecropping the land he had formerly owned.

A disastrous flood in late April, however, wiped out his cotton crop on the land that he sharecropped. Bedford Forrest was done with farming, at least for now. His dream of being a Delta planter had ended. It was now time to return to his old hometown and try another way to make a living, which, after moving to Memphis later in 1866, he undertook.

His earlier venture in the brokerage business had failed by the middle of November 1866, so Forrest entered the fire insurance business as president of a firm that he started, but that enterprise came to naught. At the same time that he entered the insurance business, he entered the railroad construction business in a venture—with others—to construct a railroad from Memphis to Little Rock, with the desire to extend it to Fort Smith subsequently. This was to be the first of several railroad ventures for Forrest, and for the railroad's construction, he began using labor from the Arkansas Freedmen's Bureau. The Arkansas endeavor required Forrest to travel, however, and he feared that travel would violate the terms of his parole. He wrote, therefore, to President Johnson and asked Johnson to expand the terms of his parole to permit travel to Washington and New York to raise capital for the railroad. Johnson granted the request.

Other events in the Deep South, however, began to draw his attention. In Pulaski, Tennessee, six young Confederate veterans—described as "a small clique of bored war veterans perhaps looking for some excitement"—started a new fraternal organization. The founders were college-educated men and were interested in social fraternities just beginning to gain traction at southern colleges and universities. Accordingly, they selected for the name of their new organization, Kappa Alpha, a fraternity founded at Washington College in Lexington, Virginia, which would soon become Washington and Lee. Kappa Alpha (or "Kuklos Adelphion") "corrupted the Greek word *kuklos*, meaning 'circle,' into the weirder-sounding 'Kuklux.'" Another suggested name had been the "Lost Clan of the Cocletz," which was derived from "an obscure Indian Legend," so to Kuklux they thus added "Klan," and thus was born the Ku Klux Klan in late 1865 or early 1866. Contrary to popular belief, Forrest had nothing to do with the Klan's founding.

The men began wearing "Halloween-style sheets" and galloped wildly down Pulaski's streets on horses. The nocturnal rides engendered terror among superstitious black citizens, who fled into their homes in terror, believing the riders to be "ha'nts" and ghosts of the Confederate dead. "The Klan had stumbled upon a power mightier than that of the law: superstitious terror, which was soon recognized, carefully cultivated and preserved."[119]

The Klan grew meteorically and quickly spun out of the control of its six founders. In April 1867, a convention met secretly in Nashville and drew up rules governing membership and officers. In the meantime, someone approached Forrest about joining the organization, and Klan tradition has it that Forrest said, "That's a good thing; that's a damned good thing. We can use that to keep the niggers in their place." Tradition also holds that Forrest left Memphis immediately for Nashville, where, through the auspices of one of his Civil War subordinates, he joined the Klan. Whether these precise facts are true will never be known because of the extreme secrecy surrounding the organization. Klan tradition also holds that the grand wizard position was first "offered to Robert E. Lee, who replied that his health would not permit him to serve, but wrote a letter approving of the Klan and saying his support had to be 'invisible.'" Lee is also purported to have endorsed Forrest—the Klan's second choice—as an outstanding man to head it. Lee scholars, however, consider this story apocryphal. Nonetheless, based on later testimony that Lee gave to Congress, Lee's views were similar to those of the Klan, and the Klan did become the "invisible empire," suggesting perhaps that the "invisible" part may have indeed been derived from Lee. Again, because of the shroud of secrecy that veils the Klan's early operations, we shall never know.

With his earlier railroad construction and fire insurance business defunct, Forrest, in May 1867, entered the life insurance business as president of the Planters' Insurance Company of Tennessee. By March of the next year, that business, too, had failed, and Forrest took bankruptcy. He then became a principal in a street-paving firm, but his business and financial misfortune continued and that firm was soon out of business.

Then came one of Forrest's most incredible ideas: mounting an invasion of Mexico. Forrest posited that he could raise an army of 30,000, conquer Mexico in six months, take possession of all mines and church property and be anointed either king or president. This arrangement, he believed, would draw 200,000 people from the southern states, as well as immigrants from Europe and settlers from the North. "He said there are at least 50,000 young men in the South who won't plow, but who would fight or dig for gold." When asked whether he thought the United States might intervene to prevent such an invasion, Forrest said that they would be glad to be rid of him.

In March 1867, Congress passed the Congressional Reconstruction Act, and the next month, the Nashville convention of the KKK promulgated rules for membership, for officers of the organization and for expansion of the Klan to other locations. It was at this meeting that the members likely elected Forrest grand wizard and subsequently confronted the realities of Congressional Reconstruction: enfranchised Republican blacks electing blacks to public offices. With black voters ascending to control of the political machinery of southern cities and even states, white Democrats like the Klan's founders feared the worst. It was, therefore, in this "political hothouse" that the Klan—now predicated on violence—spread throughout the South like the botanical cancer kudzu would later. There is evidence that Forrest was heavily involved in its metastasis.

On June 1, 1868, Forrest was a delegate to the Tennessee State Convention organized to reinstitute "constitutional authority" in Tennessee, which meant, primarily, reenfranchising some seventy thousand white Tennesseans while denying the right of black Tennesseans to vote, sit on juries and hold office. The delegates conceded only that the war had resulted in the abolition of slavery; with that declaration, they were willing to accept the Constitution and the supremacy of the federal government.

Later in June, and next in his political career, came Forrest's selection as a delegate to the Democratic National Convention in New York. Attendance at the convention gave rise to the following story:

> *One morning, according to a story apparently handed down through the Forrest family, he was in his hotel room still in his nightshirt when a knock came on the door. He told Willie to answer it, and the opened door revealed an austerely dressed woman carrying a Bible and an umbrella.*

> *She moved past Willie into the room where the just-rising Forrest, hair still sleep-disheveled, was seated on his bed. "Are you the Rebel General Forrest?" she is reported to have abruptly inquired. "And is it true you murdered those dear colored people at Fort Pillow? Tell me, sir; I want no evasive answer." The answer she reportedly received was so direct that it was remembered to have sent her screaming down the hallway into the street. Rising from his bed to his full six feet one and a half, the Butcher replied: "Yes, madam. I killed the men and women for my soldier's dinner and ate the babies myself for breakfast."*[120]

On July 17, 1868, Forrest finally received a pardon from President Andrew Johnson, whom he had supported for president while at the convention in New York. In 1868, he again entered the railroad business when he, with his partners, sought to resurrect a line not extant since before the war and combine it with other lines to create a continuous railroad from Memphis to Selma, Alabama, with a line east to the coal and iron deposits in what was to become Birmingham, Alabama, and another west into the east Mississippi cotton and grain fields. The line would connect to another line running east to the Atlantic Seaboard at Brunswick, Georgia, and eventually, the founders hoped, it would run from Selma south to Mobile.

Klan violence continued to rise all over the South, and Forrest saw it as a threat to business, so sometime in late 1868 or early 1869, Forrest, still grand wizard, issued an order abolishing robes and banning whippings and other punitive acts. Subsequently, at some point in either 1869 or 1870, Forrest resigned as grand wizard and ordered the Klan to disband. Some historians, however, question whether Forrest really ordered the dissolution of the Klan.

On March 9, 1869, Forrest encountered a reporter from the *Louisville Courier-Journal* aboard a train from Memphis to Jackson, Mississippi, and in an interview as they passed through abandoned farmland, he said that the South and Mississippi could be repopulated by black residents "gotten from Africa." He said that these blacks were "the best laborers we have ever had in the South" and told the reporter of his interest in a slave trading ship before the war and how only 6 percent of the slaves had died on the voyage to America. "They were fond of grasshoppers and bugs but I taught them to eat cooked meat, and they were as good niggers as any I ever had." Forrest also liked the idea of bringing in one thousand Chinese to work on his railroad and didn't think there would be "enmity" toward them on the part of blacks.[121]

Congress outlawed the Klan in April 1871, and the Ku Klux Committee subpoenaed Forrest to testify, which he did on June 27, 1871. For four hours, he and the committee "played a game of cat and mouse." The committee was never able to pin him down about his membership in the Klan or gain much information about the Klan itself, as Forrest claimed that everything he knew was secondhand. The proceeding closed with a greatly frustrated and highly agitated committee. Forrest's was a masterful performance.

Construction of his railroad continued, and the old problem of Forrest's temper flared up again when he chastised an Alabama construction contractor named Shepherd for failing to do the job to Forrest's satisfaction. Shepherd challenged Forrest to a duel, and Forrest accepted immediately. "He set the terms as his favorite weapons, 'Navy six' pistols, from ten paces at sunrise the following morning." That night, however, he had second thoughts, not out of fear of harm to himself, but from fear that if he killed the man, he would regret it for the rest of his life. The next morning, Forrest apologized to Shepherd, who was happy to let the dispute drop, and the matter was closed.[122]

Forrest also got cross with a former Union general named Judson Kilpatrick, who in several speeches had denigrated Forrest for his conduct at Fort Pillow. Forrest wrote a letter to the *New York Times* in which he denounced Kilpatrick as a "blackguard, a liar, a scoundrel, and a poltroon." He subsequently challenged Kilpatrick to a duel and suggested that they fight it out "on horseback with sabers." Fitzpatrick, however, refused to duel Forrest, as he said Forrest was not a gentleman.[123]

While construction of his railroad continued into 1872, Forrest traveled to New York, and subsequently to Detroit, to raise money. On the latter visit, a reporter interviewed him "and found his hair 'as white as seventy, but his face and figure look no more than forty.'" At this point, he envisioned not only the Brunswick, Georgia eastern leg of his railroad but also a western leg that would run to Kansas City and then hook up with the Northern Pacific to connect the East and the West Coasts. Neither trip was, however, successful in raising money for his increasingly impecunious railroad. Then the Franco-Prussian War and the yellow fever epidemic in the summer of 1873 brought about a financial panic that year, and throughout the United States, railroads were put under great economic stress. Finally, financial irregularities with the railroad's expenditures became an issue when it was alleged that the railroad had spent only about half of what Forrest had taken in and reported as spent. Investors began pulling out, and the municipalities—Memphis and Shelby County principally—refused further support. The railroad defaulted on its bonds, and the receivers took over and sold the railroad. Forrest resigned in March 1874 and lost his home in Memphis. His next home was to be a log house on President's Island in the Mississippi River, similar to the one into which he and Mary Ann had moved in 1845. Willie, his son, and his family also moved out of Forrest's house, and Willie, who had been employed by the railroad, went to work for the Memphis Police Department.

War clouds were on the horizon, or so Forrest thought. It appeared that the United States and Spain might fight over Cuba. Forrest was ready to go. He wrote to General Sherman, then commander of the U.S. Army, volunteering to fight and stating that he thought he could bring one thousand to five thousand of his former soldiers with him. General Sherman wrote back that he did not think there would be a war but that he would forward Forrest's note to the War Department. In his cover letter to the War Department, Sherman stated that "Forrest was one of the most extraordinary men developed by our Civil War, and were it left to me in the event of a war requiring cavalry, I would unhesitatingly accept his services and give him a prominent place. I believe now he would fight against our national enemies as vehemently as he did against us, and that is saying enough."[124]

Klan violence continued to ravage the South, and the murder of sixteen black citizens in Trenton, Tennessee, precipitated a strong reaction against the savagery. Forrest, along with Jefferson Davis, attended a meeting in Memphis to express "indignation" with the crime. Forrest, however, went further. He said that "if he were entrusted with proper authority he would capture and exterminate the white marauders who disgrace their race by this cowardly murder of negroes." His attack on the members of the organization he had once headed engendered a firestorm of criticism and vitriol aimed at Forrest, much of it in the Trenton newspaper. Forrest believed that such violence, however, was no longer necessary, as the Democrats were seizing power and would soon be able to assert it over black citizens by peaceful means.

Then, in April 1875, Forrest, earlier tarred with financial irregularities associated with his railroad, began to reclaim his reputation. He had become, once again, active in Democratic Party politics, and he began to participate in Confederate commemorative events, leading a 120-man "escort" in "a huge Memphis Memorial Day parade," then sitting on the speaker's stand with Jefferson Davis, among others. At this time, amazingly, a group of black citizens invited Forrest to speak at a barbecue, and he accepted. The event took place without incident, and Forrest expressed relief that he had not been roasted.

On President's Island, he undertook a return to farming and leased 1,300 acres that he would work with convict labor. Forrest also began cutting timber to supply the Memphis market with firewood that winter. In Memphis, people often saw him on the streets in "the plain clothes of a farmer." Nevertheless, his temper remained. Forrest became enraged when a Memphis tailor allowed moths to damage a suit of his clothes and threatened to "shoot [him] like a rat." The next day, however, he apologized.[125]

A major development occurred in Forrest's life as 1875 drew to a close. He began attending church and shortly after his first service announced, "All is right. I put my trust in my Redeemer." He had become a Christian, but his conversion notwithstanding, Forrest hired counsel and sued his old railroad, the Memphis and Selma, for debt he had incurred personally for the railroad. While farming on President's Island, he used 117 prisoners to farm that land. They were overseen by 7 guards he had hired. The malarial climate there began to affect his health, which, in the aftermath of the war, was already less than robust.

On September 21, 1876, he attended a reunion of the famed Seventh Tennessee Cavalry and gave a speech from horseback. That was to be his last reunion, as his health began to decline rapidly. His nemesis was chronic diarrhea, caused, it is believed, by a "malarial infection" that was, in turn, engendered by the swampy land and noxious night airs that produced these kinds of illnesses.

By the spring of 1877, he was no longer able to oversee his farming operations on a daily basis, and in April, he visited the first of several mineral springs resorts, this one at Hot Springs, Arkansas. Weakened by illness, with his weight now down to 120 pounds, Forrest was barely recognizable as he traveled next to Hurricane Springs, Alabama, in a fruitless effort to stem the tide of disease.

Forrest also instructed his lawyer to drop all remaining lawsuits. "He described himself as 'broken in health and spirit,' having 'not long to live.' His life, he reflected, had 'been a battle from the start…a fight to achieve a livelihood for those dependent upon me in my younger days, and an independence for myself when I grew up to manhood, as well as in the terrible turmoil of the Civil War. I have seen too much of violence, and I want to close my days at peace with all the world, as I am now at peace with my Maker.'"[126]

A friend confirmed Forrest's new demeanor: "He had about him a new mildness, a softness of expression, and gentleness in his words that appeared to me strange and unnatural.…At first I thought his bad health had brought about this change, but then I remembered that when sick or wounded he was the most restless and impatient man I ever saw." That same friend told Forrest that he did not seem to be the same man. Forrest was silent and then said, "I am not the man you were with so long and knew so well—I hope I am a better man. I've joined the church and am trying to live a Christian life....I want you to know that between me and...the face of my Heavenly Father, not a cloud intervenes."[127]

Autumn came, and Forrest next visited the mineral springs resort at Bailey Springs, Alabama, which failed to slow the inexorable decline of the old warrior, caused, the *New York Times* wrote, by "the poisonous night air of President's Island." Forrest returned to Memphis and, after a brief stay at his home on the island, moved to his brother Jesse's house in Memphis. It was late October, and the end was near. Jefferson Davis, then a resident of Memphis, visited him on October 29, 1877, but Forrest struggled to recognize him. Then, late that evening, and unlike his fellow warriors Lee and Jackson, whose last words were reportedly of battle (although in Lee's case, that is disputed), Forrest said simply, "Call my wife." And then he died.

Bedford Forrest's funeral was one for the ages. First, the *Appeal* announced his death on its front page, which was bordered in black. Then, the body lay in state—Forrest dressed in the uniform of a Confederate lieutenant general—while hundreds, black and white, streamed by the coffin to view Forrest's "emaciated corpse." The funeral took place on Halloween day 1877, and "the funeral procession was over two miles long and included hundreds of Negroes." A brass band preceded a hearse pulled by four black horses, and his pallbearers included Jefferson Davis and Jacob Thompson, a prewar congressman and former secretary of the interior. What followed was a long line of some three thousand participants, including former cavalrymen, mounted, and his soldiers on foot. They buried him at Elmwood Cemetery.[128]

The *New York Times*—not unexpectedly—published a scathing obituary based mostly on the Fort Pillow massacre. Conceding that Forrest may "have been the most formidable cavalry commander then in the armies of the south," he was, nevertheless, guerrilla-like in his methods of warfare and "hadn't the scientific daring of a Joe Wheeler." The *Times* referred to Lee's more gentlemanly cavalier betters from Virginia and posited that Forrest was typical of the "reckless ruffianism and cutthroat daring of the Southwest's rude border country: bloodthirsty and revengeful." It referred to him repeatedly as "Fort Pillow Forrest."[129]

But there were others, on both sides, who sang a different tune. Sherman, for example, "proclaimed him 'the most remarkable man' the war produced 'with a genius for strategy which was original and…to me, incomprehensible.…He seemed always to know what I was doing or intended to do, while I…could never…form any satisfactory idea of what he was trying to accomplish.'" Joseph E. Johnston, when asked who was the greatest soldier of the war, answered "Forrest" unequivocally. He said that if Forrest had enjoyed the advantages of an education, he would have been the war's "great central figure." And P.G.T. Beauregard remarked that Forrest's "capacity for war seemed only to be limited by the opportunities of its display."[130] Finally, Robert E. Lee himself said that Forrest "was the greatest genius to have emerged during the war."

At Forrest's funeral, Jefferson Davis expressed regret that senior western generals like Bragg and Joseph E. Johnston had not better utilized Forrest's talents. Davis said that he himself "never knew how to measure Forrest until, impressed by his exploits in 1864, he had gone back and reread Forrest's earlier reports and come to the conclusion that Forrest was actually a great general."[131]

What Forrest brought to the battlefield that was new and different was the concept of mounted, and thus mobile, *infantry*, his "foot cavalry." They could ride like cavalry and fight like infantry, and Britain's Viscount Wolseley, "distinguished retired commander of Britain's armies," wrote a magazine article on Forrest in 1892 in which he emphasized this element of Forrest's amazing ability to strike when and where it was unexpected and his equally amazing ability to defeat larger opponents. Wolseley went on to say that "his mind was not narrowed by military apothegms learnt by rote. His operations…seem as if designed by a military professor, so thoroughly are the tactics…in accordance with common sense and business principles."

Wolseley wrote of Forrest's recklessness in leading his troops and in attacking with cavalry in the front and the rear while his dismounted troops attacked the flanks. He could always, Wolseley concluded, find the weak point and exploit it, which he did time and again. He concluded by saying, "If ever England has to fight for her existence…may we have at the head of our government as wise and far-seeing a patriot as Mr. Lincoln, and to lead our mounted forces as able a soldier as General Forrest."[132]

In 1914, as Britain did indeed fight for its life in France, an American army observer, Colonel Granville Sevier, met a British officer in a bookstore in Piccadilly. The British officer was looking for a copy of John Wyeth's

1899 biography of Forrest—cited extensively herein—and Sevier had just noticed one in a bookcase, to which he referred the British officer. Colonel Sevier said that he had known both Wyeth and Forrest and that General Forrest had placed him on his first horse. The British officer was amazed and engaged Sevier in a conversation about Forrest.

Then it was Sevier's turn to be amazed: the British officer knew far more about Forrest than did Sevier. "How?" Sevier asked. The officer answered, "Officers of our British cavalry service study his campaigns and his methods….We regard him as one of the greatest, if not the greatest, English-speaking commanders of mounted troops." The officer left, and Sevier, on his way out, asked the proprietor the name of the British officer to whom he had just spoken. The proprietor, a Mr. Buchanan, held up a full-page newspaper photograph of a man.

"Is this the man?" Buchanan asked.

"Yes," Sevier said.

"That is Sir Douglas Haig," Buchanan said.

Haig's Corps had just fought and won the First Battle of Ypres, and he would go on to command all British forces in France.[133] A Forrest biographer noted:

> *Today military thinkers consider Forrest not just…the South's preeminent cavalryman at the end of the war but indeed the greatest American cavalryman of all time. His revolutionary fundamental philosophy was to attack even if severely outnumbered and, once the initiative had been thus seized, to pursue with a brutal relentlessness that was extraordinary in military history; this principle presaged the German blitzkrieg of 1940 and the airborne Allied behind-the-lines assaults of 1944. Revolutionary, too, was Forrest's frequent use of cannon as assault weapons accompanying his forward troops. His repeated division of forces in the presence of overpowering enemies, his cunning acumen for deceit and duplicity, his continual ability to make much of virtually nothing, his genius for employing whatever material was at hand, and his indomitable refusal to countenance effort less than total became lessons for later soldiers receiving the formal military education he never had the benefit of. His excellence as a raider was by no means all he left to military posterity, either. There were his incessant habit of assaulting from flanks and rear as well as head-on; his mastery of the psychology of the "skeer" and the intricate mechanics of inspiring it and keeping it operative; his instinctive grasp of the potentialities of terrain and weather, and such under-fire originality as the order to Morton's artillery*

> *to charge with neither cavalry nor infantry support at Brice's Cross Roads. The beating he administered to the Federals there was one of the worst ever suffered by a unit of the United States Army.*[134]

There is now, therefore, less attention devoted to Fort Pillow and more to Forrest's genius as a military commander. As noted, there are still many who—erroneously—believe that he was the founder of the Ku Klux Klan. Indeed, as Forrest aged, his views on race mellowed, as evidenced by the black barbecue he attended as well as the large number of black citizens who attended his viewing and who marched in his funeral procession.

Mary Ann died in 1893 and was interred beside her husband at Elmwood. Both were reinterred in 1905 in Forrest Park beneath an equestrian stature of Forrest, which has since been removed. Willie, their son, became a successful railroad and levee contractor. One of Willie's sons, Nathan Bedford Forrest II, became head of the Nathan Bedford Forrest Klan Number One in Atlanta, which was a capstone of the Klan that arose in the early part of the twentieth century. Nathan Bedford Forrest III, the last male in Bedford's direct line, was a brigadier general in the U.S. Army Air Corps and was the first American general to die in World War II.[135]

Perhaps the best epitaph of Bedford Forrest is this:

> *Because these soldiers of his believed in him—in his devotion to his cause and to his soldiers, in his courage which took account of dangers but was not daunted, in his immense common sense that spent effort and men only with reason—because the men who marched along with him, aching weary, staggering sleepy, starving hungry, believed in him, they would march for him a little farther and a little faster, and fight for him a little harder. His was the power, as one of his young soldiers said more than sixty years after, to "Make heroes out of common mortals"—the true power of the handfuls of truly great captains.*[136]

Chapter 5
JOHN BELL HOOD

"Sam"

BEGINNINGS

John Bell Hood was a native Kentuckian descended from ancestors who immigrated to New York in 1696 and then migrated south through Virginia into Kentucky. Hood's father, John W. Hood, was a prosperous physician who farmed about six hundred acres near Owingsville, Kentucky, "in the rolling farmland around his house and who may have owned as many as thirty slaves."[137] Hood's ancestors were Virginia planter aristocracy, and in Kentucky, they sought to replicate the Virginia plantation lifestyle. Their emphasis on the "southern way of life" was grounded in a belief that the southern lifestyle was superior. That belief arose out of a southern strain of romanticism that found voice in the "myth of Southern chivalry: the belief that white Southerners were the descendants of the feudal, Norman aristocracy of England, and, as such, were characterized by the virtues associated with aristocrats."[138] It was into this cultural milieu that John Bell Hood was born on June 29, 1831, and all of these cultural currents and cross-currents were to dramatically shape his personality and, thus, his life.[139]

John Bell Hood. *Library of Congress.*

West Point

After education in a local private school, Hood entered West Point on July 1, 1849, where he would be known for some unknown reason as "Sam." There existed at West Point a strict code of regulations governing cadet conduct: no whiskey, no smoking, no cards and even—amazingly—no chess. Enforcement, however, was lax, and cadets frequented a nearby tavern (probably the Benny Havens, immortalized to this day in song), smoked and stole chickens and geese from local farmers to cook in their rooms. They slipped out into the night to nearby dances and smuggled prostitutes into the barracks. Hood, based on his record of demerits, was likely no exception to the conduct of his peers. Indeed, the superintendent, Robert E. Lee, nearly expelled him for "an unauthorized visit to a local tavern."[140]

With 200 demerits in a year the magic number for dismissal. Hood received only 18 his plebe year but by his second year was up to 66. His third year brought 94, and in his senior year he tested the limits, accumulating 196. Hood was not an exceptional student—indeed he was not even a *good* student—finishing forty-fourth out of fifty-two graduating cadets. In fairness, however, only half of the cadets who entered West Point with Hood graduated.

The academy fostered a type of elitism among its cadets, a belief that they were—like Hood's antecedents—aristocrats. That culture was reflected in the chosen Protestant denomination of the chapel at West Point: Episcopal. Hood's classmates at West Point included future Union generals John M. Schofield, James B. McPherson and Philip H. Sheridan and Confederate generals Jeb Stuart and William D. Pender. From the class behind Hood's came Stephen D. Lee. George Thomas was Hood's cavalry and artillery instructor. He would become a Union general and face off with Hood at Nashville. It was to Robert E. Lee that "Hood formed an attachment" and whose many virtues Hood sought to emulate. Lee, however, demoted Hood from cadet lieutenant to private for a rules infraction and, as noted, almost expelled him.[141]

Post West Point

Upon graduation from the academy, Hood received a commission in the infantry and, after a furlough, headed west for California by way of Panama and San Francisco, where he met William T. Sherman, "a nervous, red-headed former army officer…with [a] piercing eye and a nervous, impulsive temperament." Hood's initial assignment was to Company E of the Fourth Infantry Regiment at Fort Jones, an isolated installation in the northern part of the state, whose troops were there primarily to watch over the Indians in the vicinity.[142] There were thirty-four officers and men at Fort Jones. The officers hunted game, which was plentiful; grew and sold crops; engaged in land speculation; and gambled heavily. Some "drank to forget their loneliness." While at Fort Jones, Hood met future Union general George Crook from the West Point class of 1852.[143]

Next, Hood transferred to the Second Cavalry, which was stationed at the famous Jefferson Barracks in St. Louis and was to become one of the most storied units in American military history, primarily because of the outstanding lineup of officers who served in it. The unit was organized in 1855 specifically for service on the Texas frontier, and Jefferson Davis, secretary of war for President Franklin Pierce, personally handpicked its officers, who were mostly West Point graduates and southerners. The regiment produced sixteen general officers in the six and a half years that it existed—eleven future Confederate generals and five Union. Four of the eleven Confederate generals became full generals, half of all of the full generals in the Confederate army: Albert Sidney Johnston, Robert E. Lee, Edmund Kirby Smith and Hood. Among the other generals who served in the Second were George H. Thomas—Hood's instructor at West Point, who would become "one of the more able Federal army commanders," as Hood would one day learn to his sorrow—William J. Hardee, Earl Van Dorn and George Stoneman, immortalized in the original version of "The Night They Drove Old Dixie Down." The Second Cavalry was Robert E. Lee's last command in the in the U.S. Army.

The most significant engagement fought by the regiment in Texas was the Battle of Devils River on July 20, 1858. On that date, Lieutenant John Bell Hood, with a detachment of twenty-five men from Company G, fought a combined force of Comanches and Lipan Apache warriors. It was estimated that of a party out of fifty warriors, nine Indians were killed and at least double that number injured. The cavalrymen counted seven casualties. Hood himself suffered a painful wound when an arrow pinned his hand to his saddle, presaging his experiences to follow in the Civil War.[144]

Robert E. Lee embodied the traits that most junior officers—Hood especially—sought to emulate. Hood, however, was rash and aggressive and did not keep his superiors informed of his movements and intentions, a trait that would haunt him, and the Confederacy, in the future. He had a fundamental belief in the efficacy of the offensive and was fortunate to avoid defeat at the hands of his Indian foes. Twenty years later, Hood said that his own fate could have been that of Custer's, whom he described as "gallant" and his cavalry as "noble." Later, his peers and superiors would say that Hood, as a fighter, had great luck; as a general, he did not.

At this point in his life, Hood was "blond, six feet, two inches tall, and was one of Lee's favorites….Lee liked his spirit. The two often rode together across the prairie around Camp Cooper, Texas [where the Second was stationed], talking about the Army and Hood's tour of duty in Oregon, where his regimental quartermaster, U.S. Grant, had ruined his career. Hood thought that Lee liked to give him advice and [he] never forgot an evening's ride when Lee earnestly told him that he should never 'marry unless you can do so into a family which will enable your children to feel proud of both sides of the house.'"[145]

Civil War Service

First Manassas through Gettysburg

After Texas seceded, and Kentucky did not, Hood cast his lot with Texas and was commissioned a lieutenant in the Texas cavalry. The great Civil War historian Douglas Southall Freeman described him as standing "six feet, two inches tall, with a powerful chest and giant shoulders. His hair and beard were a light brown, almost blond; his penetrating, expressive and kindly eyes were blue. When he spoke it was with a booming, musical richness of tone."[146]

Hood soon found himself a colonel in command of the Fourth Texas Infantry, an undisciplined outfit. Inexplicably—he had done nothing to distinguish himself—Hood became a brigadier general in the summer of 1862, a promotion deemed "the mystery of his career."[147] His brigade consisted of two thousand men from his former unit, the Fourth Texas; two more Texas regiments, the First and the Fifth; and one Georgia regiment, the Eighteenth.[148] That brigade, one of the fiercest in the Confederate army—and one of the most famous—would soon come to be known as "Hood's Texas Brigade" and its commander as "the Gallant Hood of Texas."[149]

At Gaines's Mill, one of the Seven Days Battles, Hood's Brigade was in Whiting's Division and Jackson's Corps. The brigade—after other units had tried and failed all that day—attacked a Union force on Turkey Hill in the late afternoon and routed it. This attack won the battle for the Confederates and won Hood great fame. It also helped to turn the tide of McClellan's invasion of Virginia that had carried the Union army to the gates of Richmond. "Of all the brigades of Jackson's command, including those of Whiting's Division, the most shining figure had been Hood, whose attack at Gaines's Mill was regarded as the most brilliant single achievement in The Seven Days."[150] McClellan left the Peninsula, and with his retreat, that campaign was now over. Hood's star was now ascendant.

He next took command of Whiting's Division, consisting of two brigades, Hood's and Law's, and four regiments: the Fourth Alabama, the Fourth and Eleventh Mississippi and the Sixth North Carolina. It was the summer of 1862, and the stage was set for the next great battle, the second one at Bull Run, or Manassas Junction. There, on the second day of the battle, and facing Pope's Union army, Hood led a charge that once again routed a portion of the Union army and led directly to its defeat. Lee would later report that Hood opposed the attack, but Lee ordered Hood to attack anyway. After his success, Hood was elated and told Lee that "the enemy was lying thick like roses." The dead were Zouaves who wore distinctive red uniforms. This advance, and the ensuing Confederate victory, led Freeman to term Hood "magnificent."[151] Losses in Hood's unit were heavy. This kind of slaughter was, unfortunately, to be repeated in several battles yet to come.

The invasion of Maryland followed Second Manassas. Hood, however, had been arrested for disobeying a command to turn over some ambulances that his men had captured at Second Manassas to Nathan "Shanks" Evans, who had "titular authority over Hood's troops." When Hood refused, Evans reported him for insubordination. Longstreet ordered Hood to Culpepper to await trial, but prior to Hood's departure, Lee overruled Jackson and Longstreet and let Hood stay on with his troops. He was not to exercise command, however. His men, Freeman said, became "half mutinous in resentment of Longstreet's and Evans's actions."[152]

Then, as the army approached South Mountain, Lee reinstated Hood to command, and his division once again saved the day at that battle—preliminary to the main event at Antietam Creek—when it came to the relief of D.H. Hill at South Mountain. There, Hood's Division held the line at Turner's Gap and covered the army's retreat to Sharpsburg.[153] Hood and his division then moved on to Sharpsburg and posted on the left of Lee's lines near Dunker's Church. There, on September 17, Hood's Division rushed into a breach of the Confederate lines on Lee's left, met an overwhelming number of Union troops head-on and, after a bloody fight, stopped them cold.

That evening, Lee famously asked Hood, "Where is your division?" Hood replied, "They are lying on the field where you sent them. My division has been almost wiped out." This slaughter in the east woods of Antietam was not unlike that which had taken place in the killing fields on the Peninsula Campaign and at Second Manassas. All of it was to prove a harbinger of what was to come one year later at an abattoir for the Confederate army.

Then came Fredericksburg, where Hood missed an opportunity to attack the Union right that could have led to destruction of the Union force. He missed Chancellorsville, having moved with Longstreet into southeast Virginia to meet a perceived Union threat there and gather supplies. That mission was deemed a failure.

Next was Gettysburg and all of its controversy, which remains to this day. On the first day, Hood's Division marched toward, and camped near, Gettysburg. The second day found Hood's Division on Lee's right, opposite Union general Meade's left and the two hills known as the Round Tops, as well as an escarpment that would become known as the Devil's Den by those who fought and died among the rocks and boulders of that bloody place. Lee ordered Longstreet to mount an attack up the Emmitsburg Road toward those positions. Longstreet, in turn, ordered Hood to make the attack, but Hood, relying on scouts who had surveyed the area behind the Round Tops and found those positions undefended from the rear, asked Longstreet three times to allow him to flank the Round Tops and attack from the rear. Three times Longstreet refused Hood's requests, stating that the frontal assault that Longstreet had ordered was based on a direct order from General Lee and that Hood would make the attack as ordered. Hood would later say, "I decided an attack up the Emmitsburg road would face 'immense boulders of stone, so massed together as to form narrow openings, which would break our ranks and cause the men to scatter whilst climbing up the rocky precipice.'"[154]

Regardless, at about 4:00 p.m. on July 2, Hood, as ordered by Lee and Longstreet and contrary to his own judgment, attacked up the Emmitsburg Road head-on toward the foreboding heights. As he predicted, the frontal assault failed miserably, Hood received a bad shrapnel wound in his left arm early in the attack and his division suffered heavy casualties. Hood would never again have use of his left hand.

Hood's Division was inactive on the third day, the day of Pickett's disastrous charge, although Lee initially sought its participation in that catastrophe. Longstreet, however, convinced Lee that Hood's Division was in no shape to fight on July 3, and Lee relented. On the fourth, Lee's army retreated south. The invasion of Pennsylvania was over.

After Hood recovered in a Charlottesville hospital from his wound, he spent time in Richmond, where he wooed and then proposed to Sally Buchanan Campbell Preston, a South Carolina socialite nicknamed "Buck," who spent the war flirting with Confederate officers.[155] Their courtship would last until the end of the war, when, to Hood's chagrin, it would end. Part of Hood's problem may have been his appearance. He was "a tall, rawboned country-looking man" who "looked like a raw backwoodsman, dressed up in an ill-fitting uniform." Further, "he had a long face, a long tawny beard, a large nose, and eyes with the sad expression of a hound dog."[156]

Then, with Longstreet, Hood went south to join the fight in Georgia. At Chickamauga, Hood, in the center of the Confederate lines, led a savage charge into a gap in the Union lines and drove most of the Union army from the field. Hood's bad luck continued, however, as at the peak of the charge he received a rifle bullet in his right leg. The first reports were that he had been killed, but he survived. The wound did, however, require amputation at the thigh in the field. The men of Hood's old Texas Brigade took up a collection to purchase him a "cork leg."[157]

After he recuperated, Hood was offered a promotion to lieutenant general and command of Jeb Stuart's cavalry. Stuart had garnered enormous criticism for his handling of the cavalry before and during the Gettysburg Campaign. Hood, however, declined and instead accepted the promotion to command of a corps in the Army of Tennessee, commanded by Joseph Johnston.

During the spring and summer of 1864, Johnston retreated before Sherman's relentless march on Atlanta. Davis, who was down on Johnston for the latter's failure to stem the Union tide, likely sent Hood to observe Johnston's tactics and report back to Davis, outside channels, and thus bring Johnston down.

Hood actually became friends with Johnston, at least initially, but subsequently he began to criticize Johnston for not going on the attack against Sherman. "Hood's criticisms went beyond those of most others, and some believe that he was trying to undermine Johnston to obtain command of the army for himself."[158] Finally, in July 1864, after more flanking movements and attacks by Sherman and more retreats by Johnston, as well as after a review of the situation around Atlanta by Davis's envoy, Braxton Bragg, Davis relieved Johnston and promoted Hood to full general. He took command of the Army of Tennessee with instructions to go on the attack. Hood was thirty-three years old and the youngest general in the Confederate army. Interestingly, Davis had queried

Lee about replacing Johnston with Hood. Lee replied, "Hood is a bold fighter. I am doubtful as to the other qualities necessary [for command of an army]." He also said that "Hood is…very industrious on the battlefield, careless off, and I have had no opportunity of judging his action when the whole responsibility rested on him. I have a high opinion of his gallantry and earnestness.…General Hardee has more experience in managing an army."[159] Davis, however, ignored Lee's analysis.

Hood, always aggressive, analogized the situation that he faced in the summer of 1864 before Atlanta to that of Lee before Richmond in 1862, when Lee went on the attack and drove McClellan down the Peninsula and out of Virginia in the battles of the famous Seven Days. Hood now seized the opportunity to go on the offensive with his Army of Tennessee. In July and August, he attacked and fought Sherman's army four times—at Peachtree Creek, Atlanta, Ezra Church and Jonesboro—in an effort to keep the Union army away from Atlanta. Hood suffered defeat in all four battles, and when Sherman cut the railroads supplying the city and his army, Hood abandoned Atlanta. His army emerged from those four battles greatly diminished—from 55,000 to 35,700. Hood, a great division commander, demonstrated time and again during this campaign the problems with his command of an army: poor command and control; too much authority delegated to his subordinates; an inability to manage his supplies; and rash, ill-conceived attacks on well-defended positions. The result around Atlanta was catastrophic, but unfortunately for the Confederacy, the worst was yet to come.

Davis appointed P.G.T. Beauregard to take command of the military district of the west, which, at least in theory, if not in practice, included Hood's Army of Tennessee. Hood decided to cut Sherman's supply line by moving his army into Tennessee. He did so with disastrous results. At Franklin, Hood sent his army across two miles of open terrain without artillery support, headlong into the entrenched position of Union general John Schofield, Hood's West Point classmate. Hood's thinking was that he could break Schofield and then head north for the Ohio River, attracting additional troops as he went. Schofield, however, had other ideas, and in what was later termed "Pickett's Charge of the West," Hood's men were cut down like wheat before the scythe. Hood lost six thousand men, including six generals, with five more generals wounded and one captured. After the battle, he was down to twenty-five thousand men.

Schofield then retreated to Nashville, which led Hood to call Franklin "a success." With an inferior force, Hood rashly followed Schofield and laid siege to the city. His opponent there was his old West Point instructor General George Thomas, who bided his time and prepared for battle. By December 15, 1864, he was ready and attacked Hood's left with forty thousand men. The result was predictable: another rout. With his decimated army of about nineteen thousand men, Hood desultorily moved across northern Alabama to Corinth, Mississippi. Beauregard then relieved him, and for Hood, the war was effectively over, except that for many years, Hood would continue to fight and refight those battles, blaming others for his defeats around Atlanta and in Tennessee. Hood, however, was a "disgraced general." "Sam Watkins, [a] Tennessean and the South's most famous private, would write several years after Hood's death: 'As a soldier, he was brave, bold, noble and gallant…but as a general he was a failure in every particular.'"[160] At war's end, Hood surrendered at Natchez.

Criticism of Hood followed him for the rest of his life and continues to this day among Civil War scholars. The gravamen of that criticism is that Hood, while a courageous leader, rose to a position in command of a corps and then an army for which the qualities that made him an outstanding division and brigade commander were not relevant to his success in those higher commands. Once he took command of the Army of Tennessee, his desire to emulate Lee on the Peninsula led him to undertake reckless attacks. As an army commander, he did not plan well, failed to exercise command and control of his subordinates and neglected essential details like logistics and staff work. "It was Hood's tragedy that he was an excellent soldier but a poor general."[161] Hood is often cited as an example of the "Peter Principle"—one promoted beyond the level of his competency.[162]

Hood and Johnston would spend the rest of their lives publicly blaming each other for their defeats, and Johnston would also blame Hood for engineering Johnston's relief of command. Hood, in turn, would blame Hardee for several of his defeats in Georgia. Johnston attacked Hood for his "disastrous campaign" and "the slaughter of his army." The bickering manifested in the "Battle of the Books" mirrored that of many of the other Confederate generals in defeat, a consistent theme of "Someone was to blame, and it damn sure wasn't me."[163]

The irrepressible Mary Chesnut, who knew Hood well, said, "Sam was promoted too fast, he wanted experience, was not long enough a major general, not long enough a lieutenant general." And further, "The people, now, educated by the press of the country, will not stand Hood for anything."[164]

POSTWAR

Following his surrender at Natchez, Hood made his way to New Orleans and then on to his adopted state, Texas, seeking a livelihood. He passed through Houston and then on to San Antonio. A lady who traveled with him said that "he sat opposite, and with calm, sad eyes, looked out on the passing scenes, apparently noting nothing. The cause he loved was lost—he was overwhelmed with humiliation at the utter failure of his leadership—his pride was wounded to the quick by his removal from command….In the face of his misery, which was greater than our own, we sat silent—there seemed no comfort anywhere."[165] Another woman who traveled with him said that "he was battered, beaten, discredited and a hopeless cripple."[166]

As he traveled on, however, Hood's mood gradually brightened, and in San Antonio, he received a warm welcome by those he had known before the war. They remembered him as the hero of Gaines's Mill and Second Manassas rather than the architect of the ignominious defeats at Franklin and Nashville. In Texas, he sought to convince old friends that the disastrous Tennessee Campaign was lost because of the mistakes of others and that the Tennessee Campaign had been his only viable option after the fall of Atlanta.

Hood continued to bounce from one location to the next: New Orleans, Washington, Kentucky and, at some point, Canada, to visit a colony of expatriate Confederates. He then decided to settle in New Orleans and returned there, where he would live the rest of his life. Using $10,000 he had borrowed from forty friends in Kentucky, each of whom put up $250, Hood went into business for himself, buying and selling cotton and other goods on commission. His firm was J.B. Hood and Company, Cotton Factors and Commission Merchants, with its office at Common Street, where Canal Street meets the Mississippi River.

New Orleans was home to a number of former Confederate generals. Besides Hood, they included from time to time Jubal A. Early and full-time residents P.G.T. Beauregard, Simon Bolivar Buckner, "Fighting Joe" Wheeler and James "Old Pete" Longstreet, who came there to serve as president of the Life Association of America, an insurance company. Old Pete wrote a letter to the *New Orleans Times* urging reconciliation with the North, acceptance of radical Reconstruction and acknowledgment by southerners that they were "a conquered people." His position, set forth in his letter, was, of course, anathema to southerners and the beginning of Longstreet's undoing.

New Orleans hoped to regain its former glory as a great cotton port, and Hood hoped to be a part of its renaissance. With his two partners, John C. Barelli and Fred N. Thayer, Hood sought business from former Confederate officers such as Stephen D. Lee, a farmer in Mississippi, and Nicholas A. Davis, chaplain of the Fourth Texas, who was farming in Texas. Notwithstanding those relationships, however, Hood's business did not prosper. Soon, much of the cotton from the Deep South was riding the rails to the North rather than shipping on boats out of New Orleans. Hood's business closed, and in 1870, when Longstreet's business failed as a result of his ill-conceived letter, soon followed by two other equally ill-conceived letters, Hood acquired Longstreet's firm and became president of the Life Association of America. He remained in that business until his death ten years later. Hood sold policies in and around New Orleans and even traveled to Canada to explore opening a business there, meeting with his old comrade Major General Henry Heth. From all accounts, the insurance business provided him with a comfortable living. The salary of $5,000 paid to him by the insurance association was more money than he had ever made.

In 1868, Hood, the longtime bachelor, married Anna Marie Hennon, member of an old and prominent Louisiana family. Anna was Catholic, and Hood, having been baptized by Leonidas Polk during the war, was Episcopalian. Armed with a special dispensation, Anna married Hood in New Orleans with Simon Bolivar Buckner as his best man. She was six years younger and had been educated in Paris. Her grandfather was a member of the Louisiana Supreme Court and her father a prosperous attorney in New Orleans. The Hennon family still owned a plantation, The Retreat, near Hammond, Louisiana, and the Hoods split time between it and the Hennon apartment in "an exclusive area of New Orleans."[167] Eventually, however, they, along with Anna's mother, moved into a grand home in the Garden District, since known as "the Hood mansion." They lived there in "comparative comfort and security with his growing family."[168]

Over the next ten years, the Hoods had eleven children, including three sets of twins.[169] These years were for Hood a happy time. The family spent their summers in the mountains, and tradition has it that when the family traveled, it was known as "Hood's Brigade" and that it was sometimes necessary to telegraph ahead for milk, just as during the war, commanders had telegraphed ahead to get supplies for marching troops.

These were also the years of the infamous Louisiana Lottery. Hood refused an offer to become a commissioner of the Lottery, a powerful and corrupt organization. The position that he was offered went to Jubal A. Early. P.G.T.

Beauregard was the other commissioner. For their few minutes of work each month, Beauregard and Early were paid handsome annual salaries variously estimated at between $12,000 and $30,000.

These indeed must have been peaceful years for Hood. A good home, handsomely furnished, a charming wife and happy children, a position of dignity in the community and what he believed to be reasonable financial security—these were his. But there were bitter memories of Atlanta, Franklin and Nashville. He was steadily working on his memoirs to show that Joe Johnston and Hardee were to blame.

From 1865 forward, Hood felt that his critics had been unjust in blaming him for the defeats around Atlanta and the two crushing defeats in Tennessee. He contended that those losses were directly attributable to a pronounced lack of manpower and resources and the failures of his subordinates. This theme would echo in his writings for the rest of his life, although his efforts in this regard seem to have diminished in the late 1860s and early 1870s, perhaps because the controversy arising out of his career was almost nonexistent during this time.

Hood, like his fellow warrior Jubal A. Early, was active in the Southern Historical Society, serving as vice-president of the Louisiana arm of that organization, with Early as its first president. He also participated in the Hood's Texas Brigade Association, the Army of Northern Virginia Association and the Louisiana Division of the Army of Tennessee Association. Hood was a popular speaker at these and other association meetings.

Then, in 1873, Hood again sought information relevant to his campaigns of 1864, contacting, among others, William T. Sherman. By that time, Hood knew that Joseph Johnston was about to publish his memoirs, and Hood had gotten word that he would not receive kind treatment at Johnston's hands. Johnston's work, *Narrative of Military Operations Directed During the Late War Between the States*, came out in 1874, predictably savaging his enemies. Johnston lambasted Jefferson Davis and termed Hood "a bungler."[170] Hood quickly began work on a defense.

Hood traveled to Washington in late 1878 or early 1879 in an effort to sell his papers to the War Department for $20,000. After reviewing the document, it offered him only $12,500, which he refused. For some reason, he called on General Sherman and enlisted him in his cause. Hood left the papers with Sherman and returned to Louisiana. Sherman then wrote to Congress, arguing for payment of the $20,000, and enlisted a congressman from Louisiana in Hood's cause, as Congress would have to appropriate the money. Notwithstanding these efforts, the project came to naught. The papers remained with Sherman until eventually making their way into the National Archives in 1938. They remain there today.

After Hood returned to Louisiana, his business, as the result of a yellow fever epidemic in 1878 that killed about three thousand residents, suffered severely, and Hood was soon broke. By 1879, however, the city seemed clear of the epidemic. Then there was a case across the street from the Hoods' residence, and soon Anna was infected. She died. Hood rejected advice from the family physician—Dr. T.G. Richardson, who had removed Hood's leg at Chickamauga—to take his children and leave the city; he could no longer afford such luxuries. His oldest child, Lydia, contracted the dreaded disease and also died. Hood was next. He died three days later, after receiving communion in his bed. Onlookers said that in his last moments, his eyes flashed as though he were back in combat. John Bell Hood, "Sam," was forty-eight years old.

Those around him decided on a quick and simple funeral, declining offers from various Confederate veterans' organizations to participate in the service. His friends held the service at his church, Trinity Episcopal, the day after his death and carried his casket to Lafayette Number One Cemetery. A detachment from a local company—the Continental Guards—then saluted him, adding "the military touch to his last rites" after all.[171]

After his death, General P.G.T. Beauregard secured publication of Hood's memoirs, *Advance and Retreat: Personal Experiences in the United States and Confederate States Armies.* Hood had used the book to rebut and attack General Johnston, as well as to respond to "unfavorable portrayals in Sherman's memoirs."[172] The book proved highly popular and profitable, and the proceeds, about $30,000, went to support his ten children, who, ultimately were adopted by seven families in Louisiana, Mississippi, Georgia, Kentucky and New York. In Texas, Fort Hood is named for him, as is Hood City.

It has often been said that Hood was a failure as a soldier and as businessman; measured by most standards of success, this was true. At Nashville, his military reputation was shattered, and at New Orleans, he came to the close of his life with a business disaster. It seemed almost as if he were predestined to fail—as if there in the background of his life the doleful chanting chorus of a Greek tragedy always reminding him of impending doom. Struggle as he might, he could not shake off the fate that pursued him.

To a degree, of course, he himself was to blame for his misfortunes, but there were many instances when tragic results were due to the breaks alone.[173] "Hood had incredibly bad luck at Franklin and Nashville, at Atlanta, and at Spring Hill, and a terrible yellow fever epidemic destroyed his business. Indeed there were reasons other than heredity why his face wore a look of perpetual sorrow."[174]

But some of his failures were also the result of his personality. He was emotional rather than analytical, and while that trait served him well as a leader of men at the brigade and even the division level, it did not serve him well at the corps or army levels. His failure at that level to analyze and weigh various courses of action against the probabilities of success or failure did him in. "He was much inclined to be impetuous in his decisions, trusting his intuition and his blind optimism to see him through."[175] That, then, is his epitaph.[176]

Chapter 6

JOSEPH EGGLESTON JOHNSTON

"Old Joe"

BEGINNINGS

Another in the seemingly endless line of controversial Confederate generals, Joseph Eggleston Johnston was born at Longwood plantation near Farmville, Virginia, on February 3, 1807, of impeccable Virginia lineage. Johnston's grandfather Peter Johnston settled in Petersburg in 1726. His father, also named Peter, had served with distinction in the American Revolution under Henry "Light-Horse Harry" Lee, Robert E. Lee's father. His mother, Mary Valentine Wood Johnston, claimed Patrick Henry as an uncle. Father Peter served thirteen terms in the Virginia legislature from Prince George County, but seeing greater opportunity elsewhere, he accepted a judgeship and moved in 1811 to Abington in the southwestern part of the state. There, Peter continued his participation in politics and became a member of the area's gentry. Through his political connections, he was able to "get one son elevated to the federal Congress."

Young Johnston received his education at the prestigious Abington Academy, and at home, he learned of his father's military exploits so that he leaned toward a military career, which his father encouraged. Thus appointed by Secretary of War John C. Calhoun in 1825, Johnston entered West Point, where he would have as a classmate and lifelong friend Robert E. Lee; Jefferson Davis would be a fellow member of the Corps of Cadets,

Joseph Eggleston Johnston. *Library of Congress.*

though not a classmate. Fellow future Confederate general Albert Sidney Johnston, no relation, was a senior when Joseph entered and served as adjutant of the corps. At the time that Joseph entered West Point, he stood five feet, seven inches tall and was described as "rail thin," with deep brown eyes, a broad forehead and close-cropped brown hair. Johnston received only 14 demerits in four years—as compared to the 716 that Jubal A. Early rang up and the zero that Robert E. Lee and five others in his class received—and Johnston finished 13th in a class of 46 and out of 105 who started with him. He graduated in 1829 and received his commission as a second lieutenant in the artillery.

Johnston participated in the Black Hawk Indian War of 1832 and, subsequently, in the First Seminole War of 1835. In 1836, he received a promotion to first lieutenant, but believing that promotions came too slowly, he resigned in 1837 and joined the Topographical Bureau in Florida as an engineer. The Second Seminole War began in 1838, and as a civilian, Johnston accompanied the army on a raid against the Seminoles. The raid failed, and as the army retreated, Johnston took command of a unit that protected the raiding party's rear and saved the party from likely annihilation. He was cited for bravery in that action. Later that year, disillusioned with civilian life, Johnston returned to the army.

For Christmas 1840, Johnston accompanied Second Lieutenant Robert McLane to his home on the eastern shore of Maryland. There he met McLane's sister, Lydia, who was at the time eighteen years old—Johnston was thirty-one—and was described as handsome rather than pretty, of "sweet disposition" and "quiet and reserved." Lydia and Robert were children of Delaware senator Louis McLane, a powerful politician and plantation owner who would have a positive influence on Johnston's military career. His and Lydia's was to be an outstanding—albeit childless—marriage of forty-two years, and Johnston would say after her death that she was "my love, my life, my soul."[177]

MEXICAN-AMERICAN WAR

The Mexican-American War began in 1846, and Johnston, like so many of his West Point contemporaries, served with distinction at Vera Cruz, Cerro Gordo, Contreras, Churubusco, Molino del Rey, Chapultepec and Mexico City and was brevetted a major, lieutenant colonel and, finally, a colonel in that conflict. In Mexico—a training ground for the far larger conflict that would follow—Johnston served with his old friend and classmate Robert E. Lee, as well as future Confederate commanders Jubal A. Early, Braxton Bragg, Thomas J. Jackson, P.G.T. Beauregard and Jefferson Davis. Later to serve on the Union side and also in Mexico were U.S. Grant, W.T. Sherman and George Meade. Johnston was wounded early at Vera Cruz but recovered sufficiently to participate in the attack on Mexico City. He emerged from the war a hero "bathed in military glory."

After the war, Johnston returned to the Topographical Engineers, his prewar assignment, but in 1855, bored, he transferred into the U.S. Cavalry. As storm clouds gathered, Johnston, with Lydia accompanying him, served in Kansas, most notably at Fort Leavenworth. It was here that he began to demonstrate his penchant for engaging in disputes, especially with superiors. A lieutenant colonel, Johnston contended that he should be a full colonel and thus applied repeatedly to Secretary of War Jefferson Davis for a promotion. Davis turned him down each time, and after Davis left that position, Johnston applied to two more secretaries of war for promotion. Finally, the third secretary, John B. Floyd, who was from Johnston's hometown, promoted him; however, the dispute with Davis would set a table fraught with long-term consequences.[178]

CIVIL WAR

April 1861–July 4, 1863

As the Civil War rolled toward the United States like an inexorable tidal wave, Johnston received from Secretary Floyd the position of quartermaster general of the U.S. Army and a promotion to brigadier general. He would be the only officer of the future Confederate States Army to achieve that rank in the U.S. "Old Army." Johnston did not own slaves and believed that a war with the North would be ruinous for the South, but he also believed that if Virginia seceded, he, too, must leave the army and go with the South.

Lydia did not want him to go. She told him that Jefferson Davis hated him and would ruin him. General Winfield Scott, his old commander in Mexico, also urged him directly and indirectly through Lydia not to go. "Get him to stay with us," he told her. "We will never disturb him in any way."

Lydia replied that "my husband cannot stay in an army which is about to invade his native country."

Scott said, "Then let him leave our army, but do not let him join theirs."

"This is all very well," Lydia replied, "but how is Joe Johnston to live. He has no private fortune, or no profession but that of arms."[179]

Then came the first battle at Bull Run Creek—First Manassas to the Confederacy. Historians have argued through the ensuing years about what happened there in July 1861. McDowell attacked Beauregard's army along a broad front. Beauregard issued a welter of confusing, often conflicting orders and in the end faced disaster on his left. Then, fortuitously, Kirby Smith and Jubal A. Early arrived, flanked McDowell and crumpled his right into what became a rout. Johnston, the senior Confederate officer on the field, gets credit for saving the Confederate left, although at the time Beauregard received the lion's share of credit for the Confederate victory. Indeed, it *was* Johnston who, after stabilizing the Confederate left, ordered Early and Smith to counterattack, but it was nothing but luck that put Early and Smith in the right place at the right time.

Jefferson Davis arrived on the field and later claimed that he ordered Beauregard and Johnston to pursue the retreating Union troops, but no pursuit ever materialized. There is confusion as to why that pursuit never took place. The public blamed Davis, but both Johnston and Beauregard were the recipients of Davis's ire for failing to pursue and destroy McDowell's disintegrating army, and in the 150 years since the war, historians have argued incessantly about that issue, just as those three men did in the immediate aftermath of the battle and the war.

Indeed, in the years after the Civil War, as Confederate generals played the blame game, Johnston and Beauregard blaming each other for the Confederate failure to pursue McDowell's defeated army. The truth is, however, that the three principals—Davis, Beauregard and Johnston—met and did nothing, because the Confederate army was in no position to pursue *anyone*: it was exhausted from the July heat and the two days of battle, was disorganized with soldiers separated from their units and lacked the command and control, food and ammunition necessary to support another attack.[180]

Nevertheless, Davis promoted Johnston to full general and assigned him command of the Army of the Potomac. During the six-month period following Manassas, Johnston and his army first remained at Manassas and then moved closer to the District of Columbia at Centerville and Fairfax Court House. First Manassas and the six months following that battle unfortunately exacerbated Johnston's already toxic relationship with Jefferson Davis. There were disputes over the organization of the army and over the number of troops that Johnston needed to attack across the Potomac, an attack that, as a result, never came.

Johnston became embroiled in a dispute with the acting secretary of war, Judah P. Benjamin, which added fuel to the Davis fire. Johnston also continued to complain to Davis about his rank relative to other senior

Confederate generals, citing a law passed by the Confederate Congress holding that rank in the Confederate army was to be a function of rank in the Union army before the war. Under that law, Johnston contended that he, as a Union brigadier general—the only Confederate general to have attained general officer rank in the "Old Army"—should be the senior officer in the Confederate army. Davis, however, took a somewhat attenuated position that as quartermaster general, Johnston had held a *staff*—as opposed to a *line*—position and that a staff position did not count under the law. Further in support of his position, Davis argued that Lee and Johnston were in the same West Point class and that Lee deserved seniority because he had finished ahead of Johnston. In addition, Mary Chesnut reported that a "spat" between Lydia Johnston and Varina Davis may also have influenced Davis's decision. Davis thus established the order of seniority in the Confederate army as Samuel Cooper, Albert Sidney Johnston, Lee, Joseph Johnston and Beauregard. Johnston was furious, and this issue would remain a hot one with him for the rest of his life. It would also cause more tension between Davis and Johnston, tension that would prove deleterious to the Confederacy for the remainder of the war.[181]

Those tensions increased when Davis ordered Johnston to pull back from Centerville; Johnston did so but, as he had earlier in a retreat from Harper's Ferry, left behind military supplies that the Union captured. Johnston's old friend George McClellan then began what would become known as the Peninsula Campaign when he landed his army at Fortress Monroe below Richmond and began an inexorable advance up the Peninsula toward the capital of the Confederacy. This maneuver gave rise to another of the seemingly endless disputes between Johnston and Davis: Davis wanted Johnston to take on McClellan down the Peninsula, but Johnston wanted to allow McClellan to come up the Peninsula closer to Richmond, where he would have left his gunboats and supply base behind and where his army would be bisected by the Chickahominy River. Davis, however, prevailed and forced Johnston to move his army—outnumbered two to one—down the Peninsula to meet McClellan.

Notwithstanding Davis's wishes, Johnston, after moving toward McClellan, almost immediately began withdrawing before the Northern horde, and at Yorktown, he once again left critical military supplies—powder and cannons—behind. Johnston stood and fought successfully at Williamsburg, where Jubal A. Early was wounded, but after the battle, McClellan's advance brought the Union army within sight of Richmond.

Then, at Seven Pines—called Fair Oaks by the Union—Johnston attacked. He failed, however, to coordinate the attack with all of his division commanders, and in the confused melee that followed, Johnston managed to get only 14,000 of his 55,000 men into battle against only 15,000 of McClellan's more than 100,000. Johnston sent out a flurry of confused and confusing orders. Command and control on the Confederate side were nonexistent. Two of Johnston's generals, Longstreet and Huber, lost precious time arguing about who was senior. Johnston sent John Bell Hood into the fight, but his division got lost in the woods and missed the battle. Late in the day, Johnston took personal command of three brigades and led them into battle. It was here that he was wounded by a musket ball and shrapnel in his right shoulder, unhorsed and incapacitated. The battle deteriorated into a disjointed fight among disorganized small units. It being tactically inconclusive, Confederate generals present at the battle would once again argue about who was responsible for the failure of the South to achieve a signal victory. In spite of Johnston's failure to win a tactical victory, however, the draw had the salubrious effect of stopping McClellan's advance on Richmond. Another general would have to drive him back down the Peninsula, and the arrival of Johnston's relief—Robert Edward Lee—would constitute one of the watershed events of the war.[182]

Johnston's convalescence from his wound at Seven Pines lasted six months, and in November 1862, he reported to Richmond that he was ready to return to the army. He hoped that he could be restored to command in Virginia, his home state, but Davis instead shipped him west to command Confederate forces caught up in actions against Grant and Sherman, who were after Pemberton in Mississippi, and against Rosecrans, who confronted Bragg in Tennessee. Johnston didn't understand the functions of a geographical commander, and neither did his two subordinates, who disregarded both his advice and his commands. Davis and Seddon in Richmond wanted Johnston to defend both states by switching troops between Tennessee and Mississippi, while Johnston correctly thought that strategy not only impractical but also logistically impossible. Thus the stage was set for another Confederate debacle.

Gradually, Rosecrans shoved Bragg out of Tennessee, and gradually, Grant and Sherman drove Pemberton into Vicksburg. Johnston urged—and occasionally ordered—Pemberton to save his army and not the town so that he would lose only one of the two. Pemberton, however, after a resounding defeat at Champion Hill, did just as Johnston had urged him *not* to do and retreated into Vicksburg, where Grant surrounded him and eventually—on July 4, 1863—starved him out. Johnston, in command of a small force at Jackson and urged by Davis and Seddon to link up with Pemberton, never did, earning once again the opprobrium of his Richmond betters. Sherman, on the other hand, respected Johnston "and others of the Federal armies marveled as the Confederate general's ability to forestall their every maneuver."[183]

July 4, 1863–April 1865

After Bragg's various failures in Tennessee and Kentucky, Grant maneuvered him into Georgia, and Bragg asked to be relieved of command of the Army of Tennessee, with Johnston taking his place. Thus, Johnston faced off against Sherman, who had twice as many men. Johnston took command of the Army of Tennessee at Dalton, Georgia, and immediately began to retrain and restore that army's morale, which he did. The troops liked Johnston, and gradually, they developed confidence in him. Nevertheless, they, and he, faced overwhelming odds, and it would be those odds that would prove decisive in the controversial campaign to follow. That controversy would be fueled by Davis's incessant demands that Johnston stand and fight Sherman's horde, by the surreptitious criticism of Braxton Bragg (now Davis's military advisor) and by John Bell Hood's back-channel communications with Seddon, Davis and Bragg. Between Sherman and those four, Johnston faced impossible odds.

Sherman's strategy was simple: use three-quarters of his army to pin down Johnston and then flank him with the other quarter. It worked time and again, driving Johnston from Dalton to Resaca to Calhoun to Adairsville; to Cassville to Cartersville to Lost Mountain; to Kennesaw Mountain; and, finally, across the Chattahoochee, the last natural defense before Atlanta. There were battles along the way at New Hope, Dallas and Pickett's Mill, all of which Johnston's army won. Still, he could not handle the flanking movements that, in spite of Johnston's tactical victories, forced him to withdraw again and again. Moreover, Johnston's subordinates—Hood in particular—continued to undermine and disobey him. The handwriting thus appeared on Johnston's doleful wall.

Finally, at Kennesaw Mountain, Sherman had enough of the flanking maneuvers and decided to attack head-on. There took place one of the strangest incidents of the war. Sherman's men came in waves across an open field toward Johnston's men, entrenched and elevated. The men in blue were cut down like cornstalks. A fire started in the field and threatened to roast the wounded Union soldiers alive. Then, a Confederate officer called a truce and shouted for the Union troops to retrieve their wounded, which they did. The fighting then resumed. Cheatham and Cleburne repulsed two heavy attacks, and Sherman would forever after regret his decision to come at Johnston directly.

Sherman's major problem was that Johnston, as soon as he took up a defensive position, would send troops to the rear to prepare his next line of defense. In addition, his retreats were masterful, and he made Sherman pay with blood for every mile that he advanced. As a result, Sherman and Grant both considered Johnston the ablest of all Confederate generals. Their respect and admiration would not, in the end, be enough to save Johnston's job from the insidious forces at work in Richmond, as well as one cancerous tumor at work in Johnston's own army. Finally, that cancer, Hood, replaced Johnston in command of the Army of Tennessee. Hood, of course, would go on to waste Johnston's army in four futile attacks around Atlanta and then, finally, completely destroy it at Franklin and Nashville. Of Hood, following the destruction of his army, Mary Chesnut would write that he was "a target of public vituperation. [He] cannot be sufficiently abused." And he was not *then* sufficiently abused, but he has certainly been since.

Johnston and Lydia lived in Alabama during the winter of 1864–65. Then, under pressure from the Confederate Congress and at the urging of Lee, Davis reluctantly gave Johnston command of Confederate forces east of the Mississippi River except for Virginia. Therefore, in February, at Charlotte, North Carolina, Johnston took command of the Army of Tennessee, which was only faintly reminiscent of its former self. He had only seven or eight thousand troops and five or six thousand more under Bragg at Wilmington, which predictably fell on February 25. Bragg retreated with his shadow army, and Johnston sent D.H. Hill to reinforce him. Approaching from the south, Sherman said that he had to be more careful with his "special antagonist back." Bragg then attacked at Kinston on March 8 and, as usual, enjoyed a victory on the first day but a defeat on the second day, for which Johnston and Bragg—true to their traditions—each blamed the other, laying the foundation for the "Battle of the Books" that was to follow the war. Another battle followed at Bentonville, Grant flushed Lee out of Petersburg, and defeats at Five Forks and Sayler's Creek followed. Then the war was effectively over, although Johnston had not surrendered his army.

Johnston and Bragg met with Jefferson Davis and his entourage in Greensboro. Davis wanted to fight on, but Johnston told him that the

South was defeated and that further loss of life was futile and a waste of blood. Bragg supported Johnston, and while Davis fled south to Georgia, Johnston met with his old adversary Sherman at Durham Station and signed the document of surrender. Jefferson Davis, Craig Symonds has written, considered the surrender by Johnston "an act of treachery." Subsequently, Kirby Smith surrendered the South's forces west of the Mississippi. The war was over.[184]

POSTWAR

Initially, Johnston thought that he might go to Canada as other expatriate Confederates did—Jubal A. Early for one—and he secured permission from federal authorities to do so. However, the requirement to obtain permission if he desired to return was a deterrent, and he decided to remain in the United States. He and Lydia left North Carolina in early June for a resort near Danville. It was an effort to restore Lydia's health, which had been ravaged by the war. She suffered from neuralgia, and Johnston suffered from rheumatism and vertigo; while his illnesses were manageable, hers was not.

In the immediate aftermath of the war, and thereafter, Johnston did not mourn the passing of slavery, which, as an institution, he thought to be unsustainable. As a career army man, he had not owned slaves and cared little for the institution. He had fought for Virginia, not for slavery, although the two—Virginia and slavery—are inseparable with the benefit of hindsight.

Johnston was faced with the daunting prospect of making a living. Initially, Lydia inquired of Colonel Ben Ewell concerning the prospects in Richmond for an engineer. Ewell did not encourage Johnston, and so he, with other Confederate veterans, formed the National Express and Transportation Company in November 1865. Unable to raise capital in the penurious South, however, that business quickly folded.

Johnston then became president of the Alabama and Tennessee River Railroad Company, and he and Lydia moved to Selma, Alabama. There, he renewed his interest in the church—he had been baptized by Bishop Leonidas Polk during the war—and Bishop Wilmer of Alabama confirmed him on Good Friday of 1867. Again, however, his business was unable to raise sufficient capital to fund the venture, and it folded as well.

Johnston was still troubled by his conflicts—not with the Union but with other Confederate commanders—during the war, beginning with Jefferson Davis's failure to rank him as the senior Confederate officer based on his seniority derived from his position as the senior Union officer to "come south." His relief by Hood still galled him, as did the betrayal by Hood and Bragg that led to his relief. Johnston absolutely hated Davis, and he wanted to clear his name and the historical record with his memoirs. But Davis was still in prison and thus a martyr to the South. It was, therefore, not a good time for him to blast Davis. Instead, Johnston decided to bide his time and gather materials in preparation for his book.

After Johnston had gathered materials for what he considered to be his correction of the record that had been distorted by other Confederate generals, he contracted with D. Appleton Company of New York to publish his book. Then followed many drafts and many annoying edits before his book, *Narrative of Military Operations Directed During the Late War between the States*, came out. Not unexpectedly, he condemned those who, he believed, had conspired against him, and he argued forcibly that the South's failure in the war came not just militarily but also rested in part on its failure to create "a strong financial structure based on cotton in the early stages of the war."[185]

The book, however, received limp acceptance in the South, where a majority now saw the need for unity in the face of Congressional Reconstruction, and Johnston's book, with its attacks on his old adversaries, did not promote that unity. He attacked Davis for everything from his failures at First Manassas to his relief of Johnston during the Atlanta Campaign. He attacked Beauregard for his failure to follow up at First Manassas—Beauregard would later say that reading Johnston's memoirs, it was as if Beauregard were not even at the battle—and he attacked Hood for losing the Army of Tennessee at the four battles around Atlanta and the suicidal attack at Franklin, followed by the abortive Siege of Nashville. Beauregard, in reply, termed Johnston a "dissatisfied and disappointed officer." Johnston also blamed Hood for failing to carry out the attacks during the Georgia Campaign that Johnston ordered when he was in command of the Army of Tennessee.

Johnston's book was just one of many in which Confederate officers took up the pen to attack one another. Jefferson Davis, Hood and Bragg were Johnston's antagonists in the Battle of the Books. In his memoirs, Johnston defended his conduct and strategy at Manassas, Seven Pines and Vicksburg, blaming others for the failures in those battles, especially Davis for Manassas and Vicksburg. Johnston blamed Richmond for failing to send cavalry to cut Sherman's supply line in the Atlanta Campaign. Forrest, he maintained correctly, could easily have done it.

Johnston's book sold poorly and made no profit for the publisher. It also failed in Johnston's attempt to win support for his cause throughout the South. The book naturally offended Hood and Beauregard, and Hood, now living in New Orleans, wrote a response that was published in 1879. In it, he said disingenuously that Johnston had ruined the Army of Tennessee before Hood ever took command, basing that contention on Johnston's retreats at Dalton, Resaca, New Hope Church, Cassville and Kennesaw Mountain. In the meantime, Davis had come out with the *Rise and Fall of the Confederate Government* in 1877 but did not attack Johnston. Now viewed in the South as a martyr, Davis's refusal to roll in the muck with Johnston caused Johnston's attacks on Davis to backfire and led to Johnston's condemnation throughout the South.

Johnston then wrote an article for *Century Magazine* as part of its "Battles and Leaders" series. The article was another diatribe against Davis, once again beginning with Davis's failure to rank Johnston appropriately at the beginning of the war and assigning him blame for his other alleged failures during the war. His four articles covered First Manassas, Seven Pines and the Vicksburg and Atlanta Campaigns; the series led historians Govan and Livingood to wonder "as in many other of the articles in this enlightening series who the greater enemy of the Confederates actually was, the Federal opponent or they themselves." With these articles, Johnston's star in the Confederacy once again dimmed.

As for Johnston's military reputation, Sherman and Grant praised him. Sherman said he was "dangerous and wily opponent," and he criticized Hood and Davis. Grant ten years later said that Johnston's decision not to break the siege of Vicksburg and his North Georgia tactics were correct. If Johnston, Grant argued, could have prolonged the war another year, the North might have abandoned it.

In the autumn of 1868, Johnston went alone to London, Liverpool and Paris, where he met with expatriate Confederates. Upon his return to Richmond, he organized the Joseph E. Johnston Company, the general agent for the Liverpool, London and Globe Insurance Companies, which would operate in several southern states. With this opportunity, the Johnstons moved to Savannah, where Robert E. Lee would visit him in the spring of 1870, a few months before Lee's death in Lexington, Virginia. Johnston invited other Confederate officers to join him in his business, and within four years, he had 120 agents in Georgia, Alabama and Mississippi. He and Lydia spent Christmas at her home in Baltimore and their summers at Warm Springs, Virginia.

In 1876, Johnston became interested in politics and supported Democrat Samuel J. Tilden for president against Republican Rutherford B. Hayes. Tilden won the popular vote, but Republicans challenged the results from Louisiana, Florida and South Carolina. A Republican-dominated Congressional committee, not surprisingly, ruled in Hayes's favor, but as a sop to the South, it declared the end of Congressional Reconstruction. Disgusted, Johnston said of Tilden, "If he had the heart of a dung-hill hen, he would have claimed the Presidency, and been inaugurated…it is as certain as any matter of opinion, that if he had been resolute he would have been backed by the whole Democrat party against which Grant would not have attempted to use his little military force."[186]

At the beginning of 1877, the Johnstons moved to Richmond, where he became Virginia agent for the Home Insurance Company. In 1878, Democrats—mostly Confederate veterans—asked him to run for Congress as the Democratic candidate. He was seventy and coy about the offer. After deliberation, Johnston said he wouldn't campaign for the nomination but would accept the "will of the people." He won the Democratic Party nomination after having his disqualification for public office removed by Congress on February 23, 1877.

Johnston did campaign in the general election and was elected to the House from Virginia, but he would refuse a second term. As a congressman, Johnston served on the Military Affairs Committee and visited his alma mater at West Point as a function of the committee's military oversight. Johnston was "an unremarkable Congressman." He introduced no legislation, seldom spoke on the floor and voted the straight Democratic Party line. Johnston's decision to run only once was because he believed that campaigning was expensive and demeaning. Moreover, he was disturbed by the apathy of southern voters and the corruption involved in the party nominations, which could be purchased for $1,500. He longed for the days when a gentleman could offer himself for nomination and be elected.[187]

In the summer of 1880, he and Lydia took a trip to New York and Narragansett Bay. Johnston admired greatly the neat farms and villages, in particular Pittsfield, Massachusetts, "the most beautiful little town in the world, in a little tract of country like the greenest parts of England." While on this trip, he attended a meeting of the Aztec Club for veterans of the Mexican-American War.[188]

Even though he had refused a second term, Johnston and his wife decided to keep their home in Washington, although he maintained legal residence in Richmond and regularly visited there. Before the year's end, after the expiration of his term in Congress, he became involved in a controversy that spread quickly throughout the South. This was the famous (or infamous) "Confederate Gold" issue, and Johnston's involvement arose out of what he thought was a private conversation, off the record, with a reporter for the *Philadelphia Press* named Frank A. Burr, whom Johnston knew. Burr wrote that Johnston believed Davis had failed to account for $2 million in gold that had accompanied Davis on his flight south after the fall of Richmond in 1865. Johnston immediately responded that he had thought the conversation private and that the article was filled with inaccuracies, but he never firmly denied that he had said those things about Davis and the gold. The South rallied around Davis, and Johnston was soon and once again pilloried by friend and foe alike, and there were plenty of the latter.

Johnston then became president of a company called the Pan-Electric Company, which was to manufacture and distribute electrical inventions, but the venture was apparently ahead of its time and failed. With time on hand, he read military history from Rome to the American Revolution and recounted his own past battles and campaigns. Johnston considered Napoleon above all others except Julius Caesar and believed that Marlborough was England's greatest soldier. He told a young South Carolinian that he considered Sherman the ablest of the Union generals, although he believed that his friend George McClellan "was the best organizer in the Federal Army." Grant, he said further, was "the best fighter, but Sherman was the genius of the Federal army." Finally, he said that "Robert E. Lee was their superior in any capacity." Nevertheless, he stated firmly that "Forrest was the greatest soldier of the war" and "expressed regret that Virginians had known so little…of the ability and the exploits of the great cavalry leader."[189]

Grover Cleveland was elected president over Republican James G. Blaine in 1884—the first Democratic president since the outbreak of the Civil War—and he appointed "the aging general" commissioner of railroads, a position that required that Johnston travel considerably to all parts of the country. While in Portland, Oregon, in July 1885, he received word to return east at once to act as one of the pallbearers at Grant's funeral. It was a fitting assignment, as each man held great respect for the other. Grant had singled Johnston out as the ablest of Confederate commanders and the one who had given him the most anxiety. Shortly before his death, Grant had written of the campaign in Georgia that neither the great defensive soldier

Thomas, nor the ingenious Sherman, "nor any other soldier could have done it better" than old Joe.[190]

As the nation stopped to mourn Grant's passing, the errors of his presidential career were forgotten, and writers and orators paid tribute to his military achievements. In New York, around the first small tomb in Riverside Park, a great crowd gathered. Among them, four men stood erect as the personification of the growing spirit of reunion. Simon Buckner and Philip Sheridan stood arm in arm along with Sherman and Johnston. Their appearance together, a reporter for *Harper's Weekly* wrote, "gives a picture of American fraternity astonishing almost to ourselves who remember terrible conflict within the present generation."[191]

On February 22, 1887, Johnston's greatest fear was realized when Lydia, whose health had continued to decline, died suddenly in Washington. Childless, the couple had been extremely close. She was his confidante and his sounding board, and she had supported him openly in his conflicts with Jefferson Davis when she was in Richmond during the war. Johnston was devastated. "For the rest of his life he could not bring himself to write or speak her name." He kept the house as she had left it and lived alone, a suddenly old man who enjoyed the company of the dwindling circle of old friends. The next year, 1888, Benjamin Harrison defeated Cleveland, even though he lost the popular vote, and Johnston was out of office.

After his federal career ended, Johnston—and the others who fought in the bitter conflict that was the Civil War—gradually connected with one another in a feeling of comradeship. Veterans' reunions were frequent on both sides, so in 1890, in response to an invitation, Johnston attended a reunion of the Army of Tennessee in Atlanta. An amazing experience followed. Johnston and Kirby Smith were in a carriage pulled by horses when men in the crowd recognized him. Swirling around the carriage, they unhitched it from the horses, and among cries of "Old Joe" and attempts to touch him, the veterans, in an extraordinary demonstration of respect and affection, pulled the carriage themselves for the remainder of the parade. A newspaper, upon seeing Johnston passing by, reported that he possessed "all the old-time grace and dignity." Nevertheless, Johnston wept in response to the men's spontaneous burst of devotion to their old commander.[192]

The next month, he was invited to Richmond to participate in the unveiling of the equestrian statue of Lee. Veterans from all over the South attended this event, and it was Johnston who pulled the cord to unveil the statue of the beloved Lee, Johnston's friend and classmate from West Point days. Undoubtedly, the moment engendered memories of their time together on the Plain, in Mexico and during the war. His old friends and comrades noticed, however, that the general tired easily and that his age showed more and more.

William Tecumseh "Cump" Sherman died on February 8, 1901, and Johnston went to New York to attend the funeral as an honorary pallbearer. It was a cold, raw day, damp and windy, and out of respect for his old adversary, Johnston refused to wear a hat. When encouraged to do so by a spectator, who said that Johnston might become ill from the weather, he replied that if he were in Sherman's place and Sherman in his, the latter would remove his hat.

Johnston did just what the spectator warned against: he got sick with a severe cold. On top of a bad heart, he began to fail in spite of the best efforts of his physician. Johnston lingered into March, but on March 21, 1901, in Washington, he died, with his brother-in-law by his bedside. The funeral was the next day, and Lydia's family buried him in their Baltimore family plot next to her. He is the only full Confederate general without a memorial on his grave.[193]

Tributes poured in, but perhaps the greatest was from one of his men, Sam Watkins, an infantryman in the First Tennessee, who said, "Such a man was Joseph E. Johnston, and such is his record. Farewell old fellow. We... loved you because you made us love ourselves."[194]

Chapter 7
JAMES LONGSTREET

"Old Pete"

Another member of the Confederacy's capacious pantheon of controversial generals is James Longstreet. The controversy surrounding Longstreet did not begin, however, until seven years *after* the war, and it was largely—if not entirely—a function of his postwar politics. Indeed, in the years immediately following Lee's surrender at Appomattox, Longstreet enjoyed a reputation as one of the South's leading generals, slotted in the competence hierarchy just below the sainted Robert E. Lee and the martyred Thomas J. "Stonewall" Jackson. That would, however, change dramatically beginning in 1872.

CHILDHOOD

General James Longstreet's New World progenitor was Dirck Stoffels Lange Straet, a Dutchman who immigrated in 1657 to what was then New Netherlands, which included parts of New York, New Jersey, Maryland, Connecticut, Delaware and Pennsylvania. His new country eventually anglicized his name to "Longstreet." William Longstreet, the future general's grandfather, moved to Augusta, Georgia, where he invented a steamship, but for want of capital, the venture failed, leaving the field to

Robert Fulton. The ever-creative William subsequently invented a steam cotton gin before buying a plantation in Edgefield, South Carolina, where the general was born.

General Longstreet was born on January 8, 1821, the fifth child and third son born to James and Mary Ann Dent Longstreet. The elder James called his son "Peter," for his "rocklike" personality that reminded him of St. Peter, the rock of the church. That appellation would eventually be his sobriquet in the Confederate army: "Old Pete," they would call him.

The elder James subsequently bought a cotton plantation in the northeast Georgia hill country near what was to become Gainesville, Georgia. There, in that recent frontier area, young James learned to ride, shoot and hunt—learned, in short, to be an active outdoorsman. When James was eight, his father decided that he would seek an appointment to West Point for James at the appropriate age; to qualify, the boy would need an education that was unavailable in and around Gainesville. The elder James thus sent his young son to Augusta, Georgia, in 1830 to live with his illustrious uncle, Augustus Baldwin Longstreet, Yale College graduate, lawyer, judge, newspaper editor, author and educator. Augustus Baldwin Longstreet would eventually serve as the president of Emory College and South Carolina College (later the University of South Carolina) and as chancellor of the University of Mississippi. Bigger than life, Augustus reputedly weighed seventeen pounds at birth. From him young James would acquire a lifelong fondness for whiskey and card games.[195]

WEST POINT

Longstreet, at six feet, two inches in height and weighing two hundred pounds, entered West Point in 1838 at the age of seventeen. He would be a member of the outstanding class of 1842. Longstreet, however, was anything but outstanding, finishing fifty-fourth out of fifty-six—third from the bottom of his class. In fairness to Longstreet, however, eighty cadets began West Point in his class, and twenty-four washed out. Longstreet was an indifferent student, preferring "the school of the soldier, horsemanship, sword exercise, and the outside game of foot-ball [more] than the academic course."[196] He failed "Mechanics" in his third year; however, in keeping with academy custom, Longstreet took the examination again two days later and passed.[197]

James Longstreet. *Library of Congress.*

At West Point, Longstreet formed a friendship that would endure for a lifetime, even though the two cadets would find themselves facing off on opposite sides in the conflict to come. His name when he arrived at West Point was Hiram Ulysses Grant, but a clerical error by an administrator changed his name to Ulysses Simpson Grant. To the cadets, he became "Uncle Sam Grant," and then just Sam. Among the Corps of Cadets, Grant was regarded as the finest horseman at West Point, and of him, Longstreet, in his memoirs, would say that Grant was "of noble, generous heart, of lovable character, a valued friend…a man who was to eclipse us all."[198]

PREWAR ARMY SERVICE

Upon Longstreet's graduation and commissioning as a brevet second lieutenant, the army assigned him to the infantry at Jefferson Barracks in St. Louis, where he would serve for two years, an exception to the rule that sent most West Point graduates west to remote forts in Indian country. After a year, in 1843, his good friend Sam Grant joined him in St. Louis. Through Longstreet, Grant met Julia Dent, Longstreet's cousin who lived near the post. Grant and Julia established a relationship that he hoped would lead to marriage, but it was not to be at that time.

In 1844, Longstreet met Louisa Maria "Louise" Garland, the seventeen-year-old daughter of Longstreet's regimental commander, Lieutenant Colonel John Garland from Lynchburg, Virginia. Louise was described as "slender, petite and quite attractive, with high cheekbones and black hair."[199] Longstreet soon asked for Louise's hand in marriage, but because of her age, her father declined and told the couple to wait until Louise was older.

That same year, Longstreet's posting at Jefferson Barracks came to an end when the Fourth Infantry, Longstreet's regiment, received orders to join General Zachary Taylor in Natchitoches, Louisiana, on the Red River near the Texas border. Their mission was to monitor the situation in Texas, which the United States had annexed earlier that year, to Mexico's chagrin. There was little to do at what was named "Camp Salubrity," so Longstreet indulged his lifelong love of poker.

The next year brought a permanent promotion to second lieutenant and orders to join the Eighth Infantry at Fort Marion in St. Augustine, Florida. That unit soon transferred to General Taylor's army in Corpus Christi, Texas, however, as relations between the United States and Mexico deteriorated. It was the autumn of 1845, and war with Mexico loomed large on Longstreet's horizon. Nevertheless, in the intervening months, there was little to do, and Longstreet, now reunited with Sam Grant and other officers and friends from West Point and Jefferson Barracks, transferred to Corpus Christi. There, he hunted and played cards. Corpus Christi provided many delights for the men—prostitution and gambling, among others—and Taylor's hands were full trying to keep his 3,800 men out of trouble.[200]

MEXICAN-AMERICAN WAR SERVICE

But war with Mexico did come, and Taylor's small army, with Longstreet, immediately moved into action along the Mexican border. After victories at Palo Alto and Resaca in disputed land that was to become a part of Texas—those battles gave Longstreet his first taste of combat—Taylor took his army south to Monterrey, where, leading a numerically inferior force, Taylor's army captured the city after heavy fighting. Longstreet led several attacks that were critical to Taylor's success at Monterrey, and he emerged from that battle regarded as an outstanding young officer. After the battle, Longstreet received a promotion to first lieutenant and became adjutant of the Eighth Infantry.

Subsequently, he participated in the Siege of Vera Cruz, where Winfield Scott—who had taken command from Taylor—used naval guns that sailors had rowed ashore. The big guns brought naval officer Raphael Semmes into action, and those guns coupled with army artillery to pound the city into submission. Longstreet participated with distinction in the battles at Cerro Gordo Pass, Churubusco, El Marino Del Rey and Chapultepec, which led to the capture of Mexico City and the end of the war.

The lessons from the Mexican-American War for Longstreet, as for many who would become general officers on both sides during the Civil War, were numerous. As adjutant of the Eighth Infantry, he learned the importance of supply and transport across large distances, and as a company commander, he saw how strong, professional leadership could transform citizen soldiers into a successful fighting force. He also learned how artillery, in whose range and accuracy there had been many advancements in the years leading up to the war, could destroy soldiers trying to move across open terrain and could pound a besieged army into submission. And he saw the command qualities of two generals of different style and substance: Zachary Taylor and Winfield Scott—from the latter he learned the value of maneuver and flanking movements with a numerically inferior army. And finally, he learned that his physical strength, stamina and leadership on the battlefield were of a quality that would serve him and the men he led well. He emerged from the Mexican-American War regarded as an outstanding soldier and leader of men.[201]

SERVICE BETWEEN THE WARS

After the war, Longstreet finally married Louise Garland, now twenty-one, in Lynchburg, Virginia, and the next month, he and Louise attended the wedding of Sam Grant and Longstreet's cousin Julia Dent in Missouri. That marriage, and his friendship at West Point with Grant, provided the glue that would hold that friendship together through the savage war and the tumultuous peace to follow. Longstreet's second wife, Helen Dortch, would later write that Longstreet never kissed Louise until they were married.

Longstreet's father-in-law, John Garland, was now a general, and there is no doubt that Longstreet's career benefited from his patronage. It was said at the time that a letter from Louise Garland Longstreet to her father could make or break the career of a one of Longstreet's fellow officers.

With the conclusion of the Mexican-American War, Longstreet eased into a peacetime career that took him to Fort Marion Scott near Fredericksburg, Texas, and then on to Fort Bliss near El Paso. These were happy years for the Longstreets. Their family grew to include four children, and Longstreet's career took him to Fort Leavenworth, Kansas, where he again ran into Grant, then a civilian and struggling as a farmer. Longstreet would later say that Grant "was poorly dressed in civilian clothes." Longstreet gave Grant a five-dollar gold piece to repay a loan Grant had made to him at West Point, and after a year at Leavenworth, he moved farther west to Albuquerque, where he, now a major, served as paymaster. His father-in-law, General Garland, was stationed there, and that posting did nothing to hurt Longstreet's career. Albuquerque, however, would be his last assignment as an officer of the United States Army. As Longstreet put it in his book: "I was stationed at Albuquerque, New Mexico as paymaster in the United States army when the war-cloud appeared in the east. Officers of the Northern and Southern States were anxious to see the portending storm pass by or disperse, and on many occasions we, too, were assured by those who claimed to look into the future, that the statesman would yet show himself equal to the occasion, and restore confidence among the people."[202]

Such, of course, was not to be, and as events "in the east" carried from 1860 on into 1861, secession among the southern states proceeded apace. Longstreet finally resigned his commission on May 9, 1861, and with his family headed east to join the new Confederacy, whose capital was Montgomery, Alabama, and whose newly elected president was Jefferson Davis. Longstreet would later say, however, that it was "a sad day when we took leave of lifetime comrades and gave up a service of twenty years." It was a sadness that descended on an entire nation split in two, both sides now preparing for war. On June 22, Longstreet met with President Davis at the executive mansion in Montgomery, where he was offered a commission as a brigadier general in the Confederate army. He accepted that commission on June 25, 1861.[203]

WARTIME SERVICE

First Manassas to Gettysburg

On July 18, Longstreet's Brigade met a Union division trying to cross Blackburn's Ford at Bull Run and successfully repulsed that attack. His brigade did nothing on the first day of the First Battle of Manassas, however, but provide artillery support on the twenty-first, when Joseph Johnston arrived on the field by railroad from the valley and, along with Jubal Early on the Confederate left, attacked and broke the Union line. That attack initiated the rout that drove McDowell's army and its horde of onlookers back to Washington. Here, once again, it is unclear what happened next, but there was no pursuit of the fleeing Union army. We do know that Longstreet tried to pursue and that he, who either received an order not to pursue or thought he had received such an order, was so angry that he stomped his hat. Nevertheless, Longstreet emerged from First Manassas with a reputation for stability and acumen during battle and received a promotion to major general in October 1861.

Next up was Union general George "Young Napoleon" McClellan's invasion of the Peninsula, a campaign designed to take Richmond. Longstreet, now commanding a division, distinguished himself at Williamsburg, but at Seven Pines, when Joseph Johnston finally attacked McClellan's divided army, Longstreet became confused by Johnston's vague verbal orders and took his division in the wrong direction down the wrong road, where he became entangled with another Confederate unit. That mistake cost Johnston the power of his counterattack, which, although it drove McClellan back, could have been the basis for a decisive victory for the Confederacy. In terms of his performance in battle, Seven Pines would be the low point of Longstreet's career.

With Johnston wounded at Seven Pines, Davis turned over command of what was then the Army of the Potomac to Robert E. Lee. In attacks on

McClellan's army at Oak Grove, Mechanicsville, Gaines's Mill, Savage's Station, Frayser's Farm and Malvern Hill (the battles collectively known as the Seven Days), Lee drove McClellan back down the Peninsula. Longstreet made up for Seven Pines during the Seven Days, in which he distinguished himself and his corps by vigorous attacks at Gaines's Mill and in a rearguard action at Frayser's Farm. Ironically, Stonewall Jackson's performance during the Seven Days, on the other hand, was considered "lethargic." Lee then reorganized his newly christened Army of Northern Virginia into two corps: Longstreet would command the First Corps and Jackson the Second. Lee at this point in time regarded Longstreet as his second in command, and the two became fast friends. Telling in this regard was Lee's assignment of five divisions to Longstreet's Corps and only three to Jackson, who had emerged from the Seven Days with his reputation tarnished, contrasted to Longstreet, whose star was ascending.

Lincoln changed generals, replacing McClellan with Longstreet's West Point classmate John Pope, who brought his Army of Virginia south toward Richmond. Lee split his two corps and sent Jackson north to meet the threat, while Longstreet remained around Richmond. A sharp fight ensued on August 28 at Groveton between Jackson's Corps and part of Pope's army, and Lee brought Longstreet up from Richmond on the run. Jackson was now entrenched west of the First Manassas battlefield and under heavy pressure from Pope. Longstreet's Corps covered thirty miles in twenty-four hours and arrived at midday on August 29. Lee wanted Longstreet to attack immediately as his forces arrived, but Longstreet thought that piecemeal attacks against an unknown foe over unknown terrain would be hazardous. Lee yielded on this point, establishing a precedent that would haunt him in battles to come: acquiescing to Longstreet on critical command decisions. Longstreet conducted a reconnaissance the afternoon of the twenty-ninth; on the thirtieth, Pope attacked Jackson head-on, but Longstreet was ready. Pope, however, was not. It was a classic hammer and anvil situation: Jackson was the anvil and Longstreet the hammer, and hammer he did. Longstreet's Corps delivered a devastating flank attack, rolling up Pope's army and once again sending it reeling back toward Washington. It was Longstreet's finest moment, and he emerged from Second Manassas a Confederate hero for his hard-hitting attack that had routed Pope's army.

Nevertheless, Longstreet's twenty-four-hour delay in the face of Lee's order to attack immediately engendered criticism among Lee's officer corps. Lafayette McLaws said, "James Longstreet is a humbug and a man of small capacity who is very obstinate, not at all chivalrous, exceedingly conceited and entirely selfish."[204]

Following Second Manassas, Lincoln again changed generals, this time bringing back McClellan. In Richmond, Davis and Lee decided that Lee would invade Maryland in an effort to draw the Union army away from Richmond and bring Maryland into the war on the side of the South. Moreover, Lee hoped that he could recruit soldiers in Maryland and finally gain recognition by the countries of Europe. In September 1862, he crossed the Potomac and headed north. Lee sent part of his army under Jackson to capture Harper's Ferry and remove any threat of a flank attack from that location. Longstreet and Jackson, however, were dismayed by this move, because even with the two corps united, Lee's force was still outnumbered, perhaps by fifty thousand. Nevertheless, with Longstreet's Corps in tow, Lee moved north into Maryland, and McClellan shadowed him every step of the way.

After some preliminary jockeying, when McClellan (now armed with Lee's battle plan, which had been dropped by a Confederate officer and then found by one of McClellan's men) failed to attack and destroy Lee's army, the two opposing forces met at Antietam Creek near Sharpsburg, Maryland. There Longstreet's Corps held Lee's line against one of McClellan's piecemeal assaults. While that battle was a tactical draw, it was a strategic victory for the Union, as Lee was forced to withdraw and Lincoln promulgated the Emancipation Proclamation, which changed the war from one about secession to one about slavery, thus co-opting European nations that had already abolished slavery and the slave trade.

Longstreet emerged from Antietam a hero. He had held the Confederate left and center against savage attacks and had inflicted heavy losses on the Union forces attacking him. After the battle, Lee dubbed him "my old Warhorse."

Next up was Fredericksburg, in December 1862. There, the Union army, now led by Ambrose Burnside of "Burnside's Bridge" fame, confronted Lee's Army of Northern Virginia. Lee's army occupied the heavily fortified Marye's Heights and a sunken road at its base, and that terrain and those fortifications would be the great equalizer in the battle in which Burnside's army outnumbered Lee's by more than 30,000 men. And equalize it did: Lee's—and especially Longstreet's—men repelled fourteen foolhardy attacks with horrendous losses. When the battle ended, Burnside had lost 12,700 men to Lee's 5,300, and that night, as the Northern Lights appeared over the battlefield, the pitiful moans and cries of the wounded rose into the cold winter's air in a doleful chorus.

Longstreet's star, ascendant in the Southern press after Second Manassas and Antietam, remained so, and many observers now rated him the finest combat general in the Confederate army, primarily because of the outstanding command and control that he exercised over his corps. In addition, Longstreet had devised a new form of defensive field fortification—the traverse trench—that took the long, straight slit trench and divided it into compartments so that a shell bursting in one compartment would not cause casualties in the compartments on either side. Those trenches were the forerunner of the system of trenches employed in World War I.

Finally, Fredericksburg reinforced Longstreet's belief that the Confederacy, with its smaller armies, was and would be better served by fighting on the defensive. That belief would have deleterious consequences for the South in the future—not because it was wrong, but because it would hamper Lee's ability to take the offensive at a critical moment in what would be the decisive battle of the war.

In February 1863, Lee assigned Longstreet and two of his divisions—Pickett's and Hood's—to southeastern Virginia, where there were troubling reports of large Union forces in both Virginia and North Carolina. An ancillary reason for the excursion was to gather supplies for Lee's forces. Although there is a conflict of opinion among historians, a majority hold that the mission was a failure and that Longstreet neither collected supplies nor conducted any effective action against Union forces in that theater, whose number, especially in Virginia, was greatly exaggerated and whose force posed no threat to Lee's rear. That assignment, however, caused Longstreet and the roughly forty thousand men under his command to miss Lee's greatest but costliest (he lost Jackson) victory at Chancellorsville. The majority view is also that if Longstreet been present at Chancellorsville, Lee would have had sufficient numbers to complete the annihilation of the Army of the Potomac. Lee did not have enough men, however, and the Union army escaped to fight another day, which next would be at Gettysburg.[205]

Gettysburg to Appomattox

Gettysburg is, and always has been, the most controversial battle of the war, and it would ultimately prove to be Longstreet's, well, Gettysburg. Lee, in preparation for the invasion of Pennsylvania and following the death of Jackson, divided his army into three corps: Longstreet with First Corps, Richard Ewell with Second Corps and A.P. Hill with Third Corps. The battle at Gettysburg was fought over three days, with the South winning the first two days and General George Gordon Meade, who had relieved Hooker and was now in command of the Army of the Potomac, winning the strategically dispositive third day.

Much has been written, and argued, about Longstreet's performance at Gettysburg. The criticism of Longstreet primarily arises out of his performance on the second day, when he failed to execute an attack ordered by Lee until so late in the day that Union forces had occupied the two Round Tops and were able to repulse Longstreet's attack. Longstreet had wanted to flank Meade on his left—the Confederate right—and force him to fight them on more favorable terrain between Gettysburg and Washington. Lee, however, refused, saying that he would get them where they were: on Cemetery Ridge. History has not judged Longstreet kindly on his performance here. A number of historians argue that Longstreet was pouty and thus did not carry out Lee's orders when he was supposed to do so.

But there is more, and if true, it would be more damning. The criticism is that Lee issued Longstreet a "dawn order" to attack Meade's left early on the second day. The truth is, however, that Lee never issued such an order—as stated by his staff officers who were with him at the time—but instead issued an order the morning of the second day to attack at noon. Longstreet, however, did not attack until late that afternoon, and the outcome of the attack on the two Round Tops was thus preordained.

The third criticism is that Longstreet was supposed to support Pickett on the third day—the disastrous Pickett's Charge—with two more divisions. Again, however, there simply is no proof that Lee ordered such support. Indeed, both the "dawn order" and the "two divisions" arguments arose seven years after the war, propagated by Jubal Early and William Pendleton, the latter claiming to have heard the dawn order and the former angry with Longstreet for becoming a Republican.

In September 1863, Lee dispatched Longstreet and two of his First Corps divisions south to join Braxton Bragg around Chattanooga, where Bragg was engaged with Longstreet's West Point roommate, General William S. "Rosey" Rosecrans. Rosecrans had maneuvered Bragg out of Chattanooga and into North Georgia, and Bragg was crying for more troops. Bragg, after several retreats before the Union army, decided to attack his foe at Chickamauga Creek and did so on September 19, 1863. Longstreet and his men, traveling by train, arrived that evening and took up their position on Bragg's left.

The next day, Bragg attacked but in piecemeal fashion—like McClellan at Antietam and Lee at Malvern Hill—starting on his right. Then came

Longstreet's turn, and just as he prepared to attack, Rosecrans shifted troops along his front, creating a half-mile gap, into which John Bell Hood's division roared, shattering a third of the Union army. Rosecrans took what was left of that third and retreated rapidly into Chattanooga, but George H. Thomas took the other two-thirds and made a stand on Horseshoe Ridge that saved the Army of the Cumberland from complete destruction and earned him the sobriquet the "Rock of Chickamauga." It was here that Hood, who had led his division into the gap, was wounded and lost his leg at the hip during his assault.

Longstreet launched repeated but unsuccessful and costly attacks against Thomas's position, and that night, Thomas orchestrated an orderly retreat into Chattanooga. Thus, the Union army had once again escaped to fight another day. In the meantime, Bragg's army had suffered high casualties—eighteen thousand out of sixty-three thousand—and Longstreet's Corps had lost eight thousand out of twenty-three thousand. For all of those losses, the South had won but a tactical victory. Thus, from a strategic standpoint for the Confederacy, Chickamauga was a non-event, because Bragg did not follow up his victory of the twentieth with an attack on the twenty-first. Such an attack likely would have caught Rosecrans's army unprepared and in transition from offense to defense.

Longstreet had requested additional troops from Bragg on the evening of the twentieth so that he could renew his attacks on the twenty-first. Bragg refused, which engendered bitterness and anger in "the Bull of the Woods," as Longstreet was termed by Bragg's army at Chickamauga. That bitterness and anger would lead Longstreet in a new direction in the weeks to come.

Historians are split on Longstreet's performance at Chickamauga: many give him credit for the Army of Tennessee's only victory up until that point. Others say that he failed to properly exploit another half-mile-long gap that later appeared in Thomas's line that, they contend, he could have used to cut that part of the Union army in two. Nevertheless, newspapers at the time credited him with the victory, and he stood after Chickamauga at the apex of his career. Mary Chesnut wrote, "Bragg, thanks to Longstreet and Hood, has won Chickamauga."[206]

After his success at Chickamauga, Longstreet was caught napping when the Army of the Cumberland, trapped in Chattanooga, crossed the Tennessee River at Brown's Ferry. Longstreet's Corps was supposed to be defending that crossing but did not. The Federals established a beachhead there that enabled them to construct a supply line over which they funneled the men and supplies into Chattanooga that would eventually spell doom for

Bragg and his army. Mary Chesnut, ever ready with a quip, now changed her tune: "What a slow old humbug is Longstreet." Also, "Jackson's men had gone half a day's march before Peter Longstreet waked and breakfasted.… And Stonewall, could he come back to us here."[207]

In April 1864, Longstreet returned to Virginia to join Lee again. In the meantime, Grant had taken command of all Union forces, including the Army of the Potomac. In theory at least, Meade headed that army, but in actuality, Grant ran that show. When Grant took command, Longstreet, speaking of his old friend and the husband of his cousin Julia Dent, said, "We must make up our minds to get into line of battle and to stay there; for that man will fight us every day and every hour till the end of the war. In order to whip him, we must outmaneuver him, and husband our strength as best we can."[208] His words would prove prophetic.

The first clash between Lee and Grant occurred on May 5, 1864, at a place that included the old battlefield at Chancellorsville, where skeletons still lay. They would call it the Wilderness, and over two days, the armies relentlessly slammed into each other through what was tantamount to a Virginia jungle. Longstreet missed the first day, failing to march over the road that Lee had ordered and—as he had done at Second Manassas—once again freelancing so that he was late for the battle. The two armies slugged it out that day, with the Union forces driving the Confederates back off the Orange Road, and then, with a vicious counterattack, the Rebels restored the original line. The next day, with reinforcements, Hancock routed the Confederate right, and a disastrous defeat loomed for Lee's outmanned and outgunned troops. Then, at the eleventh hour, up came Longstreet's Corps and slammed into the Union army in one of the great counterattacks of the war. His men, led by the famous Texas Brigade, rolled up the Union left like "parchment" and then continued forward, on the verge of destroying a large portion of Grant's army. Fate, however, intervened, and Longstreet took a bullet in the neck and shoulder from his own men. His counterattack lost steam, and the two armies settled into defensive positions for the night.

Longstreet missed the next two battles—Spotsylvania Court House and Cold Harbor—while he recovered from his wound. He rejoined Lee on October 16, 1864, at Petersburg and assumed command of First Corps, dug in along the Confederate perimeter. Longstreet and Union general Philip Sheridan squared off at Cedar Creek on October 19, 1864, shortly after Longstreet's return to First Corps, and Sheridan won "a stunning victory" over Longstreet, capturing forty-three pieces of Confederate artillery and taking numerous prisoners, including Confederate general Stephan Dodson. Still, the siege sputtered on.

Finally, Grant broke the Siege of Petersburg at Five Forks on April 1, 1865—famously remembered for the shad bake that drew Fitzhugh Lee and George Pickett away from their troops at the time of Sheridan's attack—and Lee retreated from Petersburg to Appomattox, where, with Longstreet, he surrendered to Grant on April 9, 1864.[209]

POSTWAR

1865–1870

After the surrender, Longstreet joined Louise on April 13 in Lynchburg, where she was staying with her Garland family. On May 31, she gave birth to James Jr., their eighth child and second named for his father. The first had died of scarlet fever in January 1862. Doctors who examined Longstreet in the aftermath of the war and his Wilderness wound told him that he could expect to live about eight more years. He would defy those predictions and live four more decades.

Longstreet arrived in Lynchburg with $100 in gold, his share of a large sum of money that ended up in the hands of the Army of Northern Virginia. He intended to settle in Texas, where he and Louise had enjoyed several good years in the army. Accordingly, with one of his sons, Garland; his aide, Tom Goree; and a servant named Jim, he started south, leaving Louise behind in Lynchburg. Garland and Goree rode on horseback, while Longstreet traveled in an ambulance driven by Jim. They moved steadily, but slowly, through the Carolinas to Longstreet's brother's house in Cleveland, Georgia, and then on into Alabama in early August, witnesses to the savage desolation and mindless destruction that Sherman's army had left in its wake.

Longstreet's brother, William, joined them, but Tom Goree left them at this point; the Longstreet party moved on to Texas by way of Canton, Mississippi, where Longstreet's sister lived. After a visit there, Longstreet—riding alone now—headed for Mobile, where he likely caught a steamer headed for New Orleans. He arrived there at about the end of September 1865. New Orleans was already home to five Confederate generals: Hood, Beauregard, Simon Bolivar Buckner, John Magruder and Cadmus Wilcox.

Longstreet had a particular affection for the Washington Artillery, a famous unit out of New Orleans that had fought by his side for four years, and he thus decided to join a cotton brokerage firm being formed by two of its former officers, Edward and William Owens. The two Owens brothers were natives and had "good business connections" in the city; with that, Longstreet decided that he would make New Orleans home.

He returned to Lynchburg to fetch his family and seek a pardon from the U.S. government, but after meeting with Secretary of War Edwin Stanton and Grant, who agreed to write a letter to the president on his behalf, Longstreet met with President Andrew Johnson, who said, "There are three persons of the South who can never receive amnesty: Mr. Davis, General Lee and yourself. You have given the Union cause too much trouble."[210] In the meantime, a federal grand jury in Norfolk indicted General Lee and others for treason. That Damoclesian sword overhung many of the Confederacy's senior officers, and Lee's petition for amnesty was, like Longstreet's, denied.

Back in New Orleans, Longstreet busied himself with preparation for the opening of the cotton brokerage—Longstreet, Owen and Company—on New Year's Day 1866. Next was to visit cotton planters and line up crops, and over the next few weeks, Longstreet traveled through Louisiana, Alabama and Mississippi seeking clients. In March 1866, Longstreet became president of the Great Southern Fire, Marine and Accident Insurance Company Board. Between the two businesses, Longstreet likely earned between $10,000 and $15,000 per year, roughly $250,000 to $350,000 in today's dollars. He also sought opportunities in the fast-growing railroad business, but when nothing came of these efforts, he settled into the cotton and insurance businesses. He also became president of the Southern Hospital Association. His former comrade, Lieutenant General D.H. Hill, said that at this point Longstreet was "a genial, whole-souled fellow, full of fun and frolic."[211] Those traits, however, would soon be tested.

The Longstreets, like the families of most Confederate generals, were at the apex of New Orleans society and enjoyed the company of the most prominent New Orleans families. In addition, he and the Owens brothers bought a hunting cabin outside New Orleans in which to entertain friends and business acquaintances. For the Longstreets, as 1867 approached, life was good. This, however, was about to change—and change dramatically.

With Lincoln's death and the passing of his desire to reintegrate the defeated South into the Union, radical Republicans passed what would become known as Congressional Reconstruction, which placed the heavy heel of military occupation on the recalcitrant Confederacy's throat, with the exception of Tennessee, which had already reentered the Union. An underlying issue for white southerners was black voting power, the straw that stirred the racial-divide drink. Accordingly, in March 1867, the *New Orleans Times* solicited input from eighteen prominent citizens concerning the course that white southerners should take in the aftermath of the South's defeat and with the advent of Reconstruction. Longstreet did not shy away from the task at hand: in a letter that the newspaper published, he urged acceptance of, and acquiescence to, the new rules, in support of which he said, "let us accept the terms we are…duty bound to do, and if there is a lack of good faith, let it be upon others." Longstreet's point was that the South should participate in the electoral processes in force and then, through the restoration of constitutional government in the states, regain the political control that whites had exercised before the war.

What he said was not dissimilar to what other Confederate generals—Lee, Beauregard and Wade Hampton, for example—had said and were saying, and if he had quit then, he would have quit ahead. But he did not quit. On April 6, 1867, he wrote a second letter to the *Times* that was reprinted by the *New York Times* one week later. In it he said that the North won the war and that its interpretation of law must prevail. He urged the South to accept the postwar laws, including the right of blacks to vote.

Once again, however, enough was not enough for Longstreet. Inexplicably, he wrote a third letter urging cooperation with the Republican Party. Before sending it, however, Longstreet wisely sought the counsel of his uncle, Augustus Baldwin Longstreet, then chancellor of the University of Mississippi, in Oxford. Chancellor Longstreet read the letter and then said, "It will ruin you, son, if you publish it." John Bell Hood also told Longstreet, "[T]hey will crucify you." Undeterred, Longstreet sent the letter. Both men were correct in their assessments of the storm to come.

That storm broke immediately. Indeed, the afternoon of the letter's publication in New Orleans, an editorial appeared calling Longstreet a "traitor." It was one thing to urge cooperation with the federal troops then occupying the South but quite another to urge cooperation with the party that had defeated the South in the late war and had freed the slaves—the Party of Emancipation.

The letter received favorable reviews in the North, but southerners and their newspapers savaged its author. Overnight, Longstreet became a pariah. Old comrades turned away from him on the street, and old friends refused to sit with the Longstreets in church. His business, and that of the Owens's, was severely affected. Longstreet was stunned, thinking that what he had written made good sense. It did not, however, make good sense in the Deep South, and the firestorm—predictable to everyone but Longstreet—engulfed him and his family.

In August 1867, Longstreet and his family left the furor of New Orleans for the relative calm of Lynchburg, Virginia, and for the next two years, Longstreet would be out of New Orleans and out of work. He used this time to travel to New England and New York and spoke often to groups of Union soldiers. In June 1868, Johnson pardoned him, and that autumn, Longstreet supported his old friend Grant in his successful run for president. Longstreet attended Grant's inauguration on March 1, 1869, and ten days later, Grant appointed him surveyor of customs for the port of New Orleans at a salary of $6,000 per year. This appointment, however, gave even greater credence to his status as a scalawag—a southerner who supported the forces of Congressional Reconstruction.

In 1869, Early gave up on his exile in Canada and returned to Virginia, where he quickly assumed leadership of the various Lost Cause organizations. Then began the final leg of Longstreet's sad descent into Confederate purgatory. The South had fought with the belief that God was on its side. When it lost the war, southerners began to search for reasons. Longstreet supplied a major plank to the proponents of the Lost Cause catechism: he had defied Lee's order to attack at dawn on the second day at Gettysburg, his defiance had cost the Confederacy victory there and the Confederacy's defeat at Gettysburg lost the war for the South. Based almost entirely on Longstreet's politics, this mantra thus transformed Longstreet into the South's Judas and, in New Orleans, made lepers of him and his family.[212]

1870–1880

Most of the controversy surrounding the dawn order arose out of the assertions of William Nelson Pendleton, one of Lee's staff officers who claimed to have been present the evening of the first day meeting when Lee purportedly gave Longstreet the order. But the report that Pendleton authored in 1863 made no mention of such an order, and other of Lee's staff members present at that meeting stated that Lee gave no such order. Nevertheless, in the charged atmosphere of Radical Reconstruction, Pendleton's assertion—and Early's subsequent writings—combined to torpedo Longstreet's military reputation.

On May 30, 1873, Longstreet became president of the Levee Commission at a salary of $6,000 per year. Longstreet's next appointment, however, was disastrous. Republican governor Henry C. Warmouth placed him in command of the Louisiana State Militia, a mixed-race group that was—like anything that smacked of Republicanism—anathema to white southerners. What followed sealed Longstreet's fate in New Orleans. A group known as the Crescent City White League—largely comprising Confederate veterans—began fighting the forces of Reconstruction, and those conflicts finally came to a head on September 14, 1874, when some 8,400 White Leaguers marched on the statehouse in New Orleans. Longstreet met them with a force of 3,600 and, foolishly overestimating his capital with the Confederate veterans, rode into their midst. The White Leaguers promptly pulled Longstreet from his horse and attacked his little army, overwhelming it with 38 killed and 79 wounded. Federal troops then came in and restored order, but Longstreet's place in the southern hall of shame had been cemented when he had used black troops against white southerners.[213]

This incident gave impetus to those who would attack his military reputation and blame him for the South's defeat: William Nelson Pendleton, Jubal A. Early, Charles S. Venable, A.L. Long, Walter H. Taylor and Charles Marshall—some from Lee's staff—as well as John B. Gordon, Braxton Bragg, Wade Hampton, William Preston Johnston, Cadmus M. Wilcox and, worst of all, Jefferson Davis. Lee, however, had made only one criticism of Longstreet at Gettysburg: he said that Longstreet should have stopped him from ordering and executing Pickett's Charge. Now, of course, Lee was dead, and Longstreet's critics had an open field on which to run—and they were off to the races. Early ignited the controversy in a speech at Washington and Lee College in 1872, and Pendleton added fuel to the fire when he repeated the charges—now expanded to include the purported failure of Longstreet to send two extra divisions with Pickett—the next year in the same place.

Once again, Longstreet took his family and left New Orleans, this time for good. In the summer of 1875, they moved to his old hometown, Gainesville, Georgia, where he bought for $6,000 the Piedmont Hotel, a three-story boardinghouse. He also began farming two miles outside of town, a vocation that he would love for the rest of his life. Gainesville was a northwest Georgia trading center and somewhat of a resort town noted for its salubrious mineral springs. Planters moved their families there in the summer, and in the 1870s, a railroad reached the town, giving impetus to the summer trade.

Longstreet's scalawag reputation accompanied him to Gainesville. Fellow churchgoers would not sit in the same pew with him at church and would cross to the other side of the street to avoid meeting him. In spite of the move to Gainesville, Longstreet returned to New Orleans in 1876–77. He served on the board of directors of the New Orleans city schools in 1878 and as an ex officio member of the Board of Tulane University (then the University of Louisiana), and in March 1877 he converted to Catholicism. His move away from the Episcopal Church had begun in New Orleans when he was shunned by Episcopalians and accepted by Catholics.

Rutherford B. Hayes became president in 1877, and Longstreet applied for the position of U.S. marshal in Georgia. He did not get the job, but in September 1878, he became deputy collector of internal revenue in the United States Treasury Department at a salary of six dollars per day. In January 1879, he was appointed postmaster in Gainesville. A newspaper reported that he was somewhat diminished from his wartime statue, and the old beard was gone, replaced by heavy sideburns and a moustache. He had no use of his right arm, a legacy of his great counterattack at the Wilderness.[214]

1880–1890

Somewhat amazingly, in 1880, Hayes appointed Longstreet ambassador to Turkey at a salary of $10,000 per year. Longstreet, leaving his wife and children behind in Gainesville, left the country on November 1, 1880, for his new post. In a largely ceremonial position, Longstreet used sixty days of his time abroad to travel through battlefields of the Franco-Prussian War before returning in 1881 to Georgia, where he had finally been named U.S. marshal, a post he assumed on July 1, 1881. A reporter described him as "then sixty years old…a fine-looking man whose auburn hair had turned almost completely white."[215] He now became active in Georgia politics, involving himself in internecine struggles within the Republican Party for control of the northwest Georgia area. Longstreet sought to establish rule by traditional, native-born whites, interestingly, against the scalawag wing of the party, which sought to exploit the black vote. President Chester A. Arthur, however, supported the scalawag wing of the party, and Longstreet, with other problems, was doomed in terms of his tenure in office.

Longstreet's predecessor as marshal had been O.P. Fitzsimmons, who had run a corrupt office with corrupt deputies. The financial records were a disaster, and for some reason, the naïve Longstreet retained most of Fitzsimmons's deputies and then installed his own son, Garland, as chief deputy. Those decisions proved to be major mistakes, and a Justice Department investigation—along with Longstreet's failure to support Arthur in his reelection bid—led to his removal from office in 1884.

After leaving office, Longstreet once again retired in Gainesville, where he and his family spent the winter months at his hotel and the summer months at the joy of his life, his farm. There he had the hilly ground terraced and raised, among other things, turkeys and grapes; he made wine that he sold to the locals, who called his place "Gettysburg." From time to time, Longstreet fired his musket to scare off boys who were menacing his grapes. Of himself he said, "My arm is paralyzed; my voice…is gone; I can scarcely speak above a whisper; my hearing is very much impaired, and sometimes I feel as if I wish the end would come, but I have some misrepresentations of my battles that I wish to correct, so as to leave my record correct before I die."[216]

The controversy over Gettysburg rolled on. D.H. Hill, who had been blamed for the "lost order" incident of the 1862 Maryland Campaign, rose to Longstreet's defense for his role at Gettysburg. Hill wrote to Longstreet, "The vanity of the Virginians has made them glorify their own prowess & to deify Lee. They made me the scapegoat for Maryland and you for Pennsylvania. I told old granny Pendleton to his face in Charlotte that his charges against you were foolish."[217]

Hill, correctly so, wanted to correct the record to reflect the strong bonds of friendship between Lee and Longstreet, about which he wrote, "You were [Lee's] confidential friend, more intimate with him than anyone else. I know that he would be grieved at such talks as Pendleton & Jones have made. I am willing for you to use anything written by me in regard to Lee's implicit trust in you or anything to your own credit that does not disparage others."[218]

That opportunity soon presented itself. *Century Magazine*, in the summer of 1884, began running articles by various Civil War generals about their wartime experiences, and Longstreet quickly jumped into the cauldron. As noted, Confederate generals used that forum to attack and blame one another for bungling various battles. Joseph E. Johnston and Braxton Bragg went at it about First Manassas, Johnston went after G.W. Smith about Seven Pines and Beauregard and Preston Johnston—Albert Sidney's son—went back and forth about Shiloh. "The pages virtually trembled with the blows of aging warriors more interested in presenting arguments with former comrades than in past strife and erstwhile enemies."[219]

Longstreet wrote five articles, beginning with Fredericksburg and then moving on to the Peninsula Campaign, Second Manassas and the Maryland and Pennsylvania Campaigns. In these articles—an attempt "to set the record straight"—Longstreet appeared cross and vindictive with both the sainted Lee and the martyred Jackson, capital offenses in the South. In particular, he criticized Jackson for being slow and "sluggish" at Seven Pines. He also gave Jackson no credit for Second Manassas and criticized him again for his performance during the Maryland Campaign. It was evident that Longstreet thought little of Lee as a strategist, and as he would in his autobiography, he criticized Lee in *Century* for his various failures at Gettysburg. Perhaps correctly, he argued that his own "offensive-defensive" plan would have saved countless lives and won the battle. Once again, Longstreet had poured highly flammable fuel on the already blazing fire, and *Century* fanned the flames when it took all of the articles and compiled them in a four-volume set, *Battles and Leaders of the Civil War*.

Much of Longstreet's criticism was orchestrated by Lee's Virginia coterie, which had viciously attacked Longstreet, beginning with Early's seminal "Longstreet blame" speech at Washington and Lee in 1872 and who had, of course, deified Lee and Jackson. Longstreet disapproved of Jackson as a "Field Marshall," and that, coupled with his criticism of Lee, continued to relegate him to the lowest point in the hierarchy of Confederate generals. Nevertheless, Longstreet did have his supporters. Besides Hill, Lafayette McLaws, "who labeled Early the 'Confederate Falstaff,'" recognized the minefield that confronted anyone who tried to write Confederate military history. "As for Malvern Hill," McLaws wrote, "who is going to tell the truth about it? The whole truth? If I was to write what I saw concerning the total want of a plan in the attack...I would be denounced by our own people as a calumniator....We attacked in the most desultory, harum scarum way. The same thing occurred at Gettysburg." Instead, it was Longstreet who was attacked as a "calumniator."[220]

As historian Douglas Savage wrote, Longstreet, Lee's "Old Warhorse," had committed "three cardinal sins": he had joined the Republican Party, he had accepted employment from Republicans and, worst of all, he had taken on the myth of the Lost Cause by publicly criticizing its godhead, Robert E. Lee. Indeed, of Lee's performance at Gettysburg, Longstreet wrote, "When the smoke cleared away, Pickett's Division was gone. Mortal men could not have stood that fire." Longstreet further enraged southerners when he wrote that he had protested the charge to Lee, who sent the two divisions across the field and up Cemetery Ridge anyway. "That day at Gettysburg," he would write, "was one of the saddest of my life."[221] His opponents in the South—especially among Lee's apostolic successors—would ensure that he had many more sad days.

In 1885, Grant died of cancer, against which he had struggled while trying to finish his memoirs. Longstreet was the only major southern figure to testify to Grant's greatness as a general and to "endorse his military genius without reservation."[222] During these years, Longstreet continued to farm and run the Piedmont Hotel. His physical health, however, was poor. Besides his paralyzed right arm, he suffered from arthritis and could speak only softly. In addition, his hearing was bad, and he had to use a hearing trumpet. In spite of these ailments, however, the Longstreets enjoyed a comfortable life, especially from a financial standpoint.

Longstreet spoke extensively—beginning in 1883 at the Chicago World's Fair—at reunions of Union soldiers, where he told them what they wanted to hear: "They fought well under a hero worthy of every man's respect." In 1886, he attended a Confederate reunion in Atlanta, riding "uninvited and unexpected" in a parade of some ten thousand Confederate veterans in full uniform. The passage of time had ameliorated much of the animosity toward Longstreet, and when the old soldiers recognized him, they shouted the Rebel yell and cheered their old commander. Longstreet reached the reviewing platform, dismounted his horse and mounted the platform, where he shook hands with his old adversary, Jefferson Davis.

In 1888, Longstreet attended the twenty-fifth anniversary of the Battle of Gettysburg. One of his old adversaries, Dan Sickles—a Tammany Hall Democrat of somewhat questionable reputation—had become a friend and was there. And in 1890, he attended another reunion and parade for the unveiling of Lee's statue in Richmond. Gradually, his old critics were dying, and the Confederacy had begun to set aside the old internal animosities and welcome Longstreet back into the southern fold. But Longstreet was a stubborn old cuss, and as with the three newspaper letters, he could not leave well enough alone.

Two unfortunate events intervened in 1889. On April 9, the twenty-fourth anniversary of Appomattox, Longstreet's home burned, and with it all of his papers, his uniforms and his sword. Then, at the end of 1889, Louise died. Beginning in 1890, Longstreet immersed himself in writing his book. It would take five years to complete, and finally, in 1896, J.B. Lippincott Company of Philadelphia published Longstreet's *From Manassas to Appomattox*. One historian characterized it as "defensive in tone, with numerous inconsistencies, contradictions, half-truths and outright lies." It is today, however, viewed as "an important insight into the Civil War and Longstreet himself."[223]

Once again, Longstreet criticized the deified Lee, and once again, that criticism engendered denunciation of Longstreet throughout the South. He simply would not let go of the old battles and the old controversies. In his memoirs, Longstreet also said that Early was "the weakest general officer in the Army of Northern Virginia."[224] Early, however, had died in 1894 and was no longer around to take up the anti-Longstreet cudgel and respond with the vitriol he had spewed at Longstreet during his lifetime. Longstreet, thirty years earlier given only eight years to live, was enjoying the ultimate revenge: he was outliving all of his old adversaries.

Longstreet continued to appear at Civil War reunions and parades and continued to speak to veterans' organizations. In 1889, he was Georgia's delegate when a commission designated Chickamauga as a national monument. He would appear there again in 1895, when the battlefield was dedicated as a national park. In 1889, he attended a parade in New Orleans as a guest of the Washington Artillery in connection with the unveiling of a statue of Lee, and in March 1892, he and Sickles spoke to the Irish Society, where they got "pie-eyed drunk" together. That same year, Longstreet attended the third annual meeting of the United Confederate Veterans, which was headed by his old adversary John Gordon. Again, Longstreet was well received by the Confederate veterans, except by Gordon, who responded to Longstreet with cold disdain.[225]

1890–1904

In 1893, Longstreet went to Gettysburg for Memorial Day ceremonies and then on to Antietam. At Gettysburg, he was accompanied by some of his old adversaries, Dan Sickles and Oliver Howard, whose troops were routed and driven through the town on the first day. Billy Mahone, a friend and ally, rode the train from Philadelphia with Longstreet. Earlier, Longstreet had spoken in Philadelphia at a Union League dinner, where he spoke warmly of Ulysses S. Grant, late husband of his cousin Julia Dent. All of the participants were perhaps bound by a contention that "they shared some onus of error in the battle."[226] The "onus" was, for Longstreet and Billy Mahone, an outgrowth of two main factors: both had joined the Republican Party after the war, and both had criticized the sainted Robert E. Lee. Longstreet had become "a welcome guest at

Northern commemorative ceremonies," having appeared at the dedication of Grant's tomb in New York, with its parade on Broadway and a reception afterward given by President William McKinley.[227]

These kinds of activities continued on into 1894, 1895 and 1896, but it was 1897 that brought a major change to his life: Longstreet married Helen Dortch (she was thirty-four; he was seventy-six) in the Governor's Mansion in Atlanta. His children opposed the marriage, but Longstreet said, "Old men get lonely and must have company." Helen would live until 1962, outliving Longstreet by fifty-eight years. She wrote a book titled *Lee and Longstreet at High Tide*, defending Longstreet, whom she rightfully thought history had mistreated. As Longstreet biographer Gordon Sawyer noted, "She is a book unto herself."[228]

That same year, Longstreet sought a job as U.S. railroad commissioner, held at one point by Joseph E. Johnston and, at the time that Longstreet applied, by Wade Hampton. President McKinley nominated him for that position on October 29, 1897, with confirmation following on January 2, 1898. Hampton, who hated Longstreet, refused to assist him with the transition. Longstreet's new job was a position that involved lots of travel and little work. He and Helen took a honeymoon in Mexico, where they visited the scenes of some of his Mexican-American War exploits and, using railroad passes and an expense account, toured the West. As a *Baltimore Sun* reporter described the job, "It pays handsomely, and is an extremely pleasant position in every way; but from the time of its creation it has never been anything but a sinecure. The hardest work the incumbent has ever had is to 'tote' around the railroad passes showered upon him…and to sign for his month's pay." Longstreet and Helen took an apartment in Washington, D.C., and in 1901, he attended McKinley's second inauguration.[229]

Longstreet continued his attendance at reunions and northern commemorations on into the new century. He appeared at West Point for its centennial in 1902. There Longstreet ran into his old cavalry commander from the western theater, Joseph Wheeler, who had served in the United States Army during the Spanish-American War and was, therefore, wearing a blue uniform. Longstreet said to him, "I hope Almighty God takes me before he does you, for I want to be within the gates of hell to hear Jubal Early cuss you in the blue uniform."[230]

Those words were prophetic. He and Helen returned home to Gainesville in time for Christmas 1903. By this time, Longstreet was suffering terribly from his Wilderness wound in the shoulder and neck, and he now had cancer in one of his eyes. His weight dropped from more than 200 pounds to about 135. On New Year's Day 1904, the Bull of the Woods, Lee's Old Warhorse, developed a terrible cough and began expelling blood, probably from his throat wound. He died, mercifully, the next afternoon, saying, "Helen, we shall be happier in this post."[231] He is buried in Gainesville, and for many years, other than his grave, there was no indication that he ever lived there; however, a statue of him now marks the place where his house was located.[232]

Chapter 8
RAPHAEL SEMMES

"Old Beeswax"

BEGINNINGS

Raphael Harcourt Semmes, a sea dog whose exploits would become legendary, was born on September 27, 1809, in Charles County, Maryland, where his father, Richard Thompson Semmes, was a tobacco farmer. Richard was descended from Benedict Semmes, who accompanied Lord Baltimore's 1634 expedition to Maryland, and Raphael's mother, Catherine Middleton Semmes, was descended from Arthur Middleton, one of the signers of the Declaration of Independence.

Raphael's mother died in 1811, when he was only two, and his father, Richard, died in 1823, when Raphael was fourteen. Upon the death of his father, his uncle Benedict took legal custody of Raphael and his brother, Samuel. Benedict Semmes was a prominent physician who had just been elected to the Maryland House of Delegates. Although Benedict had legal custody of the boys, actual custody rested with Benedict's brother, Raphael, a prosperous Georgetown merchant with several businesses that ranged from the sale of liquor to banking to an import-export trading company and a wholesale grocery business.

Taylor described the younger Raphael's education as "sporadic." He attended Charlotte Hall Military Academy for a few years, but from his later writing, one can conclude that he was a well-educated young man.

Raphael Semmes.
Library of Congress.

When Raphael was sixteen, his uncle Benedict secured an appointment as a midshipman for him. The Naval Academy had not come into existence at that point in time, so on April 1, 1826, Semmes entered service as a midshipman aboard the USS *Lexington*. What followed were six hard years at sea for the slim, dark-haired young man aboard the USS *Brandywine* and the USS *Porpoise*. On April 28, 1832, Semmes passed the examination to become a "passed midshipman," the step before commissioning as a naval officer. He was twenty-three years old.

The navy had too many officers for too few assignments, so officers, including passed midshipmen, spent much of their time "awaiting orders." Semmes was no exception, but he used his leave time to "read law" with his brother, Samuel, in Maryland, and in 1834, he was admitted to the Maryland bar. It is not clear why, but subsequently, he—still awaiting orders—moved to Cincinnati to practice law. There he took a room in the home of Oliver and Elizabeth Spencer and almost immediately began courting their daughter, Anne Elizabeth, described as "as stately, handsome girl with regular chiseled features, brilliant brunette complexion and hazel eyes."[233]

In March 1835, Semmes received orders to report to the USS *Constellation*, a renowned naval vessel on which he was to serve two years. On October 18, 1835, the navy detached him from the *Constellation* and sent him to Florida, where the Second Seminole War was in progress. There Semmes, attempting to take a small steamer, the *Lieutenant Izard*, up the Withlacoochee River, ran his ship aground. In the navy of that day—indeed of *any* day—running a ship aground could spell the end of a career, but the navy did not even convene a board of inquiry. Semmes returned to the *Constellation*, his career unscathed.

In 1837, he left the *Constellation*, and that year finally brought his promotion to lieutenant. A few months later, he married Anne, and for the next five years he alternated his time between the practice of law and surveying the Gulf coast for the navy. In 1841, he bought land along the Perdido River in Alabama and built a home he named Prospect Hill. He also became a citizen of Alabama.

In 1843, Semmes assumed his first command afloat when he took command of the USS *Poinsett*, which was one of the navy's first steamers. In 1845, he moved to the USS *Porpoise* as first officer. The Mexican-American War broke out in 1846, and aboard the *Porpoise*, Semmes headed for Mexico.[234]

MEXICAN-AMERICAN WAR

The Mexican-American War was a land war, with only a minor role for the navy, which was directed to blockade Mexican ports along the Gulf of Mexico. Semmes went aboard the USS *Raritan* first; then, in October, he took command of the USS *Somers*, a small, fast brig, about 133 feet in length. The *Somers* earlier had experienced the only documented mutiny in U.S. naval history, which had resulted in the hanging of three mutineers, including Heddie Philip Spencer, the son of the secretary of war.

Semmes and the *Somers* were assigned to a squadron commanded by Matthew Perry with orders to blockade the Mexican port of Vera Cruz. Somehow, a Mexican ship slipped by the *Somers* and into port. Chagrined, Semmes sent a party in a small boat at night, and the men burned the offending ship. Subsequently, while patrolling offshore, the *Somers*—a top-heavy vessel—caught a large wave abeam and rolled over, resulting in the loss of life of thirty-nine of its seventy-six crewmen. Semmes narrowly escaped drowning, and later he faced a court of inquiry, which not only exonerated him but also praised him for the manner in which he had handled his ship. Back on the *Raritan*, Semmes's roommate now was a young naval officer named John R. Winslow, who would later come back to haunt Semmes.

In a portent of things to come in a later, larger war, Semmes took in six naval guns to support operations ashore. There he encountered and interacted extensively with Robert E. Lee, who was chief engineer to General Winfield Scott. Semmes also worked with another army officer, Thomas J. Jackson, in placing naval artillery at Vera Cruz. Subsequently, at Mexico City, he worked with Ulysses S. Grant. Eschewing a return to the small U.S. fleet, Semmes instead finagled a position as an aide on the staff of Brigadier General William J. Worth, who cited him three times for bravery.[235]

SERVICE BETWEEN THE WARS

Following the Mexican-American War, Semmes returned to Mobile, where he would once again await orders. Mobile had now become his permanent home, and there he practiced law and wrote a memoir of his experiences in the Mexican-American War with the somewhat cumbersome title of *Service Afloat and Ashore During the Mexican War*. The book was well written and extremely well received. Foreshadowing an issue that would arise in connection with his later career, he argued that if Mexican ships had preyed on U.S. merchant vessels, their crews would be treated as pirates. In addition, Semmes—a proponent of Manifest Destiny—argued presciently that the United States would eventually become the dominant commercial power in the Western Hemisphere and that it would not be Britain that ruled the waves, but the United States.

A few months after his return to Mobile, he took command of the USS *Electra*, a store ship in Pensacola. Semmes did not endear himself to *Electra*'s crew. He applied the lash liberally—sixteen floggings in his first forty days onboard—then took command of the USS *Flirt*, a curiously named schooner. In October 1849, Semmes requested shore duty and, returning to Mobile, moved his residence from the Perdido River into Mobile proper. From 1849 to 1855, Semmes moved in and out of the navy, until finally, that year, he was promoted to commander and took command of the USS *Illinois*, a mail ship. That would be his last U.S. Navy seagoing command. He then joined the navy's Lighthouse Service in Washington, D.C.

Semmes's beliefs included one holding that southerners were cavaliers descended from England's Norman overlords and that northerners were "roundheads" descended from Puritans, whom he despised. Moreover, he viewed the U.S. Constitution as a compact that allowed states to withdraw from the Union at will. Those views, coupled with his "antipathy" toward the election of a Republican president in 1860 and Semmes's belief in states' rights, led to his resignation from the navy on February 15, 1861.[236]

CIVIL WAR SERVICE

Following Alabama's secession from the Union and Semmes's almost immediate resignation from the navy, the Confederate provisional government in Montgomery, Alabama, offered him a naval commission. His wife, Anne, was in Cincinnati with her family, who were Unionists, as were some of Semmes's family. Nevertheless, Semmes headed for Montgomery. As he rode the train through Alabama, he would later recall:

> *This night ride through the burning piney woods of Alabama afterward stood as a great gulf in my memory, forming an impassable barrier, as it were, between my past and my future life. It had cost me pain to cross the gulf, but once crossed, I never turned to look back. When I washed and dressed in Montgomery the next morning...the labors and associations of a lifetime had been inscribed in a volume that had been closed, and a new book, whose pages were as yet all blank, had been opened.*[237]

Semmes would soon begin to fill those pages with exploits that would become the stuff of legend and part of the Southern catechism underpinning the Lost Cause catechism.

In Montgomery, Semmes, who had met Jefferson Davis earlier, called on the new president of the Confederacy. Davis dispatched him on a curious—and ultimately unsuccessful—mission north to purchase military supplies for the South from munitions brokers. While on this March 1861 mission, Semmes became a commander in the nascent Confederate navy, and in April, he returned to Montgomery. An assignment to head the

Lighthouse Bureau followed, much to Semmes's chagrin, but after Fort Sumter, he requested sea duty.

Semmes persuaded Confederate secretary of the navy Stephen Mallory to allow him to convert a packet steamer, the *Havana*, into a commerce raider. Semmes believed that commerce raiders could bring the Union's oceangoing commerce to its knees and lead to Southern independence. Mallory agreed, and Semmes immediately traveled to New Orleans to purchase and begin the *Havana*'s conversion into the CSS *Sumter*. Thus would begin Semmes's "adventurous career" as captain of his first commerce destroyer.

On June 30, 1861, with the *Sumter* now ready for sea, Semmes ran the l'Outre Pass to the Gulf of Mexico past a Union blockade, barely escaping the USS *Brooklyn*. As he ran free into the Gulf of Mexico, Semmes broke the Confederate flag on his ship and later wrote that the crew "gave three hearty cheers for the flag of the Confederate States."[238]

The *Sumter* would roam the shipping channels of the Caribbean and the Atlantic for only six months, but during this period, it brought to bay eighteen Union cargo ships, beginning with the inexplicably named *Golden Rocket*, which Semmes burned. During this period, it eluded numerous U.S. warships, and a British naval officer said of Semmes, "There is no doubt he will do an enormous amount of damage before he is taken, for he seems a bold, determined man and well up to his work."[239] He would indeed prove to be both.

Semmes did not, however, hold his crew in high regard. He referred to them collectively as "Jack" and considered them lazy, liars, thieves, drunkards and rascals who were incapable of managing their own affairs, right down to proper maintenance of boots and underwear. Semmes maintained these under strict control and issued those stores to the men as needed, docking their pay as the paymaster doled out those items of clothing. His opinion of the enlisted men is perhaps summarized in this statement: Jack "is as big a drunkard and as great a villain as ever."[240] Jack was not the only rascal at sea. In what was then known as Suriname, the U.S. Consul referred to that "rascally steamer sailing under the name *Sumter*." Semmes's and the *Sumter*'s reputations were growing.

Of Semmes himself, it was said that he was a "high strung commander," an austere and formal man, and with the exception of Dr. Gault, the surgeon, and Mr. Kell, his first lieutenant, he rarely held any intercourse with his officers except officially. He waxed the ends of his moustache (which his sailors called his "st'unsail booms"), and he would pace the quarterdeck alone, twisting and retwisting those long ends.[241] His waxed moustache would give rise to the name that Jack gave him: "Old Beeswax."

Badly in need of repairs, Semmes took the *Sumter* across the Atlantic to Gibraltar. By this time, a number of Union warships were in hot pursuit, including five under future admiral David Porter. At Gibraltar, a British visitor said:

> *I could scarcely believe that so poor a vessel could have escaped so many dangers. She is a screw steamer with three masts, a funnel strangely out of portion to her size, and a tall, black hull, so high out of the water that she gives you the idea of being insufficiently ballasted....She is crank and leaky. Her engines are partially above the lower deck, and are surrounded by a cylindrical casing of 6-inch wood covered with half-inch bars—very poor protection against a 9-inch shot.*[242]

Gibraltar was to be the last port of call for the *Sumter*. Three Union warships arrived and blockaded the port, among them Semmes's future opponent, the USS *Kearsarge*. With *Sumter* under repair and with half of his crew having deserted, Semmes sought and received permission to abandon it. He paid off his crew and, with Kell, left Gibraltar for Southampton.

Lionized in England, Semmes took passage to the Bahamas as he made his way back to the Confederacy. However, in Nassau, a promotion to captain came through for him, along with orders to return to England to take command of a new ship still under construction at the John Laird Sons and Company in Birkenhead. There, the Confederacy's agent, James Dunwoody Bulloch, who would be Theodore Roosevelt's uncle, had ordered two ships that he had designed and that were to serve as Confederate raiders, one to become the CSS *Alabama*, which Semmes would command, and the other the CSS *Florida*.

The *Alabama* was built with oak to enable easier repairs to its hull in foreign ports; it was 220 feet long and 32 feet wide amidships. Fully loaded, it drew 15 feet of water. Bulloch had installed several innovative features: a freshwater distiller that would produce a gallon of water per man per day and two engines rated at three hundred horsepower each. *Alabama* carried a year's worth of parts, two sets of sails and enough coal for eighteen days steaming. In addition, *Alabama* was driven by a twin-bladed retractable screw that could be raised up and out of the water and into a well in about fifteen minutes, when steam was not necessary, and the ship could move under sails hoisted on three masts, with its "chimney stack" stored. It was described as a "barque." *Alabama* carried six six-inch thirty-two-pound cannons, two eight-inch "pivot" guns and a one-hundred-pound Blakely rifled gun. Its complement was twenty-five officers, and "Jack" on this ship consisted of eighty-five enlisted men. It cost the Confederacy about $237,000, a handsome sum indeed in those days.

A skeleton crew spirited it to sea out of Liverpool and on to the Azores, where Captain Semmes, Kell and the ship's surgeon, Lieutenant Galt, subsequently arrived. When Semmes saw it there, he said, "I had surveyed my ship…with no little interest, as she was to be not only my home, but my bride, as it were, for the next few years, and I was quite satisfied with her external appearance. She was, indeed, a beautiful thing to look upon."[243] On August 24, 1862, Semmes put the *Alabama* into commission with a ceremony that had his crew lower the British "merchant colors," under which it had sailed to the Azores, and raise the Confederate ensign. Semmes then read his commission and orders to take command of the *Alabama*, and the band played "Dixie." *Alabama*'s motto was *Dieu t'Aidera*: "God helps those who help themselves."[244]

For the next two years, *Alabama* terrorized Union merchant ships, sailing in the Gulf of Mexico, the Atlantic as far north as Newfoundland, around the Cape of Good Hope into the Indian Ocean, the South China Sea south to Singapore, through the Malacca Straits and on into the Pacific as far east as the East Indies. During these voyages, it captured sixty-five Union merchant ships and, in a short sea battle off Galveston, quickly sank the USS *Hatteras*. With the Northern press all over the Federal government to corral *Alabama*, the secretary of the navy dispatched nineteen ships—and at one point up to fifty—to catch *Alabama*. When Semmes learned of the size of this fleet at sea, he proposed to raid New York Harbor, but low coal scuttled that mission. When Semmes captured a ship and burned it, he carefully removed the crew and any passengers first and then treated them with the utmost courtesy and civility. That aspect of Semmes's behavior would serve him well after the war.

A sailing captain whose ship Semmes had burned said of him in the *New York Herald*, "He sports a huge mustache, the ends of which are waxed… and it is evident that it occupies much of his attention. His steward waxes it carefully every day, and so prominent is it that sailors on the *Alabama* call him 'Old Beeswax.' His whole appearance is of a corsair, and the transformation appears to be complete from Commander Raphael Semmes, United States Navy, to a combination of Lafitte and Kidd."

But all good things must come to an end, and the end for *Alabama* loomed large on the nautical horizon. Semmes sailed it back into the Atlantic and then to Cherbourg for needed repairs. There, three Union ships—including its old foe, the USS *Kearsarge*, commanded by Semmes's Mexican-American War roommate (and now captain), John Ancrum Winslow—blockaded *Alabama*, keeping it in port. Faced with a choice of atrophying in port or fighting, Semmes challenged *Kearsarge* to a duel, which took place on June 19, 1864. Unbeknownst to Semmes, who thought the ships evenly matched, Winslow had fortified *Kearsarge* with steel chains hung over its sides that he had covered with wood, and the outcome was thus preordained. In just over an hour, and before a large crowd of onlookers who manned the French coast around Cherbourg, *Kearsarge* sent *Alabama* to the bottom. Semmes and some of his officers, however, escaped to England on an English yacht, the *Deerhound*, owned by a Southern sympathizer named John Lancaster. For Semmes, his career as a blue-water raider was over. The redoubtable Mary Chesnut would say of him, "Semmes, of whom we have been so proud—he is a fool after all—risked the *Alabama* in a duel of ships! He has lowered the flag of the famous *Alabama* to the *Kearsarge*. Forgive who may! I cannot."

From England, where he remained for the remainder of 1864, Semmes made his way back to the Confederacy through Cuba and Mexico, then traveled into Texas, across the Deep South and up into Virginia. He saw firsthand what Sherman had wrought on his march through Mississippi, Alabama, Georgia and South Carolina. In Richmond, Semmes became commander of the James River Squadron based on his flagship, the ironclad CSS *Virginia*. Richmond, however, fell on April 2, 1865, and Semmes ordered his squadron scuttled. He then took the 450 men from his small navy and joined Lee's Army of Northern Virginia in its escape from Petersburg. Semmes and his "Naval Brigade" took the train to Danville, where Jefferson Davis appointed him a brigadier general in the army, even though Semmes thought a major general's rank would be more commensurate with his navy rank. At Danville, his "brigade" had melted away from 450 men to roughly 250 because of desertion, but he gamely divided his men into two regiments and manned the guns defending the town. Word then came of Robert E. Lee's surrender, and Semmes abandoned Danville and marched his troops to Greensboro, North Carolina, where he joined forces with General Joseph E. Johnston, who surrendered the Army of Tennessee shortly to General Sherman. Thus ended the war for Admiral/Brigadier General Raphael Semmes.[245]

POSTWAR

Semmes was clever. Fearing that he would be tried as a pirate, he finagled a parole document whose terms were legally broad enough—yet specific enough to him—that it would allow him to avoid trial if he did not "take up arms against the Government of the United States." Semmes was further "permitted to return to his home, not to be disturbed by the United States authorities, so long as he observes this obligation, and obeys the laws in force where he may reside." The document was signed on April 30, 1865, by Semmes and U.S. Army brevet brigadier general William Harstuff.

It took him two weeks to travel to Montgomery, Alabama. There, he and his son Raphael took a riverboat to Mobile, where Anne (who may have spent the last two years there, though it remains unclear) awaited him. In Mobile, Semmes spent the last half of 1865 trying to establish a law practice. He bought a "rambling 2-story, frame house" four miles west of Mobile and named it the Anchorage.[246]

Semmes persisted in his beliefs that the Constitution was a pact between the states and that it thus allowed a state, or states, to withdraw at will. He viewed the South as the "injured party" and was bitter and angry in defeat, angry like those victorious Northerners who wanted the South's leaders tried as traitors, Semmes included. Union troops had arrested Secretary of the Navy Stephen Mallory, but in most cases, the Federal government honored the paroles issued to military leaders at the end of the war. The line of demarcation between those up for arrest and those not seemed to be that *senior* military commanders were subject to arrest and trial. Accordingly, they were excluded from the first presidential amnesty proclamation issued on May 29, 1865. Semmes knew that Union officials would consider him a Blackbeard or a Captain Kidd and that no specific pardon could be expected, especially in the aftermath of Lincoln's assassination.

Some of his officers—undoubtedly feeling the pinch after the war—wrote to him asking if they were due any prize money. While there was no prize money, Semmes's agent sold sixty-odd chronometers in England for $4,142. Semmes took half of that money based on the rationale that he had paid off the other officers of the *Alabama* in London after the *Kearsarge*'s deadly work and, moreover, had himself incurred substantial expenses on behalf of the *Alabama*. That left about $2,000 to be divided among seven officers, not a bad haul in the penniless postwar South.

In mid-1865, Semmes put out feelers to be a commercial agent in South America but got no takers. Through all of the remainder of 1865—indeed, through all of the rest of his life—Semmes, like Jubal Early, remained an angry, unreconstructed rebel. He considered Northerners "barbarous peoples" and said that he would not accept a pardon even if one were offered. Later, however, he would change his mind as a matter of economic necessity.

Meanwhile, forces in the North were moving against "the pirate Semmes." Then, on the night of December 15, 1865, a party of U.S. Marines surrounded the Anchorage and arrested Semmes on a charge of violation of "the usages of war" by leaving the scene of his loss to the *Kearsarge*. The officer in charge told Semmes that they would leave with him in the morning, Semmes, apparently unruffled, slept the whole night through.

The next day, Semmes and his captors boarded the steamer *Louise* and sailed for New Orleans. General Dabney Maury was aboard the *Louise* and, in the light of Semmes's arrest, feared that Nathan Bedford Forrest, the "Butcher of Fort Pillow," would be arrested next; however, Gideon Welles, the secretary of the navy, had targeted Semmes—Forrest, though indicted, would escape prosecution.

Semmes's captors put him up at the St. Charles Hotel, one of New Orleans's finest, where a stream of sympathetic visitors called on him. Semmes requested his Baltimore son-in-law to retain an attorney for him. On February 20, he boarded a ship for New York, and he was treated with "great courtesy" by the ship's officers. In New York, Semmes spent a night at the Astor House and then, with his escort, boarded a train for Washington. In Washington, his escort took him to the navy yard, where he would await trial on what now consisted of five charges: 1) using false colors—usually British—to approach his victims; 2) seizure of vessels in neutral waters; 3) illegal destruction of captured vessels; 4) treason; 5) and violation of the rules of war by escaping on the *Deerhound* after the *Kearsarge* had sunk the *Alabama*.

Semmes, through his son-in-law, hired attorney James Hughes to represent him. Hughes was a friend of President Andrew Johnson's and thus enjoyed access to the president. Semmes wrote to Johnson, arguing forcefully that his arrest constituted a violation of the terms of the parole granted to him by General Harstuff. Upon consideration by various federal authorities, the five charges were eventually reduced to one: leaving the scene of *Alabama*'s sinking without being paroled. Then, a second charge was added: cruelty to prisoners. This charge evaporated when former prisoners stated publicly that Semmes had treated them with courtesy and kindness. Again, Semmes's future rested on the *Deerhound* charge, pressed stridently by Secretary Welles.

Johnson was tiring of the case. He complained that Anne Semmes visited him regularly, "crying and taking on about her husband."[247] Then, in the case of *In re Milligan*, the Supreme Court held that military courts had no jurisdiction where civilian courts were available. Because Welles and his colleagues wanted to try Semmes in military courts, that decision eviscerated their cause of action. Thus, on April 7, the authorities released Semmes from prison. This particular legal ordeal was over.

The next legal issue arose upon his return to Mobile, whose citizens had lionized him and urged him to run for city probate judge, which he did successfully. President Johnson stated, however, that no "unpardoned rebel" could hold elected office. Semmes then applied to Johnson for a pardon, but the president denied that request. Semmes denounced Johnson as a "charlatan" and "a traitor to his state [Tennessee]." Next came the Fourteenth Amendment to the United States Constitution, which prohibited former officers of the Confederate States Army or Navy from holding public office unless permitted to do so by an act of Congress approved by two-thirds of each chamber. Such a vote was extremely unlikely for "the pirate Semmes."[248]

Seeking work, Semmes applied for and was granted a position on the faculty of the Louisiana State Seminary, later to become Louisiana State University. Semmes became the professor of moral philosophy and English literature. Leaving his family in Mobile, Semmes traveled to Alexandria, Louisiana, where, for a $3,000 annual salary, he would take up his faculty position. Next, he accepted an offer to be editor of the *Memphis Bulletin* for an annual salary of $5,000, and in March 1867, Semmes relocated to Memphis. That arrangement disintegrated when the owners refused to grant Semmes full editorial control and objected to his anti-Johnson polemics. When he did not get his way, Semmes, true to his tradition, called the publishers "a set of political scoundrels" and resigned after only seven months.

Next came a lecture tour on which Semmes told of his experiences on the *Alabama*. A member of one of his audiences described him at this time as "a small, dark-looking man; thin, wiry, weather-beaten in his face with a fierce-looking mustache twisted outward at the ends and a dangerous look about his…eyes." The man thought that Semmes was uncomfortable as a speaker because he twisted the ends of his mustache. Jack would not, however, have been surprised. Semmes told of capturing Union vessels, but it was his colloquy about the *Alabama* that sent his audience members to their feet: "No enemy's foot ever polluted her deck. No splinter of her hull, no shred of her flag, remains as a trophy in the hands of the enemy!"[249]

The lecture tour was a financial success, and while other Confederate leaders such as James Longstreet accepted the South's defeat and tried to move on, Semmes, like Early and Jefferson Davis, remained an unreconstructed and bitter rebel. In 1868, Semmes began his memoirs, which covered more than just his wartime experiences at sea. Indeed, *Memoirs of Service Afloat During the War Between the States* was a defense of the South's right to secede pursuant to his reading of Constitutional law. The war had been, he posited, a struggle "against barbarism." Semmes argued forcefully on behalf of the Southern states and their conduct in seceding from the Union and then fighting for their independence over four years. He saw the war as a struggle between good and evil, with the South on the side of the angels and the North a collection of "cowards, hypocrites, and prevaricators." Once again, he denounced Northerners as "Puritans" and "roundheads," with Southerners analogous to the Cavaliers of the English Civil War. To Semmes, damning someone as a "Puritan" was the greatest insult of all. The book, published in 1869, became a pillar of the Lost Cause movement.

On race, Semmes viewed free blacks as "nearly worthless" and feared miscegenation: "[T]he mulatto, as the name imports, is a mule, and must finally die out."[250] The book, in short, was a philippic against the North and Northerners, and Semmes's hatred of both seared its pages, which were boiling with vitriol and scorched with bitterness, all in keeping with the beliefs and behavior of Early and other Lost Cause adherents. Whatever else the book was, it was not a book designed to foster national reconciliation. Nonetheless, the citizens of Mobile continued their adoration. In 1871, they bought a house for him and his family in downtown Mobile, and then the mayor appointed him city attorney. Still, Semmes, a staunch Catholic, "lived in a world of villains. The values that he prized most were threatened not only by Yankees but by Protestants."[251]

In 1873, Semmes sought Congressional approval to remove his impediments so that he could hold public office. Twice a measure to do so passed the House but failed in the Senate. Semmes, however, remained "the first citizen of Mobile": "While…not given to words, he was easy of approach, affable and pleasant in conversation, and kind and agreeable in his intercourse with his fellow man.…He had the esteem and confidence of every one, and his practice was good considering the times, the scarcity of money [and the] unsettled conditions."[252]

Anne was a rapid talker, and Semmes rarely spoke when she was present. They built a cabin on Point Clear in 1876, across the bay from Mobile, and in the warm months, they spent most of their time there. Semmes was bothered by a "chronic intestinal disorder," and after a meal of seafood he became gravely ill. After dictating his last will and testament, by which he bequeathed everything to Anne, he died on August 30, 1877.

Mobile paid him its highest honors the next day at his funeral. Guns fired from dawn to sunset, and after a service at the Catholic Cathedral, four white horses pulled his hearse through the streets of the city to the Catholic Cemetery. A crowd of several thousand followed in the rain. Obituaries referred to him as "the Nelson of the Confederacy" and "the Stonewall Jackson of the sea." Thus eulogized, Semmes moved quickly into the pantheon of Southern heroes, and by the 1880s, he was firmly ensconced in the temple of the Lost Cause. His fame, however, extended far beyond the South. Kaiser Wilhelm II, soon to attain fame—or infamy—in World War I, told the U.S. ambassador to Germany in 1894, "I reverence the name of Semmes. In my opinion, he was the greatest admiral of the nineteenth century. At every conference with my admirals I counsel them to read and study Semmes's *Memoirs of Service Afloat*."[253]

Considering other nineteenth-century admirals—Nelson, for example—there is perhaps no higher praise.[254]

Chapter 9

ROBERT E. LEE

"Marse Robert," "Uncle Robert," "Bobby Lee," "Bob Lee," "Rob Lee"

CHILDHOOD

Robert E. Lee was born on January 19, 1807, at Stratford in Westmoreland County, Virginia, to Richard Henry Lee III, known as "Light-Horse Harry," and Ann Hall Carter Lee, who was known as "Nancy" and was a member of the wealthy and distinguished Carter family. Nancy's great-grandfather was Robert "King" Carter, who owned 300,000 acres of land and more than one thousand slaves. Her father, Charles Carter, owned Shirley, a plantation of some 25,000 acres of land that had been in the Carter family since 1720. Harry and Nancy married in 1793. He was thirty-six and she was nineteen. As Harry Lee's wife, Nancy was not to enjoy the lifestyle or the happiness to which she had been accustomed at Shirley.

At Robert's birth, Harry Lee was in possession of Stratford as a legacy—though not an inheritance—from his first wife, "the divine Matilda" Lee, a distant cousin who had inherited Stratford and six thousand acres from her father. Concerned about Harry's profligacy and myriad speculative investments—mostly in land—at her death in 1790, Matilda bequeathed Stratford in trust to their three children: Phillip, who would die at age ten; Lucy Grymes; and Henry Weddon, who possessed many of the same bad proclivities extant in his father, except perhaps more. Henry Weddon would later—while his wife was ill—impregnate his sixteen-year-old sister-in-law, who was his ward, and he was thought to have murdered the infant. Henry Weddon would become infamously known in Virginia as "Black-Horse Harry Lee."

It was said that Nancy Carter was happy in her new marriage for all of two weeks, as Light-Horse Harry's fortunes began an inexorable decline about the time of his second marriage. Light-Horse Harry was, in short, a rogue, albeit a *charming* rogue, who lost money in one bogus venture after another. One story about Harry perhaps best illustrates his character. He went to a neighbor's house claiming that he had lost his horse. The neighbor agreed to lend him a horse and sent along a slave to bring the horse back when Lee was done with it. Several weeks passed: no horse, no slave. Finally, the slave returned, much worse for wear. His master asked him what had happened. The slave said that Harry had sold the horse. Asked why *he* had not returned, the slave replied, "He sold me, too."

In 1798, Harry parlayed his famous name into a successful run for Congress and moved his family to Philadelphia. There he managed to alienate a number of important people, including future president Thomas Jefferson, and he passed a bad check to George Washington. But it was he who said of Washington in a eulogy, "First in war, first in peace, and first in the hearts of his countrymen." To complete the Light-Horse Harry saga, he finished his book, *Memoirs of the War in the Southern Department of the United States*, in Alexandria and then was beaten almost to death in a Federalist/Anti-Federalist fracas in Baltimore. (Harry was an avowed and outspoken Federalist.) Finally, in 1813, during the War of 1812, Harry left Virginia for Barbados. He attempted to return to Virginia in 1818 but became ill on the return voyage; he was put ashore on Cumberland Island, Georgia, and there died at the home of his deceased Revolutionary War commanding general, Nathanael Greene, where he was cared for by Greene's daughter. Thus, from the age of six, Robert never saw his father again.

Robert attended school first at Eastern View in Fauquier County and then at Alexandria Academy, which was free to local boys. His two older brothers were gone: Charles Carter Lee attended Harvard and later became a lawyer in New York City, and Sidney Smith graduated from the Naval Academy and served until the Civil War as a career officer in the U.S. Navy. Robert thus by default became the oldest son in Nancy Lee's house and eventually became male head of the household. At Alexandria Academy, Robert excelled in mathematics, and although there is debate

Robert E. Lee. *Library of Congress.*

among historians as to whether family economics drove him to the United States Military Academy at West Point—a questionable theory because his mother tried to talk him out of going—that is where he decided to go. Lee thought that if he did not like the army after graduation, he could instead embark on a career as an engineer, since West Point's curriculum was essentially that of an engineering school.[255]

West Point

Robert's cousin William Fitzhugh wrote to Secretary of War John C. Calhoun requesting an appointment for Robert to West Point. Lee hand-delivered the letter to Calhoun, who, after receipt of additional letters from a number of prominent men, granted the appointment—though not in 1824, as Lee sought. Because he had appointed too many candidates from Virginia for that class, Calhoun delayed Lee's appointment until the summer of 1825, as he did with another Virginian, Joseph E. Johnston. After a year at what was tantamount to a prep school, run by a Quaker named Benjamin Hallowell, Lee and 105 classmates entered West Point in 1825. Brevet Lieutenant Colonel Sylvanus Thayer was superintendent of West Point and had reshaped the school into a rigorous engineering regimen that would wash out about half of each entering class. In Lee's class, only 46 out of the 106 who entered would survive to graduate and be commissioned.

Lee, however, excelled, finishing second in his class academically behind Charles Mason of New York, who would leave the army after only one year. Lee was one of six graduates in the class of 1829 who received no demerits, and he attained the highest position in the Corps of Cadets, Cadet Adjutant. The combination of his academic (second in his class) and military (first in his class) records was extraordinary.

Jefferson Davis was one year ahead of Lee, and Joseph E. Johnston, who would be a lifetime friend, was a classmate. When he graduated, Lee was approximately five feet, eleven inches tall and was "powerfully built," but strangely, his shoe size was only four and a half. He was described as "incredibly handsome," with "a military bearing and posture"—a man who "moved with grace and poise." Lee had dark-brown eyes and black wavy hair that "was thick and full." His classmates called him "the Marble Model" because he was so handsome that he looked like the model for a marble statue.[256]

Army Career, 1829–1846

Newly brevetted second lieutenant Robert E. Lee, who was assigned to the prestigious Corps of Engineers, headed south for Cockspur Island, Georgia, where he was to assist with the construction of what would become Fort Pulaski, which was to guard the approaches to Savannah. Plagued by heat, humidity and swarms of mosquitoes, Lee sought refuge in Savannah at the home of his good West Point friend and classmate Jack Mackay, who happened to have five attractive sisters living at home. They embraced Lee, and he embraced them, striking up a flirtatious relationship with Eliza Mackay. The Mackay girls had other suitors, however, and Robert soon realized that his relationship with Eliza would lead to naught.

In the summer of 1830, Robert left Cockspur on furlough when the semitropical island's climate halted work on the fort. He returned to northern Virginia to spend his furlough in the company of various family members, including George Washington Parke Custis; his wife, Mary "Molly" Custis; and their daughter, Mary Anne Randolph Custis, at Arlington, their large home across the Potomac from Washington.

Parke Custis was a wealthy planter who owned thousands of acres of land spread over three plantations—Arlington, White House and Romancoke—and about two hundred slaves. Custis greatly indulged his daughter, his only child, producing a spoiled, self-indulgent, hot-tempered, careless girl. Moreover, she said exactly what she thought, when she thought it, and that predilection produced a sharp-tongued, sharp-featured brat of a girl. In today's usage, she would be said to have no filter.

Following Robert's return from Cockspur Island, he and Mary spent time together during the summer of 1830. Initially, Parke Custis opposed a marriage between Robert and Mary because of Robert's kinship with the two Harrys: Light-Horse and Black-Horse. Eventually, however, Parke Custis relented, and the two became engaged in September 1830. Mary and Robert married at Arlington on June 30, 1831. Robert, who would all his life enjoy the company of women and children more than men, had, however, in choosing *this* woman, married his absolute antithesis. The union produced a marriage that would prove difficult and, at times, unhappy for both of them.

Prior to his marriage, Robert had reported to his next duty station, which was at Fortress Monroe, located on the Atlantic at the tip of the Virginia Peninsula formed by the James and York Rivers, where the fort guarded the approaches to Newport News and Norfolk. Mary joined him at Fortress Monroe, but there she would have only one or two servants instead of the small army that had waited on her at Arlington. Living in small, cramped quarters instead of the enormous Arlington, she would face the strictures of army life, with its rigid command structure that spilled over to the officers' wives.

At Fortress Monroe, Lee began a platonic but very close relationship with Harriett Talcott, the wife of one of his fellow officers. Lee biographer Emory

Thomas called it a "mock love affair."[257] It was one of many relationships with various women that Lee maintained after he married Mary Custis. He did not, however, hide those relationships—or even his correspondence—from Mary, and there is no evidence that he ever acted on his (and his partners') feelings. Perhaps as close as he ever came to unfaithfulness was with Mary's young first cousin—and likely a distant cousin of Robert's—Mary Custis "Markie" Williams, with whom, in 1844, when she was eighteen and he was thirty-six, he began and maintained a lifelong correspondence and, through it, a love affair. Their correspondence is filled with expressions of love and affection, and at times, their communications became outright sensual, as biographer Elizabeth Brown Pryor stated. The letters, and Markie's diary, were loaded "with sentiments that surpassed the bounds of close cousinly affection." "Oh Markie, Markie, when will you ripen?" Lee had written to her when she was just fifteen and he was thirty-three.[258]

Upon his Savannah friend Eliza Mackay's marriage, he wrote to her of her wedding night, "And how did you deport yourself My child? Did you go off well, like a torpedo cracker on Christmas morning?"[259] Another woman in his life was Tasy Beaumont, "My beautiful Tasy." To a male friend, Henry Kayser, Lee confided in 1845, "You are right in my interest in the pretty women, & it is strange I do not lose it with age. But I perceive no diminution."[260]

Lee addressed a movement in the Anglican Church known as "Puseyism," which was a proponent of the "high church" movement. Lee was a low church man, and to a group of fellow officers he said, "I am glad to see that you keep aloof from this dispute that is disturbing our little parish.... *Beware of Pussyism! Pussyism* is always bad, and may lead to unchristian feelings, therefore beware of *Pussyism*!"

Lee biographer Emory Thomas noted that while there were "pussy-cats" in that era, "the vulgar meaning of 'pussy' was in vogue too."[261] Lee was not, then, the straight-laced, taciturn man Lee aficionados have made him out to be. He was funny, liked ribald humor, had a vibrant sense of humor and adored women, especially *young* women.

Over the next fifteen years, Lee, occasionally accompanied by his growing family but often not, received assignments to Washington, D.C., Baltimore, St. Louis and Fort Hamilton at Brooklyn, New York. He was promoted to first lieutenant in October 1836 and to captain in July 1838, after only two years as a first lieutenant, at that time a very rare event for an army officer in peacetime. But Mary's health steadily declined during the years between their marriage and the Mexican-American War in 1846, and she would be an invalid by the Civil War. During those years, "Lee experienced increased frustration with his wife. He gave vent to his concerns and continued to seek emotionally fulfilling relationships beyond his marriage. Those relationships, probably 'innocent,' tended to focus upon bright young women as Lee moved into midlife."[262]

In spite of it all—his "mock love affairs" with Markie Williams and Eliza Mackay—Lee remained a loving husband to Mary. "Indeed, he took pains to inform and even involve his wife in his correspondence with young women. To a degree, Mary and Robert Lee developed some sort of understanding on the subject. And whatever arrangement, spoken or unspoken, the Lees adopted, Robert remained a faithful spouse and a sensitive, warm, sensuous man at the same time." Nonetheless, he always preferred to be with women rather than men, around whom he was far more reserved, preoccupied and indeed somewhat shy. With women, on the other hand, he was outgoing, playful, funny and a flirt of the first magnitude.[263]

In the first fourteen years of their marriage, Robert and Mary produced seven children, all of whom had nicknames that were assigned to them by their father, whom they called "Pa'a." Custis Lee was "Boo" or "Mister Boo." Mary Custis was called "Daughter." Fitzhugh—as opposed to Lee's nephew, also named Fitzhugh—was called "Rooney" or "Roon." Anne Carter was known as "Annie." Agnes was "Wigs" or "Wiggy." And Robert E. Lee Jr. was "Rob," "Robertus" or "Brutus." The youngest, Mildred, was called "Precious Life" by her father. Rob would later write of his father, "Our greatest treat was to get into his bed in the morning and be close to him, listening while he talked to us in his bright, entertaining way."[264] Of the four daughters, none would ever marry, which biographer Pryor attributed as much to "personality and circumstances" (the Civil War) as to their father, although other historians disagree, believing that Lee *was* an obstacle to their matrimony.[265]

Rob also recalled that Lee "'was very fond of having his hands tickled, and…it pleased and delighted him to take off his slippers and place his feet in our laps in order to have them tickled.' In the evening Lee told stories to his younger children while they tickled his feet. And if they became so absorbed that they neglected their task, Lee stopped to declare, 'No tickling, no story!' With the older children Lee ran family races and entered high-jumping competitions at the standard he set up in the yard. He played with his children and when he kissed them, he kissed them on their mouths."[266]

THE MEXICAN-AMERICAN WAR

A boundary dispute with Mexico led to war. Lee requested field duty and received orders to Mexico in August 1846. He served in northern Mexico and then joined General Winfield Scott in central Mexico for his campaign to take Mexico City. Lee joined Scott's staff—his inner circle—but was a field officer, who, with artillery assistance from Raphael Semmes, oversaw the blasting of Vera Cruz's walls, which led to its surrender.[267]

Scott then moved toward Mexico City, and Lee distinguished himself at Cerro Gordo—where Scott cited him for gallantry and called him "indefatigable"—and then received a brevet promotion to major. At Contreras, he found a route around the enemy's lines, which Scott exploited and which led to a brevet promotion to lieutenant colonel for Lee. At Chapultepec, Lee again led troops in a flanking movement. Scott said that Lee was "the very best soldier I ever saw in the field."[268]

Lee learned from his experiences in the Mexican-American War, which was a training ground for the leaders on both sides of the Civil War, much as the Spanish Civil War would be for World War II. First, he learned that a smaller force could defeat a larger force by using maneuvers to make flanking moves. Second, he learned that a leader must take chances and accept the risks inherent in difficult movements, but he must calculate those risks based on thorough and accurate reconnaissance such as that provided by Lee to Scott in Mexico. And third, there was a lesson that would come to haunt Lee—and the South—at Malvern Hill and, most importantly, in the Pennsylvania Campaign. That lesson was the almost exclusive efficacy of offensive action, of the attack, above all else. In Mexico, however, the success of the attack was predicated on two important factors: the inefficiency of the musket, with its range of only one hundred yards, which allowed an attacking force to overcome defenders while taking only one round of hostile fire, and the fecklessness of the Mexican commanders and the ineptitude of the Mexican soldiers. Neither of those factors would be present in the war to come.[269]

THE PEACEFUL INTERLUDE, 1848–1860

What followed the Mexican-American War was for Lee a series of peacetime assignments, beginning with three years at Fort Carroll in Baltimore Harbor and a surveying expedition to Florida; in 1852, he became superintendent at

West Point, an appointment that he did not want. Here, however, he was able to move his family with him and enjoy their company for an extended period of time. As superintendent, he oversaw cadet James McNeil Whistler—who flunked out—and future generals Philip Sheridan; Joe Wheeler; Lee's nephew, Fitzhugh Lee; John Bell Hood; Stephen D. Lee; John Pegram; W.E. Pender; John B. McPherson; and Jeb Stuart. On Lee's staff were Civil War generals George Thomas, Robert C. Garnett and Fitzhugh John Porter. During Lee's tenure as superintendent, his own son Custis also passed through West Point and finished first in the class of 1854.[270]

That halcyon time was to end when, in 1855, Lieutenant Colonel Lee transferred branches from the Corps of Engineers to the cavalry and was assigned to the Second Cavalry in Texas, under the command of Colonel Albert Sidney Johnston. As noted, the Second Cavalry had an illustrious lineup of Southern officers-to-be. Of the forty-three officers in the unit, sixteen would be generals, including eleven for the South. Among them were Joe Johnston, Kirby Smith and John Bell Hood, all of whom would be lieutenant generals.

In Texas, Lee chased Comanches and Apaches for two years, mostly to no avail. In 1857, however, his father-in-law, Parke Custis, died, leaving Mary Lee a life estate in Arlington, with Arlington to pass to her son Custis at her death. The other two plantations, White House and Romancoke, were left to Rooney and Rob, respectively. Lee took a leave from the army—he would take several leaves all together before returning in 1859—and went home to Arlington, where he took charge of about five thousand acres of land and about two hundred slaves. Parke Custis had left a tangled web of accounts and debts that Lee had to resolve.

An allegation would emerge during this time that would damage Lee's reputation in the North. It involved three slaves—two men and a woman—who escaped from Arlington. When they were recaptured, Lee, according to the report, ordered the slaves stripped and the men to receive either thirty, thirty-nine or fifty lashes and the woman either twenty, twenty-nine, thirty or thirty-nine (depending on the source), which, by one report, he administered to her bare back himself. According to the reports, Lee then ordered their backs washed with brine to intensify and prolong the pain. Supported by testimony from five sources, the allegation of behavior so contrary to Lee's nature would resurface time and again. Lee vehemently denied the allegations.[271]

In the fall of 1859, as he prepared to return to the army, an event took place that would both galvanize and define the two sides of the slavery issue. On the morning of October 17, 1859, as Lee worked at Arlington, he received a messenger from Washington. It was Jeb Stuart, and he brought an order for Lee to report to the War Department immediately. Lee, like Stuart in civilian clothes, headed for Washington.

There he learned that what was thought to be a mob of three thousand had seized the federal arsenal at Harper's Ferry. Reporting to the War Department, Lee was dispatched to take command of a company of Marines and four companies of Maryland Militia and to move on Harper's Ferry, which he did, by train, presaging another development that would blossom in the war to come. Arriving at Harper's Ferry, Lee determined that only a few insurgents had captured the armory and that they held a number of hostages within it. Lee had his men surround the armory, and the next morning he sent Jeb Stuart under a white flag to negotiate with the man thought to be a "Mr. Smith" but was really John Brown, whom Stuart recognized from his own time in Kansas. The negotiations were for naught, and Stuart signaled to Lee that he would be unable to secure a peaceful surrender. Lee than attacked with the Marines, who battered down the door, killed two of the insurgents and arrested the other two. The Marines had one man wounded and one man killed. They freed thirteen hostages. Subsequently, Brown was hanged, and Lee, with troops, was there to prevent any rescue attempt.

On February 9, 1860, Lee received orders to return to Texas to command the Department of Texas in San Antonio after two years farming three plantations and managing his slaves. The experience reinforced his belief that slavery was untenable and had to go. He disliked managing slaves and, like other slaveholders, blamed them for the problems he encountered in managing the plantations. That attitude would travel with him until his death.

Once he arrived in San Antonio, he wrote a remarkable letter to Annie that is an insight to his self-image as a father: "It is better too I hope for all that I am here. You know I was very much in the way of everybody and my tastes and pursuits did not coincide with the rest of the household. Now I hope everybody is happier."[272] Next, Lee took command of the Second Cavalry and watched as the nation began to come apart following Lincoln's election in November 1860. Texas seceded in February, and in the next few days, delegates from six of the seven seceded states—all but Texas—met in Montgomery to form a new, independent nation.

Lee received orders to Washington in April and arrived at Arlington on March 1, 1861. Three days later, Abraham Lincoln became president, and in April, when he tried to send supplies to Fort Sumter in Charleston Harbor, artillery batteries along the shore under the command of General P.G.T. Beauregard opened fire and eventually compelled the garrison to surrender.

Lincoln then called for 75,000 volunteers to put down the rebellion, and Davis responded by calling for 100,000 men. Virginia seceded.

General Winfield Scott and Francis P. Blair, a close friend of Lincoln's, offered Lee command of the Union army at a rank of major general, but Lee, who was opposed to secession and correctly thought it was "revolution" and that a "long and difficult war" would ensue, turned down the offer. He could not, he said, take part in an invasion of the southern states. Lee then resigned—after thirty-two years of service—from the U.S. Army. For him, the die was cast, irrevocably.

The Civil War

Early Travails

Lee's first assignment was as a major general in command of all of Virginia's armed forces, and he helped to raise and organize an army of some forty thousand men, mostly untrained militia. Subsequently, that force was absorbed by the Confederate army, and the Confederate Congress confirmed five full generals in the Confederate army. By order of rank, they were Samuel Cooper, who would serve throughout the war as Jefferson Davis's adjutant and inspector general; Albert Sidney Johnston; Robert E. Lee; Joseph E. Johnston; and P.G.T. Beauregard. Of that group, Johnston had been the highest-ranking officer—a brigadier general—in the prewar "Old Army." As noted previously, Johnston would never get over the lack of seniority assigned him by Davis, and the two would hate each other for the entire war and beyond, as would Davis and Beauregard, albeit for different reasons.[273]

Lee did not participate in the First Battle of Manassas, but a week after that conflict, he went to what was then western Virginia, his position laden with as much vagueness and ambiguity as his title, "senior advisor." At Cheat Mountain, Lee and two subordinates in rank, William W. Loring and Albert Rust, laid out a well-conceived plan of simultaneous attacks by the two generals, who promptly bungled the operation by failing to attack. Then, at Kanawha, General Rosecrans attacked and defeated another Confederate army under the command of General John B. Floyd. Western Virginia was thus lost to the Confederacy and soon became the state of West Virginia. Lee, the senior officer present, received the blame. He was characterized as "a general who had never fought a battle…and who wanted…victories without the loss of life." He became "Granny Lee" in the army and was called "a man too tender of blood."[274]

In November 1861, Lee assumed command of the military department of the two Carolinas and Georgia in Charleston, an assignment that set off an uproar among the officers of that department, which Davis quelled. The Confederacy was reeling from ignominious defeats at Roanoke Island, Forts Henry and Donelson in the west, as well as the loss of the entire state of Kentucky by Albert Sidney Johnston. Then Fort Pulaski fell, and Lee received the blame for its loss. His military career was at low tide, and in early March 1862, Davis invited the besieged general to Richmond as his "military advisor." Most observers assumed then that Lee's career as a field officer had ended in an ignominious collapse.[275]

Union general George McClellan assembled the largest army ever to take the field on American soil, and he landed it on the Peninsula of Virginia to begin his slow but steady march up toward Richmond. Johnston retreated but finally attacked at Seven Pines, after McClellan's horde had closed on Richmond, and was wounded there. The next day, June 1, 1862, General Robert E. Lee took command of Johnston's army and rechristened it the Army of Northern Virginia. For McClellan, the situation was about to change—and change dramatically.

Once again, however, many politicians and Confederate officers objected to Lee's appointment. Still known as "Granny Lee," he picked up the additional monikers "The King of Spades" for his work in ordering and overseeing the construction of an extensive network of trenches in front of Richmond and "Evacuating Lee" for his performance in West Virginia. An observer, Joseph Christmas Ives, responded, however, to the criticism that Lee was timid: "If there is one man in either army…who is, head and shoulders, far above every other one in audacity, that man is General Lee, and you will very soon have lived to see it. Lee is audacity personified. His name is Audacity."[276]

Christmas's words soon would prove prophetic—in spades, though not the king's spades.

The Seven Days

Lee's attacks on McClellan's 100,000-man army by his 65,000-man Army of Northern Virginia began on June 25, 1862, and in seven days, the two armies fought at Oak Grove (also known as King's Schoolhouse),

Mechanicsville, Gaines's Mill, Savage Station, White Oak Swamp (also known as Glendale) and Malvern Hill—six bloody battles in all that produced high casualty rates on both sides but especially in the Army of Northern Virginia. The battles constituted a series of uncoordinated attacks over difficult terrain by Lee's army that, taken together and from a strategic standpoint, were a victory for the Confederacy but, in several cases, were tactical defeats. The last battle of the Seven Days, Malvern Hill, is illustrative. There, Lee, believing that McClellan was retreating, ordered a general assault over terrain that favored McClellan, who was indeed *not* retreating but had instead prepared strong defensive positions. The attacks were again piecemeal and never had a chance. D.H. Hill, in the aftermath of the battle, said, "It wasn't war, it was murder."

Lee had made myriad mistakes in the Seven Days with heavy losses, especially at Malvern Hill, but he had saved Richmond and had driven McClellan back down the Peninsula. For the most part, he would not repeat those mistakes, except for one battle that would be a repeat of Malvern Hill on a larger and more devastating scale. Now, however, Lee faced another threat, this time from the north and from a Union army headed by John Pope.[277]

Second Manassas/Second Bull Run

Of all the audacious moves made by Lee during the Civil War—and there were many—none was more so than those he made at Second Manassas. Lee had reorganized his army after the Seven Days into two corps—one headed by Jackson and one by Longstreet. At Second Manassas, he split his army and sent Jackson around Pope's right. Then, the next day, he dispatched Longstreet with the remainder of Lee's forces to follow, leaving Pope's front unopposed and the road to Richmond wide open except for a small force of artillery that did just enough to make Pope think that Lee's entire army opposed him. Jackson then took up a position on Pope's right and held the line against repeated attacks until Longstreet arrived and moved over to Jackson's right and Pope's left at an angle that formed a "V" with Jackson's line. The trap was set, and Pope then attacked into the "V," just as Lee had drawn it up. Jackson held—he was the anvil, and Longstreet's hammer fell on Pope's left flank. The result was a rout. Lee's men, however, were starving and could not follow up the victory with the destruction or capture of Pope's army, which fled into Washington behind its fortifications.

An event that followed the battle provides an insight into Lee's personality. Confederate soldiers shot and killed Union general Philip Kearny, whom Lee knew, and Lee wrote the following note to Pope:

> *Sir,*
> *The body of General Philip Kearny was brought from the field last night, and he was reported dead. I send it forward under a flag of truce, thinking that the possession of his remains may be a consolation to his family.*
>
> *I am, sir, respectfully,*
> *your obedient servant,*
> *R.E. Lee*
> *General*[278]

Chaos was rampart in the Union army following Second Manassas. Pope blamed his subordinates for the disaster, but Lincoln and Henry Halleck blamed Pope, who was quickly relieved and sent west to fight the Sioux rather than the South. George McClellan, back in Washington, took command again, a sign of the desperate straits in which the North found itself in the aftermath of its devastating defeat at Second Manassas. Lee, flush with victory, decided to head north into Maryland.

One command characteristic of Lee had emerged since he took command of the Army of Northern Virginia: he viewed his role as putting his subordinates and their troops in the right position at the right time and then leaving the execution of his plan up to them. It had not worked at the Seven Days, but it worked at Second Manassas, even though Longstreet displayed for the first time a propensity to disobey or delay the execution of Lee's orders until he was ready to attack, in that case almost a day later than Lee had ordered. Lee, who was nonconfrontational and hated controversy, allowed Longstreet to get away with this conduct, and his failure to confront Longstreet then would come back to haunt him in a catastrophic way a year later.[279]

The Maryland Campaign

Lee, while conceding that his army was unprepared for an invasion of Maryland—it lacked manpower and supplies—decided to invade anyway. He saw an invasion as an opportunity to bring Maryland into the Southern camp and draw Union forces out of Virginia. Once again, Lee split his army, sending Jackson and three divisions to capture Harper's Ferry and Longstreet and two divisions to the area west of South Mountain in Maryland. Then he dispatched Lafayette McLaws and two more divisions to assist Jackson at Harper's Ferry. That left D.H. Hill and a division to protect his army's rear and placed Stuart and his cavalry along his right flank to screen him from McClellan to the east. His plan was to then concentrate his army at Boonsboro and there to give battle to McClellan if "Little Mac" had pursued him.

The Army of Northern Virginia was in sad shape: its men were exhausted from a month or so of continuous marching and fighting, and they lacked basic supplies like shoes and food. Their horses were as hungry as their riders, and an onlooker's impression of the entire army was that "they were the dirtiest men I ever saw, a most ragged, lean and hungry set of wolves, yet there was a dash about them that the Northern men lacked. They rode like circus riders. Many of them were from the far South and spoke a dialect I could scarcely understand. They were profane beyond belief and talked incessantly."[280]

Then came the famous (or, for the South, infamous) "lost order," Special Order 191, which set forth Lee's plan for the campaign and laid out how he had split his army. The order had been intended for D.H. Hill but instead—wrapped around three cigars—found its way into McClellan's hands, who now had a rare and precious opportunity to destroy the Army of Northern Virginia once and for all. Lee faced another problem as well: he had crossed into Maryland with 65,000 men but now estimated that he had lost a significant number of his troops to desertion and straggling. McClellan, on the other hand, led 71,500 well-fed, well-equipped and concentrated Union troops of the Army of the Potomac.

In the meantime, there was dissension among Lee's generals: Jackson had relieved A.P. Hill and placed him under arrest, and Longstreet had relieved John Bell Hood, arrested him and ordered him to return to Virginia. Lee intervened to keep Hood in command, and Jackson, whose dispute with Hill had festered for some time, allowed him to remain with the army.

McClellan moved slowly, but at South Mountain he overwhelmed D.H. Hill's division and began moving on Longstreet to the west. Lee realized that he stood in peril of losing his entire army, so he ordered McLaws, D.H. Hill, Longstreet and Jackson to concentrate in the hills to the west of Antietam Creek near Sharpsburg, Maryland. They did, in a line that ran from north to south. Jackson's corps held down the northern part of the line and Longstreet the southern part. A.P. Hill was still at Harper's Ferry, so Lee lined up with roughly forty thousand men against McClellan's seventy thousand plus.

If McClellan had ordered an all-out attack up and down the line simultaneously, he would have overwhelmed Lee. If, if, if.... But of course, being McClellan, he did not. Instead, he ordered piecemeal attacks similar to those Lee had used during the Seven Days, especially at Malvern Hill. The attacks began on Lee's left—Jackson's part of the line—and rolled south through places whose names would become gory legend: the East Woods, Dunker's Church, the Bloody Lane, the Cornfield. The losses were devastating to both sides, the carnage horrific.

The rolling attacks allowed Lee to move troops along interior lines from north to south and thus reinforce those under attack, much as Union general George Meade would be able to do in another Southern invasion of the North. Lee did this himself, issuing orders and placing artillery, a dramatic departure from his usual method of allowing his corps commanders to run the battle. His direct involvement in tactical operations likely saved the day.

Late in the day, after McClellan had failed to break Lee's army in the north and center, Union general Ambrose Burnside finally crossed a small bridge over Antietam Creek—now running red with blood—and almost immediately threatened to turn Lee's right flank and once again place the Army of Northern Virginia in danger of destruction. Suddenly, out of the southwest, on a dead run, came A.P. Hill's division, many of the men running barefooted, "up from Harper's Ferry," as Lee would say. It smashed into Burnside's exposed left flank. Burnside gave way and retreated back across Antietam Creek, and Lee's army lived to fight another day.

But there was to be no fighting on another day. McClellan sat—perhaps dismayed by the staggering losses he had incurred—as did Lee, and the night of the second day, Lee's army melted away into the darkness and headed back to Virginia. The losses on both sides were horrific. Lee, out of roughly 40,000 men, had lost 10,318. McClellan, out of 70,000 plus, had lost 12,410. The day of battle, September 17, 1862, would stand as the bloodiest single day of the entire war. Antietam was a tactical draw, but for Lee and the Confederacy, it was a strategic defeat.[281]

Fredericksburg

Lee used the autumn of 1862 to restore and refit his army, while McClellan, who could have destroyed him with a concerted advance and attack, did nothing. On November 7, Lincoln again sacked McClellan, and this time he replaced him with Ambrose Burnside, he of "Burnside's Bridge" at Antietam. Now Burnside moved on Fredericksburg exactly as Lee predicted. Burnside had 113,000 troops and Lee 78,000 along a six-mile front.

Lee had used his time to prepare an extensive system of defensive positions along the hills overlooking Fredericksburg. Burnside, to attack those positions, would have to cross the Rappahannock, send his men across open ground, pass over a "significant" drainage ditch and cross more open ground before confronting a sunken road backed up by a four-foot embankment. Then his troops would have to scale Marye's Heights. It would be—like Malvern Hill in reverse—"murder."

First, Barksdale's Mississippians, firing from buildings down in Fredericksburg, shot up Union troops trying to build pontoons across the river, cursing the entire time at the Union troops and delaying Burnside's army for two days. A Union officer would later say that he had never heard such profanity as that from Barksdale's Mississippians. Finally, Burnside ferried Union troops across the river to drive the Rebels away, his engineers completed the pontoons and he massed his army in Fredericksburg preparatory to the assaults on the heights.

The attack began, and at one point Lee expressed his fear to Longstreet that Union forces were about to break his center. Longstreet replied that Lee could put every Union soldier present in front of Longstreet's corps and, with enough ammunition, he would kill them all. His men didn't kill them all, but they killed many of them; the bodies piled up in front of the stone wall at the Sunken Road.

Lee's weakness was on his right, where Jackson held the line on level ground. Burnside's men there actually broke through Jackson's lines at one point, but his men—primarily Early's Division—threw them back with a savage counterattack. It was during this battle that Lee uttered those famous words: "It is well that war is so terrible or we should grow too fond of it."[282]

The battle ended. Union losses were 12,653 and Confederate 5,377. Jackson urged a night attack, and historians have long criticized Lee for not following up his victory with a counterattack against the disheartened and defeated Army of the Potomac. The victory, however, was both a tactical and a strategic success, and Lee believed that a night attack against a larger force dug in on Stafford Heights across the river would be a repeat of the day's battle, but in reverse. Thus, Burnside retreated north, and Lee established winter quarters. His greatest victory—and his greatest loss—awaited him with the coming of spring.[283]

The Spring and Summer of 1863: From High Water to Low Water

Spring came to Northern Virginia, and the two armies began to stir from their long winter's respites. In March, Lee, at Fredericksburg, became ill with a severe cough, fever, an elevated pulse rate and pain in his chest, back and arms. It was either angina pectoris or pericarditis, or both. The former involves narrowing of the arteries to the heart so as to slow the flow of blood into the heart. The latter is inflammation of the lining of the fibrous sac surrounding the heart. Lee would always refer to this episode as the "first attack in front of Fredericksburg."

Lee's believed that what he had was a "heavy cold," or a combination of arthritis and neuralgia—Lee called it "rheumatism"—like his wife, Mary. His physicians treated him with "a complete saturation of [his] system with quinine." Nevertheless—or perhaps because of this treatment—Lee remained ill into April. What he had would plague him for the rest of his life.[284]

In April, Joseph "Fighting Joe" Hooker took command of the Army of the Potomac, 134,000 strong squaring off against Lee's 53,000. In February, Lee had sent Longstreet and two veteran divisions commanded by John Bell Hood and A.P. Hill to southeastern Virginia to counter Union moves in that area and collect supplies, significantly reducing the size of his army. Lee now sent one division commanded by Jubal A. Early and one of Lafayette McLaws's brigades to Marye's Heights. There, it would counter a move by two corps of Union troops—23,000 strong—under General John Sedgwick, who had crossed the river and sat below that line of hills. Eventually, however, Early ended up with 10,000 men facing more than two times their number under Sedgwick.

Hooker then took five corps and moved up the Rappahannock, crossing the river and heading downstream toward Lee's badly outnumbered and overmatched left flank. Lee moved the rest of his army west toward the hamlet of Chancellorsville and lined the men up to face Hooker's advancing masses. Lee placed Jackson's corps on his left and divisions commanded by Richard H. Anderson and Lafayette McLaws on his right.

Hooker had seventy-three thousand men facing Lee's army of forty-three thousand, and he ordered a general attack for 2:00 p.m. on May 1. Doom overhung Lee's small army like smoke from the Union campfires. Then, inexplicably, Hooker lost his nerve and, instead of attacking, ordered his army into defensive positions facing Lee, daring *him* to attack. Lee would take the dare.

That night, Lee met with Jackson, who told him that Hooker's right flank was "in the air," uncovered and vulnerable to a flanking attack. Then occurred one of the most famous colloquies of the war:

> *Lee: General Jackson, what do you propose to do?*
> *Jackson: Go around here* [pointing at a map].
> *Lee: What do you propose to make this movement with?*
> *Jackson: With my whole corps.*
> *Lee: What will you leave me?*
> *Jackson: The divisions of Anderson and McLaws.*

And then this famous line:

> *Lee: Well, go on.*[285]

At 4:00 a.m. on May 1, Jackson took his corps and moved southwest about seven miles and then swung back to the north for about seven more miles until he was lined up against Hooker's right flank, which was indeed "in the air." Meanwhile, Lee, with seventeen thousand men, faced off against Hooker's seventy-three thousand and conducted a bravura "offensive-defensive" performance, moving troops back and forth along his front as though massing for the attack Hooker was certain would come.

The attack for which Hooker waited came late that afternoon, but not from Lee along Hooker's front. Instead, Jackson slammed his corps into Hooker's exposed right flank and rolled it up like a rug. Lee then attacked along Hooker's front to prevent him from moving troops to counter Jackson, and one of the greatest beat-downs of the war was on.

Later that night, as he tried to rest, Lee received bad news. Jackson had been wounded by friendly fire. While the wound was serious, it was not believed to be fatal, and Lee concentrated his attention on the battle at hand, which continued unabated the next morning, May 2. Back at Marye's Heights, Sedgwick finally attacked Early and drove him from that position, but Lee quickly dispatched Lafayette McLaws and his division east toward Fredericksburg, where he and Early drove Sedgwick back into a defensive perimeter. On May 6, before Lee could attack him again, Hooker and his entire army crossed back over the Rappahannock, and the Battle of Chancellorsville was over. Hooker's army had suffered a stunning—indeed historic—defeat, and it would be Fighting Joe's last battle as commander of the Army of the Potomac.[286]

Jackson would lose his arm and linger for four days after the conclusion of the battle, but strangely, Lee never went to see the wounded Jackson. Then, on May 10, the worst happened: Jackson died. Lee had sustained the first of his two great wartime losses, and this one was a loss from which Lee, and the South, would struggle to recover for the next two years. Indeed, the loss of Jackson would lead directly to, and perhaps cause, the catastrophic loss yet to come.

The Pennsylvania Campaign

Lee wanted to invade the North, and Jefferson Davis, unfortunately for the South, let him do it. At the outset, it was a bad idea. As noted, Lee, with the loss of Jackson, reorganized his army into three corps: Longstreet would command the First; Richard "Old Bald Head" Ewell took the Second and A.P. "Little Powell" Hill the Third. Ewell had required explicit instructions to perform as a division commander, and unfortunately—indeed, it would prove disastrous—Hill had gonorrhea, which rendered him at times unable to perform his duties.

In invading Pennsylvania, Lee sought a "battle of annihilation" that would end the war in a day. He presciently saw that a long war would favor the North, which, with its superior numbers and resources, would grind down the South. Unfortunately for the South, Pennsylvania would prove not to be the correct place for Lee's "battle of annihilation."

A number of factors worked against him. Jeb Stuart, stung by a rare defeat at Brandy Station, decided to redeem himself with a ride around the Army of the Potomac, now commanded by General George Meade. That act would deprive Lee of his eyes and ears for most of the invasion.

After splitting his army, as he was prone to do, Lee, upon learning that Meade was fighting one of (out--his) Lee's corps at Gettysburg, reconstituted his army there and took on Meade's legions—ninety-four thousand to Lee's generously calculated seventy-five thousand. His army won a decisive victory on the first day, but due to the ineptitude of Ewell on the left and the failures of Longstreet and Jeb Stuart to arrive on the scene, Lee missed a golden opportunity to take the hills to the left and right of Cemetery Ridge, where Meade was consolidating his army. Seizing those hills would haves rendered Meade's army subject to enfilade fire from both sides and thus forced his withdrawal from that strong defensive position on Cemetery Ridge.

Lee's army carried the second day, as Longstreet's corps almost carried Cemetery Ridge. But it did not, and on the third disastrous day, Pickett's Charge failed horribly. Lee thus withdrew his defeated—almost shattered—army back to Virginia.

There was plenty of blame to go around. On Lee's left, Ewell passed on multiple opportunities to take the hills there. On the right, Longstreet failed to mount an attack on the Round Tops until late on the second day when those positions were manned sufficiently to turn him back. Almost ten years later, Jubal Early, one of Ewell's co-conspirators on the right, would heap more blame on Longstreet for his failure to launch a dawn attack on the second day, as well as his purported failure to provide two more divisions in support of Pickett. As noted, both contentions were canards of the first magnitude, however, as no such orders ever came from Lee's mouth or pen, according to Lee's staff officers, who were with him throughout the time he was alleged to have issued those orders.[287]

Gettysburg to Petersburg

A new Union general arrived in March 1864 to take command of all Union armies, including Meade's Army of the Potomac, of which Meade would remain in titular command. He was one of Lee's comrades from the Mexican-American War and a close friend—and in-law—of Longstreet's: Ulysses S. Grant, fresh from a number of victories in the West. The war in the East was about to change. No longer would the Union army retreat after defeats. Instead, it would latch on to the Army of Northern Virginia like a snapping turtle, and it would not turn loose until the war ended.

The battle names—the Wilderness, Spotsylvania Court House and Cold Harbor—are thoroughly drenched in blood, as are the specific zones of battle: the Mule Shoe, the Bloody Angle, the Orange Plank Road and Wilderness Run. The three battles that together comprised the month-long abattoir took place along a line running roughly west–east, with Grant's army of 119,000 on the north side of the line and Lee's army of an estimated (likely too high) 75,000 on the south. In the three battles, the Army of Northern Virginia killed, wounded or captured more Union troops, roughly 54,000, than it had after the three battles concluded. Some would call Lee's army the greatest killing machine in U.S. history, but in the end it would not matter because Grant, unlike his predecessors, would not go away. As he said he would, he fought it out on that line all summer, and in the end, his war of attrition against the smaller Confederate force proved successful. After Cold Harbor, Grant again moved east, and this time he successfully flanked Lee on his right and crossed the James; by June 22, Lee and his army were dug in around Petersburg, facing an entrenched Union army with twice the number of troops. Over the next nine months, the siege at Petersburg would spell doom for the Army of Northern Virginia, and it would give the world a taste of what was to come some fifty years hence in the Great War.

Then, on April 1, while George Pickett and Fitz Lee were absent from their troops attending a shad bake hosted by General Thomas Rosser—*the* shad bake that would forever be enshrined in the Confederate hall of shame[288]—Sheridan attacked at Five Forks and broke Lee's line; the Siege of Petersburg was over. A.P. Hill died that day—joining in death fellow Confederate generals Stonewall Jackson and Jeb Stuart, who had earlier been killed at Yellow Tavern. Hill died at the hands of a Union straggler, Private John Mauck of the 138th Pennsylvania Infantry, and the next night, Lee began his long, sad retreat from Petersburg that would end at Appomattox. In the Southern collective mind, Lee's surrender thus was caused by the infamous shad bake.[289]

Appomattox

Lee's objective when his army marched in four columns out of Petersburg was to reach Amelia Court House, where supplies were waiting, and then head south for Danville and on into North Carolina to join up with Johnston's army. There, in theory, they would defeat Sherman and then head north to defeat Grant. That was Lee's plan, but it would prove impossible.

There were supposed to be 350,000 rations waiting for Lee's dwindling army at Amelia Court House. There were none, due to a not atypical Confederate quartermaster snafu. Instead, waiting for Lee's starving army were ammunition and artillery harnesses. The army had to spend a day—a *precious* day—foraging. That day gave Grant's army time to catch up. And catch up they did.

Lee wired for rations to be sent to Burkeville, but Grant cut him off, so Lee instead marched due west for Lynchburg. Supposedly, eighty thousand rations awaited his army in Farmville, so he moved in that direction. At Sayler's Creek on April 6, he lost a fourth of his army—around eight thousand men—including Generals Richard Ewell and Lee's son Custis Lee, who were captured. His ragtag, starving army continued west, and as the Army of Northern Virginia marched, it melted away to desertion and starvation. On the seventh, Grant wrote Lee of "the hopelessness of further resistance on the part of the Army of Northern Virginia in this struggle." He shifted from himself to Lee "the responsibility for any further effusion of blood, by asking you to surrender…the Army of Northern Virginia." Now surrounded, Lee considered the offer that night and asked Longstreet, who said simply "not yet." Lee, however, responded by asking Grant what the terms of surrender would be.

Grant responded that the only condition was that those men who surrendered not take up arms against the United States again. Lee then asked for a meeting with Grant on the morning of April 9. Grant got the note too late to respond, and Lee ordered John B. Gordon to attempt a breakout, which failed. At that point, Lee aide Porter Alexander proposed that the army break up into small groups and filter out through Union lines to engage in guerrilla warfare. Lee rejected Alexander's proposal, and in so doing, according to historian Jay Winik, he made "his most historic contribution—to peace." "No," Lee said. "We would bring on a state of affairs it would take the country years to recover from." With the end in sight and no more realistic opportunities for a breakout at hand, Lee said simply, and sadly, "Then there is nothing left me but to go and see General Grant, and I would rather die a thousand deaths."

The two leaders met at the Wilmer McLean House at Appomattox. Ironically, McLean's previous residence had been on the First Manassas battlefield, where it had taken a cannonball, and he had moved his family after Second Manassas to get away from the war. Now it had once again come to him at one of the most momentous occasions in the history of the country. Lee, attired in his full dress uniform and dress sword, and his aide Charles Marshall—the great-nephew of John Marshall—arrived first. Lee took a seat at a table in the corner of the room. Grant and twelve aides arrived next, and Lee rose to shake hands with his old comrade from the Mexican-American War, which the two of them discussed until Lee turned the proceedings toward his surrender.

Grant reiterated the terms set forth in his second note to Lee, and Lee accepted those terms and asked Grant to commit the terms to a writing, which Grant did: the Confederates were to make a roster of officers and men of the Army of Northern Virginia in duplicate and provide one copy to Grant's representative; officers were to sign their individual paroles, and a company or regimental commander was to sign for the enlisted men of their commands. The surrender document allowed officers to keep their horses, baggage and side arms, with all other weapons to be turned over to the Union army. "This done each officer and man will be allowed to return to their homes, not to be disturbed by the United States Authority so long as they observe their parole and the laws in force where they may reside." This last provision would prove to be one of the most important of Lee's postwar life.

But there was one more matter that was not in the surrender document: in the Confederate army, cavalrymen and artillerymen owned their own horses, so Lee asked that they be allowed to keep them. Grant replied that while he would not include it in the surrender document, he would instruct his men to allow "all the men who claim to own a horse or mule [to] take the animals home with them to their little farms." Lee replied, "This will have the best possible effect upon the men. It will be very gratifying and will do much toward conciliating our people."

Then Lee told Grant that his army held more than one thousand Union prisoners, who, like their Confederate counterparts, were starving. Immediately, Grant replied that he would send over rations for twenty-five thousand men. Lee was grateful. The two men rose, and Grant then introduced Lee to his staff while their two aides prepared the documents of surrender. Grant apologized for his appearance and later would admit his embarrassment at wearing muddy boots and no sword, especially given Lee's formal attire.

The two generals signed the formal documents, and Lee shook hands with Grant, bowed to the others and then walked out onto the porch. A crowd of Union officers had gathered to see the Confederate general, and they saluted him. Lee, seemingly oblivious to his surroundings, put on his hat and gloves, returned the salute and called for Traveller.

He mounted his horse and turned him to leave. As he did, Grant walked out onto the porch, and when Lee passed before him, their eyes met and each raised his hat to the other. The other Federal officers also raised their hats to the departing Confederate commander. Grant would later say, "I felt sad and depressed at the downfall of a foe who had fought so long and valiantly, and had suffered so much for a cause, though that cause was, I believe, one of the worst for which a people ever fought." And twenty years later, he would write that "the [Southern] men…had fought so bravely, so gallantly and so long for the cause which they believed in—and as earnestly, I take it, as our men believed in the cause for which they were fighting."[290] He would also speak of "that enemy, whose manhood, however mistaken the cause, drew forth such herculean deeds of valor."[291]

Grant later wrote of his meeting with Lee, "What General Lee's feelings were I do not know. As he was a man of such dignity, with an impassable face, it was impossible to say whether he felt inwardly glad that the end had finally come, or felt sad over the result, and was too manly to show it. Whatever his feelings, they were entirely concealed."[292]

When word reached the Union troops that Lee had surrendered, they broke out in cheering, in hugs, in items tossed into the air, in loud relief. The bands played "The Star-Spangled Banner" and marching songs. Federal artillery began firing in celebration. Grant, however, would have none of it. "He knew there would plenty of time for rejoicing, but today was not it. He sternly ordered them to stop." "The Confederates were not our prisoners," he later explained, "and we did not want to exult over their downfall."[293]

After the surrender, Lee returned to his men and told them that it was over, that he—and they—could do no more. "Boys, he said, I have done the best I could for you. My heart is too full to say more." Then, as he entered his tent, he said, "Go home now, and if you make as good citizens as you have soldiers, you will do well, and I shall always be proud of you."

Next followed the formal surrender, in which the two armies met on a simple stage road that ran alongside the village of Appomattox. Joshua L. Chamberlin, the hero of Gettysburg (and Medal of Honor winner), was in charge of the Union troops there to receive the surrender of Lee's remaining twenty-eight thousand men. Major General John B. Gordon, leader of the thwarted breakout attack, led the Confederates. Historian Jay Winik said it best:

> *Chamberlin would never forget it: "On they came, with the old swinging route step and swaying battle flags…* [the flags] *crowded so thick, by* [the] *thinning out of men, that the whole column seemed crowned with red…in the van, the proud Confederate ensign.…Before us in proud humiliation stood the embodiment of manhood; men whom neither toils and sufferings, nor the fact of death nor disaster nor hopelessness…could bend from their resolve; standing before us now, thin, worn, and famished, but erect, and with eyes looking level into ours, waking memories that bound us together as no other bond."*

Without having planned it—and without any official sanction—Chamberlain suddenly gave the order for his troops to "carry arms" as a sign of their deepest mark of military respect. A bugle call instantly rang out. All along the road, Union soldiers raised their muskets to their shoulders, the salute of honor. "At the sound of the machine-like snap of arms," Chamberlain recalled, "General Gordon started…then wheeled his horse, facing me, touching him gently with the spur so that the animal slightly reared, and, as he wheeled, horse and rider made one motion, the horse's head swung down with a graceful bow, and General Gordon dropped his sword-point to his toe in salutation." And as he did, the veterans in blue gave a soldierly salute to those "vanquished heroes"—a "token of respect from Americans to Americans."[294]

"Years later, ancient men, blue and gray, would cry as they recalled the moment of that salute, forever frozen in their memories."[295] It was the "last advance" of the fabled Army of Northern Virginia, of which Joseph "Fighting Joe" Hooker said, "That army by discipline alone, acquired a character for steadiness and efficiency unsurpassed, in my judgment, in ancient or modern times."[296]

The surrendering went on for six hours. When the last of the casualty-shrunken gray units marched up, a Confederate described what happened: "Someone in the blue line broke the silence and called for three cheers for the last brigade to surrender. It was taken up all about him by those who knew what it meant. But for us this soldierly generosity was more than we could bear. Many grizzled veterans wept like women, and my own eyes were as blind as my voice was dumb."[297]

In the days between Lee's surrender at the McLean house and the actual surrender of the Army of Northern Virginia, men from both sides met between the lines and talked. Officers who had been at West Point and served together in the "Old Army" met also, and in the immediate aftermath of Lee's surrender, some shared a bottle of whiskey outside the McLean house. Union general George Gordon Meade called on Lee at Lee's tent and introduced his son, George Jr. Lee asked him how he had gotten so much gray hair since their last prewar meeting. Meade replied, "You have to answer for most of it."

Johnston surrendered his armies to Sherman near Durham, North Carolina, on April 26, and Kirby Smith followed with his Trans-Mississippi Department in Galveston, Texas, on June 2. Finally, it was over—650,000 men had died in the war, more than 2 percent of the United States' 1860 population and more than have died in all of the country's major wars since, combined. A comparable loss today would be more than 6 million. Without question, the Civil War was an American catastrophe of the greatest and most terrible magnitude imaginable, and its scars would remain on the country for generations to come.[298]

POSTWAR

April 12–December 31, 1865

On April 13, 1865, the day after his army's surrender at Appomattox, Robert Edward Lee, commander of the Army of Northern Virginia, set out on Traveller for Richmond, accompanied by his staff members Walter Taylor, Charles Marshall and Charles S. Venable. Giles Cook rode in the ambulance, which had served as transport for the accoutrements of Lee's trade—his tent, cookware, dining utensils and uniforms—during the war just concluded. It must have been a strange feeling that the people of the Confederacy shared: theirs was the first English-speaking country to be conquered since England in 1066 by William the Conqueror.

Lee had bid goodbye to his officers, especially General James Longstreet, who, in spite of his stubbornness and recalcitrance, had remained one of Lee's closest friends. The two generals always set their tents near each other and consulted extensively about tactical and strategic affairs. Longstreet and Lee would never see each other again, and even though their views about the South's reentry into the Union after the war would be very similar, one man would be vilified and then crucified throughout the South for his views, and the other would become the apotheosis of Southern honor, courage and grace.

That night, Lee and his entourage stopped in Cumberland County to have Traveller shod. The next night, he slept in a tent for the last time at his brother Carter Lee's house in Powhatan County, as Carter Lee's house was full. The next day, April 15, Custis Lee caught up and joined the group. That afternoon, they entered Richmond, which lay smoldering in ruins. Word spread quickly that Lee was home. As he rode through the city toward his house at 707 East Franklin, which was called The Mess because its occupants had served so many soldiers' meals there, Lee passed Union soldiers, who, in silence, raised their caps and hats to him. He reciprocated. That same morning, in Washington, Lincoln died, and in the North, the acrid smell of revenge was in the air. Hanging the two most prominent Rebels—Lee and Jefferson Davis—might satisfy the need for revenge.

Lee soon came to the house, owned by a friend, John Stewart, where Lee's family lived free of charge. Stopping in front, Lee was emotional and had trouble dismounting. He gave Traveller's reins to "someone else" (the name is not recorded, although Flood said simply that it was "some soldiers"), "gave a courtly bow," went in and closed the door on both the world outside, the war and his role in it. He took off his sword, which contained the Lee family motto—"Help yourself and God will help you," in French—for the last time. Once again, Lee was in a house that he did not own. Indeed, he had never owned his own home, although Mary owned three plantations and houses, one of which, Arlington, was in Union hands and had been taken by the government for back taxes.

The Union army supplied Lee's house with an around-the-clock guard and provisions. Mary Lee, now wheelchair-bound, provided breakfast for the guard, and Lee, at least initially, slept a lot. Rooney Lee arrived three days after his father, and the family was now complete. None of Lee's children was married. They ranged in age from the youngest, nineteen-year-old Mildred, to thirty-two-year-old Custis. His family could see, among other physical changes, that Lee was losing his hair. 'He is growing quite bald, and wears one of the side locks of his hair thrown across the upper portion of his forehead, which is as fair as a woman's, marked with a line where his hat had sat."[299]

He was soon beset by visitors. Mathew Brady came to take his photograph, but Lee refused. Brady, however, contacted a mutual friend, who contacted Mary Custis Lee, and she prevailed on Robert to permit the photograph, which he did. That photograph, taken on the back porch of The Mess, to this day remains one of the most famous of the man. Thomas M. Cook of the *New York Herald* requested an interview, which Lee granted. In it, he told Cook that secession was not unconstitutional and thus not treason, and he lamented the assassination of Abraham Lincoln, an act that he deemed "beyond execration." Lee said that the South should have put out "peace feelers" two years before the end. Mary Lee wrote, "The sad truth is that our people got tired of the war, and proved unworthy of the noble blood that had been shed for their liberty. Virginia will rue the day that her sons ever laid down their arms....I cannot describe to you the agony of mind we have endured."[300]

Lee had freed his own slaves in December 1862, pursuant to Parke Custis's will, but he had a low opinion of free blacks and, indeed, hoped that Virginia's black population would migrate to the cotton belt of the Deep South. He said, however, that "I am rejoiced that slavery is abolished." Before the war, he had believed in a gradual emancipation of the slaves, thinking that sudden freedom would be "a disservice to the whole Negro race." Lee now advocated "the restoration of peace and tranquility in the country." Cook thought that Lee spoke of himself as a citizen of the United States and noted that Lee said that he would have been pleased if he had died during the war.[301]

His goal, Lee said, was to live out his life as a small yeoman farmer. It was a "bucolic fantasy," and it would never happen. For now, however, Lee was confined to his home by visitors and sightseers, so he took his exercise at night, walking the streets of Richmond among the smoking ruins.

Far to the south, at Irwinville, Georgia, Union cavalry finally captured Jefferson Davis, and a youngster named Tommy Wilson saw Union soldiers parade Davis and his family through the streets of Augusta. Later generations would know Tommy Wilson as Woodrow Wilson. Secretary of War Edwin M. Stanton ordered Davis jailed for high treason, and Davis was clapped into hot leg irons that were hammered into place around his ankles. He was confined to a dank dungeon at Fortress Monroe. This was not a time for national reconciliation; rather, in the aftermath of Lincoln's assassination, it was a time for Northern retribution, and Davis was subjected to the leg irons for five brutal days.

On May 5, George Gordon Meade visited Lee and urged him to take a loyalty oath and regain his citizenship. He said that he hoped that Lee would someday run for governor of Virginia. On May 29, President Johnson issued a general pardon, but in it, he excluded senior officers of the Confederacy. Lee urged whites to seek restoration of their full legal rights and cooperate with the United States. Only with the vote, he argued, would the South be saved. Nevertheless, a large number of Northerners wanted Lee indicted, along with Jefferson Davis, for treason, and on June 7, a federal grand jury in Norfolk did just that. The penalty for treason was death by hanging. The indictment was served, and it roiled the South, which bristled with anger and was gripped with fear that other leaders would follow. Offers of assistance from lawyers in both the North and the South came to Lee in Richmond.

With respect to the indictment, Lee contended that the terms of his parole precluded indictment as long as he abided by the laws of the United States. His old adversary, Grant, agreed, and wrote to President Andrew Johnson arguing that his (Grant's) word was embodied in the terms of the parole and that he would resign if those terms were not honored. Johnson reluctantly agreed. On June 20, Grant wrote to Lee that he should not worry about standing trial for treason. In Norfolk, prosecutors, who didn't want to argue with the commanding general of the United States Army, quit the prosecution but did not drop the charges. Lee thus remained in legal limbo.

On June 1, Lee, who wanted to farm, also wanted to get out of Richmond in the short term, so he got on Traveller and rode alone to his cousin Thomas H. Carter's plantation, Pampatike, about twenty miles northeast of Richmond. There, while Traveller grazed quietly in the front yard, Lee received a reception befitting the hero that he was, and both his host and his neighbors treated him "lavishly." At Pampatike, Lee indulged one of his favorite pastimes: playing with children. Small girls followed him around, and he spoke in baby talk to them.

Lee advised his host to hire white labor because "wherever you find the Negro, everything is going down around him, and wherever you find the white man, you see everything around him improving." Nevertheless, back in Richmond, at Lee's first communion at St. Paul's Episcopal Church, a black man went to the altar to receive the sacrament. None of the others in the congregation would go to the rail, but Lee did, and the others followed.

Lee had resurrected his correspondence with "clever young women," and on June 20, he wrote to Markie Williams, who had offered to go to Europe with him. "There is nothing my dear Markie that I want, except to see you and nothing you can do for me, except to think of and love me. It would require you to become a Fairy and turn what you touched into Gold to take me to Europe, but I would not desire you to change your nature for my benefit. I prefer you remaining as you are."[302]

Lee, upon his return to Richmond, announced his plan to move his family to Cumberland County, about halfway between Richmond and Charlottesville, to a plantation, Oakland, on the James River, about fifty-five miles west of Richmond. Elizabeth Randolph Cocke owned Oakland, and she had invited the Lees to live in a small house on the grounds. Lee was delighted to accept the invitation; Mary, however, was not delighted, as the move would take her away from friends and family. Nevertheless, Lee's family departed Richmond and traveled up the James by boat to the plantation. They stayed for a week at Oakland and then moved into the house, called Derwent, which Mary described as "small and hot." It was a "simple frame house of the type used by tenant farmers."[303] Nevertheless, they passed a quiet summer there. Lee thought about writing a history of his campaigns and began discussing that possibility with several publishers but instead decided to write a new introduction to his father's memoir of the Revolutionary War. He visited with neighboring farmers throughout the summer and corresponded with old comrades.

One of his letters was not from an old comrade but was from Union general David Hunter, who had abandoned the Shenandoah Valley to Jubal A. Early. With Hunter's departure from the Valley, Lee had sent Early to threaten Washington, providing Abraham Lincoln a ringside seat at a battle on the north side of the capital. Hunter, somewhat strangely, wanted Lee to affirm that Hunter's moves in the Valley were well done and that those moves had prevented Lee from sending forty thousand men to Joseph E. Johnston in Georgia. Lee wrote back that he had no troops to send to Johnston and was glad that Hunter had withdrawn, leaving the Valley to Early. Hunter's withdrawal, he wrote, had enabled Early to advance on Washington and had forced Grant to send troops to defend Washington instead of facing off against Lee in Northern Virginia.

For the girls, unlike for their father, Derwent was anything but ideal. Daughter Mary Custis Lee refused to stay there and instead stayed with friends in Staunton. Mildred spent her time there reading novels, which Lee deplored, instead insisting (and futilely) that she read history and "works of truth."[304] Colonel Orton Williams, Markie's brother, had courted Agnes, Lee's prettiest daughter. During the war, however, Orton had developed a drinking problem and, while serving with the Army of Tennessee, shot a private for a "disciplinary offence." Subsequently, he proposed to Agnes, but in light of his drinking and the blood of a Confederate soldier on his hands, she turned him down. Then, in a strange turn of events, Orton proposed to a married woman and, wearing a Union officer's uniform, was captured behind Union lines; after a "drumhead court martial," he was hanged as a spy. Agnes was disconsolate, and she would never marry, instead becoming a quiet and pensive spinster. Once again, there is much conjecture about the role that Lee played in his daughters' failure to marry. He once admitted that "it will require a tussle for anyone to get my children from me." Apparently the "tussle" was too much for his daughters' suitors.[305]

Mary Custis Lee attended a party in Staunton, Virginia, in the Shenandoah Valley, where she complained that "the people of the South are offering my father everything but work, and that is the one thing he will accept." That statement was to have momentous consequences, as it was overheard by Colonel Bolivar Christian of Lexington, who was a trustee of Washington College, which needed a new president. Colonel Christian told the college's board of trustees, and it voted on August 4, 1865, to offer the presidency of the school to Lee. The trustees then sent Episcopal rector Judge John N. Brockenbrough, who was also head of the Washington College Law School, to offer Lee the position. Brockenbrough had to borrow a suit and fifty dollars to make the trip to Oakland.

Washington College was in dire straits. It had only four professors and about forty students. The school was virtually broke. It had $94,000 in its endowment, but much of that was in securities that the war may have rendered worthless. And it had no president.

Judge Brockenbrough appeared at Oakland with no warning and informed Lee that the board of trustees had unanimously elected him president of Washington College with an annual stipend of $1,500 and a share of tuition paid by the students, as well as a house and a garden. Lee was familiar with the school. His half-brother, Black-Horse Harry Lee, had attended school there for a year. The board also wanted Lee to teach philosophy, but Lee declined that portion of the offer and mulled the presidency, even though he had received interest from both the University of the South in Sewanee, Tennessee, and the University of Virginia for leadership positions. Mary Lee, among others, was reluctant for him to take the Washington College job, as the move would take her even farther west and thus farther away from all she had known before the war: her family, her home and her friends.

Lee considered the offer for some three weeks. He worried that his presence at the school would do more harm than good, that his declining health might preclude the kind of effort that he deemed essential to success in the job and that he was Episcopalian and the school—and Lexington—were dominated by Presbyterians. Others, however, urged him to take the job, and finally, he accepted.

On September 15, 1865, Lee again mounted Traveller; the man who had commanded an army of seventy-five thousand men, who had engineered incredible victories against a much larger and far better-equipped foe and who had fought so long and so hard for Southern independence set out alone for Lexington, Virginia, to a small school in the Shenandoah Valley of western Virginia. Lee said that he saw the move as an opportunity "to aid in the restoration of peace and harmony."[306] He arrived in Lexington on September 18 to begin a new—and the final—phase of his life.

When he arrived at Lexington, Lee wore a brown hat and a gray suit, actually a uniform from which, in accordance with Union regulations, he had removed all of the insignia of military rank, including even the buttons. Lexington was a town of some two thousand inhabitants dominated by Washington College, the Virginia Military Institute and the Presbyterian Church. The town, like the South as a whole and Washington College in particular, was in sad shape financially. The joke in Lexington was that there were so few dollars in the town that the owners had to introduce them to one another when they met on Main Street.[307]

Lee took in his surroundings, and the next day he met with the trustees of Washington College. The president's residence was rented to a local doctor, and it was in need of repairs, so Lee decided to await completion of that work before bringing his family to Lexington. After the meeting,

Lee left for a mountain spa—the Rockbridge Baths, about eleven miles from Lexington—to "take the waters," treat his rheumatism and take "scenic rides with some of his female friends."[308]

Lee returned to Lexington at the end of September and, after a small installation service, went to work to open the school. That fall, about 50 students entered, but during the year, more arrived, bringing the total to 146 students, some of them attracted by the former commander of the Army of Northern Virginia. He called on and secured a $10,000 contribution from Lexington native Cyrus McCormick, inventor of the McCormick mechanical reaper.[309] That money obviated some of the immediate financial problems facing the board of trustees.

On October 2, 1865, Lee signed the amnesty oath required for restoration of his citizenship and sent it to Secretary of State William H. Seward—or at least it ended up with Seward—who gave it to a friend as a souvenir. It was, therefore, never acted on, and Lee would die as a non-citizen of the United States; however, in 1975, more than one hundred years later, President Gerald R. Ford signed an act of Congress that restored Lee's citizenship.

Lee had correspondence from Confederate leaders. They were everywhere: Mexico, Canada, Cuba and Brazil. Others worked for the khedive of Egypt, the prince of Rumania and the emperor of Korea. Beauregard, who, when in active service, was prone to the development of complex military plans without regard to the supplies and transport required and available, wrote to Lee. He wanted to know what Lee thought he ought to do. Lee replied that he should recognize that whatever he undertook, it would have influence on both Confederate veterans and the civilian population of the South, who held him in high esteem. He was pleased, he said, that Beauregard had no intention of leaving the South, which needed now more than ever "the aid of her sons…more than at any period in her history. As you ask my purpose, I will state that I have no thought of abandoning her unless compelled to do so."[310]

Lee concluded with a passage that would become part of the South's postwar catechism:

> *I need not tell you that true patriotism sometimes requires of men to act exactly contrary, at one period, to that which it does at another, and the motive which impels them—the desire to do right—is precisely the same. The circumstances that govern their actions change, and their conduct must conform to the new order of things.…Washington himself is an example of this. At one time he fought in the service of the King of Great Britain;*

> *at another he fought with the French at Yorktown under the orders of the Continental Congress of America, against him. He has not been branded by the world with reproach for this, but his course has been applauded.*[311]

That first autumn in Lexington saw Lee almost immediately undertake repairs to the buildings damaged by and during the war; however, his health was not good. He still suffered from angina pectoris and was developing arterial sclerosis as his arteries clogged with plaque—a condition unknown at the time—but he knew that something was wrong with him and had been since the first battle at Fredericksburg. His physicians said it was rheumatism.

Many of the students matriculating at Washington College that fall were veterans of the Army of Northern Virginia. Lee met them all, and he remembered their names. One veteran referred to his time that he had lost during the war. Lee remonstrated that he should never consider that time *lost*; rather it should be called "the most profitably spent portion of your life." Another said that "it looked as if the sorrow of a whole nation had been collected in his countenance and as if he was bearing the grief of his whole people."[312] Nevertheless, Lee soldiered on.

Custis turned up in Lexington to teach at VMI, and he would take his meals with the Lees and would "never seriously pursue a wife and family or, it would seem, his independence as a person."[313] He sometimes rode with Lee in the afternoon. Students would long remember their president: gray uniform with no insignia, boots, cavalry gauntlets, spurs and "a large, light-colored hat with a military band around it."[314]

The rest of his family arrived by packet boat on December 2, 1865. Mary was by now a confirmed invalid, confined to her "rolling chair." Lee and his family moved into the recently renovated president's house, where Lee's preeminent lieutenant, Thomas J. Jackson, had lived with his new bride, Eleanor Junkin, before the war and before she died and he remarried.[315] Custis did not live at Lee's home, however, because there was no room. Lee's nephew, Robert—his brother Smith's son—also arrived in December to resume his education, and initially he lived with the Lees but soon moved into his own quarters at the school.

Lee still had three daughters at home: Mary Custis, age thirty-one; Agnes, age twenty-five; and Mildred, age twenty. Each night, the girls entertained callers in the front parlor. At 10:00 p.m., Lee would go into the front parlor and began closing shutters, which was the signal for the callers to leave. Mother Mary Lee was "sad and lonely." She focused her thoughts on

Arlington and her childhood there and said that she was cut off from her family and "all [she] had known and loved."[316]

Lee's daughters were unhappy in Lexington as well. They had lived their early years as part of a society of landed gentry, as members of Virginia's aristocracy, where there was dancing and where their hosts served wine with dinner. Lexington, they thought, was rough and provincial, and as a result of this attitude, the townspeople thought the Lee girls haughty. Daughter Mary stayed on the road visiting friends. She had a sharp tongue like her mother and was fearless and eccentric, a quality that would increase with her years. Agnes, on the other hand, was more domestic, and Mildred totally so. In the winter, the girls ice skated and took sleigh rides in the evening. They started a reading club, but through it all, Lee's towering presence overshadowed any potential relationships for his girls. He was possessive of his daughters and wrote to Mildred that she would "never receive such a love as is felt for you by your father and mother."[317]

And there was more.[318] While Lee hoped that his sons would marry, he tried to exert control over his daughters, which worked with Agnes and Mildred but not at all with Mary. To Agnes, who was attending a wedding in Baltimore, he wrote, "I miss you very much and hope that this is the last wedding that you will attend." As Mildred would later say, all other men seemed "small in comparison" to her father. As Charles Flood stated, it was not that Lee did not want them to marry—he just did not want them to marry then.[319]

1866

On January 19, 1866, Lee wrote to Longstreet, "My interest and affection for you will never cease, and my prayers are always offered for your prosperity." And a week later, he wrote to one of Longstreet's new business partners in New Orleans, "I do not consider my partnership with him yet dissolved, and shall not let him go during life."[320] The friendship thus remained important to both men, although after Lee's death, the Lee coterie would savage Longstreet repeatedly over his affiliation with the Republican Party and his belief that the South should reconcile and reenter the Union, a view consistent with that of his friend Lee. Historian and Lee biographer Emory Thomas said it best:

> *At the surface and in public, Lee was extremely circumspect in his statements about the postwar settlement. At some level he was conscious that he had*

> *led a rebellion and lost and was very fortunate to be alive. Yet he believed that he had served in a civil war on the side devoted to traditional values and eternal verities, and he never really doubted his cause was right and good. But he was enough of a soldier to accept the verdict of arms. He also revered the old Union that his father and his father's friends founded; he wanted to restore that Union as he had known and loved it. So he counseled resignation and cooperation; indeed, he made himself a monument to making the best of a lost cause.*[321]

While living at the hotel, Lee established a daily routine to which he adhered religiously. He arose and then took breakfast at 7:00 a.m. Chapel followed at 8:00 a.m., after which he spent about six hours in his office, and then he went back to the hotel for "dinner," the southern midday meal. A brief nap followed, and then Lee made calls. Late in the afternoon, he rode Traveller. He was in bed by 10:00 p.m. after reading the newspaper and the Bible.

Correspondence from all over the South flooded his desk, and he had a secretary named Edward C. Gordon who helped with it. A group in Richmond wrote seeking permission to name a baseball club for him, but he turned it down and recommended that it use the name "Arlington." The club did, and thus was christened the Arlington Base Ball Club.[322]

People sent food to the house—large amounts of food—especially around holidays. Lee's health, however, continued its decline. In April 1866, he wrote to Markie, "I am easily wearied now, & look forward with joy to the time which is fast approaching that I will lay down and rest." She was "the cousin he loved," and he apologized for his failure to visit old friends when he was in Washington. "I am considered now such a monster that I hesitate to darken with my shadow the doors of those I love lest I should bring upon them misfortune."[323]

The school doubled his salary to $3,000 per annum, and in June, he designed a new chapel for the school. Lee, forever the old engineer, oversaw its construction. Attendance increased to 345 students in 1866, and 1867 would see another increase to 399. Washington College, under Lee's leadership, was rising phoenix-like from the ashes of the Confederacy's searing defeat.

Besides overseeing the resurrection of Washington College, Lee allowed—albeit reluctantly—the school to use his name in fundraising, which resulted in badly needed funds for the restoration of the school. Although a former superintendent at West Point, Lee did not implement a military-style code of conduct at the college. Instead, he said, "We have but one rule here, and it is that every student be a gentleman."

He recruited northern students to facilitate reconciliation and, as he would do later at the Greenbrier in West Virginia, went out of his way to ensure that they were welcomed. A professor would say that "the students fairly worshipped him, and deeply dreaded his displeasure; yet so kind, affable, and gentle was he toward them that all loved to approach him….No student would have dared to violate General Lee's expressed wish or appeal; if he had done so, the students themselves would have driven him [the student] from the college." Another time, the same professor recalled Lee saying to a student claiming special "rights," "Obedience to lawful authority is the foundation of manly character." Biographer Korda wrote that Lee was "patient, firm and profoundly respected. There was no military discipline…. [He] expected a sustained and maximum effort, absolute truthfulness and the manners of a gentleman and impressive self control."[324]

Early in 1866, Lee received a summons to testify before Congress, and on February 17, 1866, he did so before the Committee on Reconstruction and before a crowd of onlookers. Lee testified that he supported reconciliation, that he did not believe that the black man was capable of voting and that granting blacks the vote would lead to the election of unqualified people. Lee said that he had left the Union because his state had left and that his first duty was to his state. Of black citizens, he said, "They are an amiable, social race. They like their ease and comfort, and, I think, look more to the present time than to the future." Lee's views were not dissimilar to those of most white southerners.

The testimony—committee thrust and Lee parry—went on for about two hours; then Lee was done, and he left. As Lee biographer Emory Thomas said, "Circumspection, indeed refusal to write or speak publicly any sentiments except in favor of cooperation and healing the sectional breach, continued to be Lee's policy."[325] He avoided inflammatory rhetoric and avoided statements that would give his opponents an opportunity to attack him.

That spring occurred an event that the townspeople of Lexington would long remember. Authorities there captured a known horse thief named Jonathon Hughes and placed him in the county jail. Word spread quickly that Hughes had been apprehended and placed in the jail, and a mob composed of many of his victims soon formed and marched on the jail, intent on meting out immediate punishment—which, under the law, included hanging. The mob approached the jail, and the old jailer, Thomas L. Perry, faced off with them on the jailhouse steps. Hughes looked death squarely in the eyes.

Suddenly there appeared in the crowd Robert E. Lee, walking calmly through the mob. Charles Flood described it best:

> *Lee moved quietly about the crowd, addressing a few words to each group as he passed, begging them to let the law take its course. Many of the men were his veterans. Lee continued to move through the mob. Men stopped shouting and shaking their fists. Silence fell....*
>
> *Those stern Scotch-Irishmen, whose tenacity of purpose is proverbial, remounted their horses and rode out of town. They could not do a deed of lawless violence in the presence of "Marse Robert." The horse thief was duly tried and sentenced to eighteen years in prison.*[326]

Since Judge Brockenbrough had borrowed $50 to visit Lee about the presidency, the school, under Lee's guidance, had raised more than $100,000. Lee reorganized the school into ten departments, each as an independent school, and he increased the faculty from four to fifteen. In addition, the college absorbed the law school run by Judge Brockenbrough. Lee maintained a preparatory department for Confederate veterans whose secondary education had been interrupted by the war and who needed assistance in preparing for college.

The board of trustees ordered the construction of a new president's home. Lee lived now in a bedroom next to his wife's and slept on an "old camp bed." He kept five swords there: two belonging to George Washington, one that had belonged to Light-Horse Harry and two that were his. Even though he retained his wartime swords, he did not encourage the erection of monuments to the fallen Confederacy. He believed that monuments would continue to inflame passions about the war and would do nothing to promote reconciliation and a smooth reentry of the South into the Union.

That June, the Lees celebrated their thirty-fifth wedding anniversary. Mary was still in love with "the handsomest man in the army." She, however, was an invalid, but there is no indication that he was no longer in love with her. Nevertheless, Lee continued to maintain correspondence with a number of young women. For example, he wrote to his nineteen-year-old cousin, Annette Carter, about her wedding, which he would not attend:

> *I shall want so much to see you tonight my beautiful Annette, for I know how sweet you will look, and of all those that will see you, none will appreciate the happiness as I would....I wish very much I could go down*

> *today. I do not think I would take up much space, or be much in the way, but your cousin Mary won't let me go.*[327]

Earlier that year, he wrote to a niece, Jule Chouteau:

> *As there is nothing you can ask which I will not grant, so it is with much pleasure that I send the autograph you desire. I also enclose the last photograph of me. I have nine taken in uniform, but they are all alike & tempt me almost to deny myself. Do you recognize your old Uncle? You will ever live in my memory as my "beautiful Jule," and I require nothing to recall you to my recollection. You stand before me now, as you then appeared, in the broad sunlight of youth & joy, undimmed by a single shadow of the intervening years.*[328]

On September 13, Lee's second year as president began with more than three hundred students matriculating at the school. Lee rode Traveller to the edge of a "base ball field" to watch the students play this game of northern origin, which had come to the South since the war. In this era, pitchers had little skill, and batters hit almost anything that came near the plate. This, combined with the fact that the fielders had no gloves, produced such scores as 34–10 and 66–22.

Responding to an English historian, Lee wrote that the South accepted the verdict that slavery had been abolished, but he worried about the usurpation of power formerly reserved to the states by an "overly powerful Federal government." He felt that such a nation would "sure to be aggressive abroad and despotic at home." Lee thought that each state ought to be able to prescribe its rules of suffrage and "hoped that the constitution may be handed down to succeeding generations in the form we received it from our forefathers."[329]

The South, during the summer of 1866, was rife with postwar activity. There were race riots in New Orleans and Memphis, and the KKK had been formed in Tennessee. Lee, however, consistent with his feelings on the matter, urged "calm and law-abiding acceptance of reality." He told Varina Davis, "I have thought from the time of the cessation of hostilities, that silence and patience on the part of the South was the true course, and I think so still." The irascible Jubal A. Early had written to Lee from Mexico, "I hate Yankees this day worse than I have ever done. My hatred is increasing every day." Lee wrote back, "We shall have to be patient, and suffer for a while a least; and all controversy, I think, will only serve to prolong anger and bitter feelings, and postpone the period when reason and charity may resume their way."[330] He wrote in response to a manuscript that Early sent for Lee's comments that Early should "omit all epithets or remarks calculated to incite bitterness or animosity between different sections of the country."[331]

To a British visitor who considered Lee the finest soldier of the era, Lee said that "Nathan Bedford Forrest, the Confederate cavalry general from Tennessee, was the greatest genius to have emerged during the war.[332] He accomplished more with fewer troops than any other officer on either side."[333]

1867

With the new year came also Congressional, as opposed to Presidential, Reconstruction, and it came with a fury unprecedented in this country. In the time since the end of the war, the South's old guard—the men who had held office before the war—had largely reestablished themselves in leadership positions by preventing black people from voting, but with Congressional Reconstruction, that ended, and blacks took the vote. With the vote, political dominance in the South passed to them. Wife Mary Lee called the architects of Congressional Reconstruction "scum" and "cowards and base men."[334]

With Congressional Reconstruction, southern states, with the exception of Tennessee, ceased to exist and instead became parts of five military districts. Virginia was in the first. The states of the Confederacy could petition for readmission and restoration of statehood status, but the criteria for readmission included disenfranchisement of former Confederates. White northerners headed south and, among other things, ran for office. Soon, Virginia had a New Yorker as governor. Black-dominated constitutional conventions took place in the states of the Confederacy, and Lee urged white southerners not to leave the political arena. Instead, he urged participation in those conventions and then acceptance of whatever the outcomes might be. "The preservation of harmony and kind feelings is of the utmost importance."[335]

On March 22, 1867, five Washington College boys went to the Freedmen's Bureau school and became involved in an altercation with a black man. One of the students pistol-whipped the black man, and four of the boys soon found themselves in jail. Four hundred students rushed out of the dorms, intent on marching to the jail and freeing their fellow students. A Confederate veteran stood before them urging them to disband and invoking the name of General Lee, who, he said, always urged compliance with the laws. Lee expelled the pistol-whipping student and placed the other four on probation; by the time a leader of the Freedmen's Bureau had contacted Lee, the expelled offender was back in Alabama.

That year would also bring a groundswell of support to elect Lee governor of Virginia, a position that his father had held at the time Light-Horse Harry married Nancy Carter, Lee's mother. This Lee, however, was not interested in politics and politely refused. He continued to maintain a voluminous correspondence, and he urged the recipients of his letters not to publish them and to work hard to reconcile with the North.

Summer came, and with it, the school year ended; the Lees headed for West Virginia and its spas. Lee loved the "social whirl" during which he indulged his fancy for young women and the gaiety and gossip of the young. They visited White Sulphur Springs, which in 1913 would become the Greenbrier. The family traveled by carriage and coach, and Lee, accompanied by a professor, traveled on Traveller. Each night, they would rendezvous at an inn, and one night, a stagecoach arrived at the tavern where they were staying. On it was a group of Maryland girls and their chaperones, and one of the girls was "a young beauty named Christiana Bond." She and her companions had no idea whom they would encounter in the tavern. Years later, she would write:

> *We were aware of some one standing at the turn of the steep stairway above us. Looking up, at the sound of a rich, beautifully modulated voice, we knew that we were in the presence of General Robert E. Lee, the hero of our dreams.*
>
> *The man who stood before us, the embodiment of a Lost Cause, was the realized King Arthur. The soul that looked out of his eyes was as honest and fearless as when it first looked on life. One saw the character, as clear as crystal, without complications or seals, and the heart, as tender as that of ideal womanhood. The years which have passed since that time have dimmed many enthusiasms and destroyed many illusions, but have caused no blush at the memory of the swift thrill of recognition and reverence which ran like an electric flash through one's whole body.*
>
> *General Lee stood above us on the stairway, clad in Confederate grey, his wide, soft hat in his hand, which still wore his riding gauntlet. He looked very tall and majestic standing there, beaming down upon us with his kindly, humorous smile and the wonderful beauty of his dark eyes. When we recovered our wits we found a courteous invitation was being extended to refresh ourselves in the rooms which had been reserved for Mrs. Lee's party.*

It was the beginning of another relationship with a young woman, "needed by him, treasured by her."[336]

Their first night at White Sulphur Springs, there were five hundred guests in the dining room, and when Lee entered, they—with many northerners in the crowd—rose in silent tribute. That summer, Lee met W.W. Corcoran of Washington, D.C., who would later give the money to fund the Corcoran Art Gallery there. Corcoran would also give Washington College $30,000.

A rumor swept the grounds that General and Mrs. Grant would soon arrive at White Sulphur Springs. Although it was apocryphal, the rumor gained currency among the guests, especially the young guests, one of whom asked Lee what he would do when General Grant came. "Treat him with courtesy and respect, all that he is due as a gentleman," came the reply. Christiana noted, "We saw…his absolute loyalty to the allegiance he had sworn when he laid down his arms. His whole soul was engaged in the work of reconstruction, and he lost no opportunity to promote it socially."[337]

On the way back to Lexington at the end of the summer, Lee became ill at what was known as "the old Sweet Spa" and stayed there two weeks, trying to recover sufficiently to resume his journey home. He described his disability to Markie as follows: "It seems to me if all the sickness I ever had in all my life was put together, it would not equal the attack I experienced." He came back from the illness but later wrote to Rooney, "I am so feeble that I cannot attend to the pressing business connected with the college."[338]

A number of fraternities had emerged from the wreck and rubble of the Civil War, some at Washington College. One of them, founded by four Confederate veterans, was struggling by 1867. The fraternity had only twelve members when two of its members decided to make Lee their ideal, and they dedicated their fraternity to "the chivalrous warrior of Christ, the Knight who loved God and country, honours and protects pure womanhood, practices courtesy and magnanimity of spirit, and prefers self-respect to ill-gotten wealth." That fraternity survived and thrived. It became Kappa Alpha Order.[339]

That fall, students entered Washington College—now called "General Lee's College" throughout much of the country—from Massachusetts, New Jersey, Pennsylvania, Kansas and California. The faculty increased from fifteen to twenty-two, and Lee told a faculty member, "The great mistake of my life was taking a military education."[340]

That autumn brought news that Rooney was engaged to be married to Mary Tabb Bowling, known as "Tabb," in Petersburg, Virginia, at her home. Union authorities had released Jefferson Davis from captivity in

Fort Monroe in May of that year, and they now wanted to try him for treason. One of the theories of the prosecution's case was that Davis, in ordering his generals to attack the United States, had committed treason and "was ultimately responsible for the American Civil War and the death and destruction that resulted."[341] Testifying on November 27, Lee rejected the prosecution's contention and stated unequivocally that *he* was responsible for everything he had done during the war. Because Lee could not be prosecuted under the terms of his parole, the prosecution's case folded, and Davis escaped a trial for treason.

Lee and his son Custis then took the train twenty-two miles south to Petersburg for Rooney's wedding. Lee was fearful that Petersburg would still be in ruins and that he would be hated for abandoning the city in April 1865. Those fears were allayed when he was met at the station by a large cheering crowd—perhaps "thousands"—and a brass band playing "Dixie." Son Rob and daughter Mildred met their father and two brothers there—as well as Lee's nephew Fitz Lee—and attended the wedding in their company. For Lee, it was a happy return and time with family and old friends. He stayed there with General William Mahone and rode in his open carriage—pulled by four white horses—to the wedding, wearing a new suit, the first he had acquired since the war. Adoring crowds lined the street to see him, and the streets were packed for three hours.

The year ended with the family together in Lexington at Christmastime. The next year, 1868, would bring Grant to the White House and, to Lee and the South, new and different challenges.[342]

1868

This year at Washington College would be perhaps Lee's most difficult. That difficulty was compounded by his health, of which he wrote to Markie on New Year's Day 1868, "My interest in time & its concerns is daily fading away & I try to keep my eyes and thoughts trained on those eternal shores to which I am fast hastening."[343] He wrote on March 3 to General Richard Ewell, "For my own part, I much enjoy the charms of civil life and find too late that I have wasted the best years of my life."[344] There was sadness about all of his correspondence now, perhaps exacerbated by the cold that gripped Lexington and Lee.

He received job offers regularly and regularly turned them down. One came from New York City and involved the representation of "southern commerce" in the city. He would live there, and "an immense sum of money" would be his. He replied:

> *I am grateful, but I have a self-imposed task which I must accomplish. I have led the young men of the South in battle; I have seen many of them die on the field; I shall devote my remaining energies to training young men to do their duty in life.*[345]

Lee's health continued to decline. His arteries were hardening, and a visitor seeing him for the first time would have thought him twenty years older. His hair was silver now, and he had become "quite portly."[346]

There were several racial incidents that year involving Washington College students. In one, a missionary and freedmen's school founder named Erastus C. Johnston was ice skating on the North River when he was attacked by a group of young men and boys. Johnston pulled a pistol and threatened one of them, which served only to inflame the crowd. They chased Johnston from the ice—with a few scrapes and bruises—and he went to the U.S. Army to complain. The branch, in turn, went to Lee, who conducted his own investigation, found that three of his students had participated in the conflict and either dismissed them or allowed them to withdraw.

Subsequently, a schoolteacher named Julia Anne Shearman complained that she had been insulted—called a "damned Yankee bitch of a nigger teacher"—on the streets of Lexington by Washington College students. Her complaints reached northern newspapers, which excoriated Lee and the college. But there was more: a young black man shot Francis H. Brockenbrough, son of the man who had hired Lee, and almost killed him. Students from the college captured the black man and, with a rope around his neck, marched him to the courthouse, intent on hanging him. Once again, Lee intervened and urged the mob to let justice take its course. They let the man go, and he was subsequently tried and convicted but served only two years in prison.

That summer, the Lees again retired to White Sulphur Springs, and for once, Lee became involved in politics, if peripherally. At the urging of William T. Rosecrans, Lee, P.G.T. Beauregard, Alexander H. Stephens and others entered into the "White Sulphur paper" in support of Democrats running in the election of 1868. In the paper, the authors attacked Congressional Reconstruction as unconstitutional and asserted that the South was not hostile to blacks and but for Reconstruction "the relations between the two races would soon adjust themselves on the basis of mutual kindness and advantage." Lee, however, saw the alliance between "Blacks and White Republicans as a threat to white southerners." Of black people, he said further, "I wish them no evil in the world—On the contrary, [I] will do them every good in my power, and know that they are misled by those to whom they have given their confidence; but our material, social and political interests are naturally with the whites."[347]

In addition, the authors argued that "at present, the Negroes have neither the intelligence nor the other qualities which are necessary to make them safe depositories of political power."[348] Lee believed in the restoration of white conservatives to political power in the South. He had been saying and writing these things for years, but that South and the Union to which it belonged were gone. Lee wrote to his twenty-seven-year-old cousin, Annette Carter, "I grieve for posterity, for American principles and American liberty. Our boasted self Govt. is fast becoming the jeer & laughing stock of the world."[349]

When one of his faculty spoke disparagingly of General Grant when he was running for president, Lee, in spite of his Democratic Party leanings, responded, "Sir, if you ever presume to speak disrespectfully of General Grant in my presence, either you or I will sever his connection with the university."[350]

From White Sulphur Springs that summer, Lee wrote to one of his favorite young female friends, Charlotte Haxall, "My beautiful Lottie, if I were to attempt to tell you how sad your departure made us, how much we have missed you, and how depressed Lexington has since been, time and my ability would equally fail."

Later that summer, Lee sat at the edge of the dance floor, urging southern young women and men to reach across the floor to their northern counterparts and to do so in a spirit of reconciliation and kindness. A coterie of "adoring girls" surrounded him as he sat there, and once, when he decided to cross the floor himself, he asked the girls to accompany him. Only Christiana Bond would go with him.

He turned down an invitation to attend a reunion of his former officers at Gettysburg: "I think it wiser…not to keep open the sores of war, but to follow the example of those nations who endeavored to obliterate the marks of civil strife and to commit to oblivion the feelings it engendered."[351]

Back in Lexington, Lee implemented more changes at Washington College. He abolished mandatory chapel and expanded his one rule of conduct—every man must be a gentleman—to a statement that would become the basis of the honor system at Washington College: "A gentleman does not lie, cheat, or steal, nor does a gentleman tolerate lying, cheating or dishonesty in those persons claiming to be a gentleman." It was a social compact between the students and the school. Lee also prohibited the consumption of liquor.[352]

Washington College grew and prospered. Before the war, it had 83 students and a faculty of 5. In 1868, the school had 411 students, and there were more than 15 faculty members present. He changed the curriculum as well, implementing a combination of a classical education and practical coursework, including schools of law, commerce and journalism. His emphasis was on "practical education," and he added other courses in financial management, banking, insurance and even joint-stock companies. He also planned to add a school of agriculture, and he instituted a summer school, including a preparatory course of study for students not quite ready for college.

On Christmas Day, Lee mounted Traveller, took a sack of Christmas gifts, rode through Lexington and distributed the gifts to the children of Lexington. That same day, President Andrew Johnson, nearing the end of his term in office and in another Christmas Day act, issued an unconditional pardon to all those "who directly or indirectly participated in the late insurrection or rebellion." Accordingly, Lee could no longer be tried for treason, but he was still not a citizen.[353] That would have to await another century, another president.[354]

1869

Lee was concerned about Lexington's accessibility to students. No railroads served the town, and students had to take the last leg of their journey by coach. Lee went to Baltimore in April to secure financing for a new Valley Railroad connecting with other lines serving various parts of the Valley. It would be a north–south line connecting to Maryland and Tennessee through Lexington. This was to be the only commercial venture in which Lee would become involved, in spite of the myriad offers that he received during the postwar years.

That spring, Lee received an invitation to visit President Grant at the White House, and on May 1, he called there. Lee entered Grant's office and shook hands. Several people were present, but they departed; the door was closed, and that is all that is known of the meeting, as Lee and Grant were the only ones present. Grant's secretary called it "an act of courtesy." Lee's son Rob would say many years later that Lee told him that there was no discussion of politics, and Grant would say that Lee told Grant of his visit to Baltimore. Grant recalled that he said then that the two of them had done more to destroy railroads than to build them. Lee did not respond to Grant's assertion. The interview lasted only fifteen minutes or so and then was done. It was the last time the two great adversaries would meet.

On May 31, Lee took possession of the new president's home, which was at the cutting edge of home-building technology. The new home had gravity-fed running water throughout, which was pumped from two five-thousand-gallon cisterns on the grounds up to a tank on the roof and then ran down into the house. The house, remarkably, had central heat from a furnace and distributed by air ducts, as well as a connected brick wing for Traveller and Lee's other horse from the war, Lucy Long.

An aide described Lee at this point as being about five feet, eleven inches tall, modest, but with "a fierce and violent temper." He loved children and fine things: houses, china, clothing, furniture, ornaments and horses. He was religious, but in a restrained sort of way. Lee read his Bible and attended church on Sunday. If his own church did not have services on a Sunday, he went to another church in Lexington. The aide continued:

> *Intellectually he was cast in a gigantic mold. Naturally he was possessed of strong passions. He loved excitement, particularly the excitement of war. He loved grandeur. But all of these appetites and powers were brought under the control of his judgment and made subservient to his Christian faith. This made him habitually unselfish and ever willing to sacrifice himself on the altar of duty and in the service of his fellows....He was an epistle, written of God and designed by God to teach the people of this country that earthly success is not the criterion of merit, nor the measure of true greatness.*[355]

That summer brought sadness: Lee's brother Sidney Smith—the Naval Academy graduate who had served in both the United States and Confederate navies, and whom most women, including the irrepressible Mary Chesnut, considered handsomer than Robert—died, and Lee attended his funeral. On that trip east, he also visited Rooney, Tabb and their five-month-old son, Robert III. Mary Custis Lee was spending the summer at the Rockbridge Baths not far from Lexington, but after his trip, Lee headed for White Sulphur Springs, where his doctors wanted him to take the waters.

Mildred and Agnes accompanied him to the springs, and they arrived there the first week in August, "finding a flamboyant social season underway." There were around one thousand guests present from all over the country, some from as far away as California. New wealth from oil, steel and railroads covered the nation like a healing balm. Eight Confederate generals were there, as was Laura Fair of San Francisco, "whose jewelry and wardrobe were financed by the Comstock Lode silver-mining fortune."[356] One of the guests there that summer was George Peabody of Massachusetts, a wealthy benefactor of education, especially to the postwar South. Peabody, after meeting Lee, gave him "a litigation-entangled claim" for $50,000 in Virginia state bonds. It was "Yankee shrewdness" at its best: "You Southerners go fight it out among yourselves….If General Lee can't get fifty thousand dollars out of the Virginia legislature, nobody can."[357]

School opened in September. For the academic school year 1866–67, Lee had made $4,756 rather than the $1,500 at which he had started back in 1865. Financially, he was in good shape, but Lee had put on weight, and his doctors were concerned about his health. A student observed that "the impression left on me is that of a stout old man who had no…great strength." The school had students from all over, although the largest source was, of course, the South. There were twenty students from the North at "General Lee's school."

A new face appeared in Lexington near the end of September. It was Franz "Frank" Buchser, a multifaceted and talented Swiss painter who, among other talents, played the guitar and the piano and spoke five languages. He kissed women's hands and had a past that involved numerous fights and brawls and several violence-engendering sexual relationships. Buchser was also a very talented artist who wanted to do a portrait of General Lee.

Like his Union counterpart Grant—who flatly refused to sit for Buchser—Lee did not like to sit for even a photograph, but he liked Buchser and invited him to stay at his house, agreeing to sit an hour or two each day until the portrait was finished. Buchser delighted his host's daughters and their friends with hand-kissing and singing in English, German, Arabic, French, Italian and Spanish. He kept a diary of his time with the Lees.

Lee told Buchser that he blamed the war on "poor politicians," that it could have been avoided but for the avarice of the Republican Party. He spoke well of Grant but regretted that the president had allowed himself to be guided by the Republican Party. Buchser also wrote in his diary Lee's views on the hanging of Major Henry Wirz, the commandant at Andersonville Prison. Lee thought the charge against Wirz "was the world's most unjust calumny" and the subsequent hanging "pure judicial murder." Lee argued that the South had tried everything to save its Union prisoners, from offering to exchange them to asking for Union doctors and medicine to, finally, offering to release the prisoners unilaterally. All of these offers the North rejected.

The painting was the third of Lee: the first was of him as a young lieutenant, and the second was as commandant at West Point. Buchser unveiled it on October 18 at a party given by the Lees. Subsequently, he shipped the painting back to Switzerland, where its new owners refused to pay for it because they wanted a portrait of Grant. Nevertheless, in the years to come, the portrait found its legs and now resides in the Swiss National Museum on permanent display.

Lee continued to suffer from angina pectoris and had, of course, done so since the time at Fredericksburg in the spring of 1863. His physicians did not—at the time they *could not*—make this diagnosis and instead called it rheumatism. His health was declining, but few outside Lexington knew it. Indeed, offers for business opportunities continued to pour in. General John B. Gordon, whose tattered legion had received the Union salute when they surrendered at Appomattox, had become a highly successful attorney and insurance executive in Atlanta. He asked Lee to become president of the Southern Life Insurance Company, but Lee predictably refused, saying, "It would be a great pleasure to be associated with you, [Wade] Hampton, B.H. Hill [a Confederate senator] and the other good men whose names I see on your list of directors, but I feel that I ought not to abandon the position I hold at Washington College at this time or as long as I can be of service to it."[358]

That autumn, Lee came down with a "heavy cold." Nevertheless, he remained in contact with his young female friends, especially Markie Williams, who visited him in Lexington and whom he also saw at the Rockbridge Baths that summer. She told Lee that she would never marry, but Lee counseled her to do so. Eventually, she did, but only after Lee's death, when she was forty.[359] To another cousin, Caroline "Carrie" Stuart, he wrote:

> *I have been looking for you and Annette all the spring, and I believe it is the "hope deferred" that made me sick. You ought not to disappoint me, Carrie, for I cannot stand broken promises like the young men. It is a serious matter with me....You have had such experience of the ill success of my "courtships," that I hardly think you can expect any good results from them. How far has my suit with you prospered, or what encouragement do you suppose it has given me to undertake anything of the kind with another? None; nor have I attempted it.*[360]

1870

Lee became even more ill as 1870 began. He could not walk more than 150 yards at a time, and he began contemplating his resignation from Washington College. He had turned sixty-three that January, and a friend thought him in "great depression of spirits." Leaders at the school began urging him to take time off, and finally, under pressure from the faculty committee, Lee agreed to a two months' vacation and a trip south. He wanted to see the graves of his daughter Annie and his father. Thus, on March 24, 1879, he and Agnes set off for Savannah by way of Warrenton Springs, North Carolina. "Lee was thinking like a tourist, carrying train schedules and wondering about the availability of hotel rooms. The South, once it knew, would receive him as an emperor, almost as a god."[361]

The two Lees traveled by boat and train to Richmond, where three doctors examined him. They found him "a little feverish. 'Whether it is produced,' Lee said, 'by journey, or the toddies that Agnes administers, I do not know.'"[362]

In Richmond, Lee ran into Colonel John S. Mosby, who later recalled Lee as being "pale and haggard." He "did not look like the Apollo I had known in the army." Mosby visited Lee in his hotel room; then, when Mosby left, he ran into General George E. Pickett, "a struggling insurance agent of 45," who blamed Lee for the decimation of his division at Gettysburg and resented that Lee blamed *him*—but not his nephew Fitz Lee—for the shad bake debacle at Five Forks and for which Lee had relieved *him* of his command but not Fitz Lee. Mosby turned and took Pickett to see Lee, but the two men faced off in icy silence. Mosby, sensing the strain of their meeting, immediately removed Pickett, who referred to Lee as "that old man…[who] had my division slaughtered at Gettysburg." But Mosby said, "Well, it made you immortal."[363] And it had. Even though *three divisions* actually made the attack, or the "charge," the names of the other two generals, J.J. Pettigrew and Isaac R. Trimble, have faded into the thick fog of history.

After leaving Richmond by train, the Lees, late in the day on March 28, entered into North Carolina, a state that, with only 10 percent of the Confederacy's population, had supplied 20 percent of its soldiers. The bodies of their dead rested in graves located from Gettysburg to Vicksburg. One regiment at Gettysburg, the Twenty-Sixth, began the battle there with 880 men and ended with 172.

They arrived that night at Warrenton ready to find a hotel. A Confederate veteran at the station to meet his sister could not believe his eyes—before him stood Robert E. Lee. The veteran, Will White, invited the Lees to stay with his parents, and they did. The next day, they visited the grave of their beloved Annie, who had died during the war of typhoid fever at age twenty-three. Lee called her "the purest and best of his children."[364]

They boarded the train that night, headed for Augusta, Georgia. Neither could imagine what lay in store for them down the tracks. The stationmaster in Warrenton had wired ahead simply: "Lee is aboard." The news spread like sheet lightning throughout North Carolina, South Carolina and Georgia. Crowds lined the tracks. They held up babies and small children, many of them named for Lee. Veterans howled the Confederate yell. Bands played Confederate battle songs and, as it was before the days of dining cars, people sent aboard food. Lee, perplexed by it all, asked, "Why should they want to see me?"[365]

At one stop, a group of Union troops on board the train got off and purchased a basket of fruit for the Lees. Columbia, South Carolina, declared a holiday, and in a cold, driving rain, a multitude of its citizens turned out to greet the great hero of the South. Now, Lee knew that he could no longer stay on the train, so he got off and bowed to the crowd; however, he did not speak, as they wished. A band played, the crowd cheered and small girls brought bouquets of flowers to him. Porter Alexander, who had recommended guerrilla warfare before the surrender, was there, as were many of Lee's other officers. Water dripped from the brim of their—and Lee's—hats, just as it had many times before in countless places on countless battlefields.

Arriving in Augusta at night, the Lees checked into a hotel, hoping that theirs could be a quiet arrival and stay. Their hopes were not to be; a crowd gathered outside the hotel the next day. Children, again many of them named Robert E. Lee, came.

Within the crowd at Augusta was a thirteen-year-old boy who persisted until he stood next to Lee and could stare up into the old general's face. The boy was Woodrow Wilson.[366] The future president had now seen two Confederate icons in Lee and Jefferson Davis.

The next morning, the Lees boarded the train for what would be for Lee a place of happy memories: Savannah, Georgia, Lee's first duty station after his graduation from West Point. It was here that Lee had built the fort on Cockspur Island, where he had visited in the home of his friend and West Point classmate Jack Mackay; where, as "Bob" Lee, he had flirted with Jack's sisters and formed a strong romantic attachment to the lovely Eliza. At home on leave, he had become engaged to Mary Custis, but his feelings for Eliza did not abate. Indeed, writing to her about her writing him, Lee said, "It did grieve me to see the Boats coming down one after another, without any of those *little comforts* [letters] which are now so *necessary* to me. Oh, me! I do not know what I shall do for them at Old Point. But you will send some sometimes, Will you now Sweet—? How I will besiege the P. Office." That love would over the years turn into a warm friendship, but Eliza and Jack were both dead now. Other Mackays remained, however, and visiting with them would be one of the highlights of his stop in Savannah.

Lee also visited with his old West Point classmate and Civil War comrade Joseph E. Johnston. The two sat for a now-famous photograph, facing each other, "each in handsome profile, their backs straight."[367]

At home in Lexington, the trustees of the college voted a life estate for Mary in the president's home and an annuity of $3,000 per year should her husband predecease her. Lee wrote home that with respect to the trip, he was sorry he had undertaken it. The tightness in his chest persisted, and he could walk only slowly and for a short distance.

Savannah had time to prepare, and the city was ready. The largest crowd in town history greeted him at the train station. He and Agnes rode by carriage to Brigadier General Alexander Lawton's house. Crowds had gathered in front of it. Lee entered, and then went out the back door to a waiting carriage, which spirited him to Andrew Low, a wealthy cotton merchant who had been married to Eliza Mackay's now also-deceased daughter. There Lee spent a restful night.

They left Savannah for Florida, but first Lee visited Cumberland Island, Georgia, where his father, Harry Lee, had died at the home of his old commander, General Nathanael Greene. Then it was on to Jacksonville in north Florida by boat. That state had sent fifteen thousand men off to war, more than the number registered to vote. Florida's men fought all over the South. Lee's Brigade had come north as the Florida Brigade. Soon, however, because of their savage lightning attacks, they became known as the "Whirlwind Brigade."[368]

The stop at Jacksonville was for only thirty minutes. A crowd on the pier awaited the old warrior, and single file, many of them came onboard to see Lee, so many that the ship sank lower in the water. Soon, however, it was time to go, and the decks were cleared. It was obvious that the portion of the crowd that had not come aboard would have no chance to see Robert E. Lee. In deference to them, Lee appeared on deck, walked to the rail and removed his hat. Everywhere else in the South, the crowds had roared as he appeared. Here, silence. Starting at the front of the crowd, men took off

Robert E. Lee and Joseph E. Johnston. *Library of Congress.*

their hats; like a ripple through the sea of people, hats were removed until all were bareheaded. Lee gazed at them and they at him. The water could be heard lapping against the pilings.[369]

Lee and Agnes returned to Savannah for a few more days and then went to Charleston and on up to Portsmouth, Virginia. In Portsmouth, he heard the one sound that he had not heard thus far on his trip or since the end of the war: the firing of cannons. From Portsmouth it was on to Norfolk, where he visited with his highly regarded adjutant, Walter H. Taylor, and where even more cannons greeted him. Then they traveled by boat up the James River, where they visited with various relatives. A young female cousin remarked upon meeting him, "We regarded him with the greatest veneration. We had heard of God, but here was General Lee!"[370] On the other hand, there was daughter Mary, who, upon seeing him at Rooney's farm, said, "He looks fatter, but I do not like his complexion, and he still seems stiff."[371]

He returned to Lexington on May 28, and almost immediately, Lee declined the trustees' grant of a life estate for Mary Custis in the president's house, as well at the $3,000 annuity. The trustees, however, did not accede to his wishes, and the grant thus remained.

A sculptor, Edward V. Valentine, wanted to do a bust of Lee, and Lee agreed to sit for him in Lexington beginning in early June. They worked in a vacant store, and Valentine took photographs from which to complete the bust, once it was shaped. Lee gave Valentine a pair of his old boots—size 4½ c—and as the sculptor was leaving him, Lee said, "I feel that I have an incurable disease coming on me—old age. I would like to go to some quiet place in the country and rest."[372]

He presided over graduation on June 23 and was persuaded to go to Baltimore to consult with a renowned physician, Dr. Thomas H. Buckler, who lived in France but was visiting in Baltimore. Buckler diagnosed "rheumatic constitution…and prescribed 'lemon juice.'" Buckler advised him not to catch colds.[373] Lee consulted with his attorney in Alexandria about Mary Custis Lee recovering ownership of Arlington, now in the hands of the federal government, with its grounds housing some sixteen thousand graves. That story would not play out until 1882, when the United States Supreme Court would rule that the government had taken it illegally, and the government then agreed to buy it for $150,000. With the Franco-Prussian War underway in Europe, Lee wrote prophetically, "I fear we are destined to kill and slaughter each other for ages to come."[374]

On his way home, he visited with a cousin, Cassius Lee, at Seminary Hill, site of the Virginia Theological Seminary. Robert, Cassius Lee later said, told him that if Stonewall Jackson had been at Gettysburg, he would have won. If Lee said that, it is one of the rare instances in which he ever discussed the war with anyone.

School resumed on September 15, and on September 28, as he was leaving his office, a student asked him to sign a photograph for his girlfriend. Lee did and left for home. At home, he took midday dinner and then a nap, as Agnes rubbed his hands. In the next room, Mildred was playing the piano, and a soft rain fell against Lee's bay window in the dining room. After his nap, he headed for Grace Episcopal Church for a vestry meeting to discuss building a new church. In his gray military cape and broad-brimmed hat, Lee entered the parlor, where Mildred was now playing Mendelssohn's "Funeral March." Lee said that the work was "doleful." He then walked to the church through a cold rain.

The vestry met in the church sanctuary, which was unheated. Lee's two physicians were there and noted that his face was flushed, even though it was cold in the church. They discussed the money for a new church and then the last item on the agenda: a deficit in Rector Pendleton's salary. Coming up fifty-five dollars short, Lee said, "I will give that sum."[375]

He returned to the house and entered the dining room, where the family was seated for supper. Mother Mary Custis said, "You have kept us waiting a long time. Where have you been?" Lee did not answer. He stood at the head of the table to say grace. He opened his mouth. No words came out. He sat down. Mary Custis offered him tea. Lee tried to speak, but again no words came out. His face took on "an expression of resignation that was sublime," Mary Custis Lee remembered.[376] Son Custis ran for a doctor.

Lee began to speak incoherently. Drs. Barton and Madison came. They brought his "small low single bed" to the dining room and placed it in his favorite place before the bay window in the dining room. Lee now could speak a little and helped the physicians undress him. The two doctors diagnosed his condition as "venous congestion of the brain." It was, however, a cerebral thrombosis, a blood clot in the brain. It was, in short, a stroke, without paralysis. Combined with a "throat condition," his heart condition and angina, the deck was stacked against him. As a result of a cough, he was unable to expectorate; thus, water and such foods as the family gave him went into his lungs. This brought on pneumonia.

Storms came and, with them, flooding. Lee rallied and could turn over, could talk a little and knew everyone, but for the most part he communicated by nodding or shaking his head. The rain finally stopped, and on October 7, 8 and 9, the Northern Lights appeared. A Scotswoman in Scots-dominated

Lexington saw, in accordance with Scottish lore, the lights as an omen. She quoted a Scottish poem:

> *Fearful lights, that never beckon*
> *Save when kings or heroes die.*[377]

Mildred sat stroking his hands, and once he kissed her hand and said, "Precious baby." Traveller neighed in his stall. One of the doctors came and asked how Lee felt. Lee struggled to say that he felt better. But later, when Custis spoke of recovery, he shook his head and pointed to the sky. Then, when Agnes brought his medicine, he shook his head and said, "It is no use." On October 10, he was in constant pain and could no longer speak. Colonel William Preston Johnston, the son of Albert Sidney, was a constant visitor and came now to sit with his old commander.

The rain began again. Agnes woke Mildred around midnight and took her to the dining room, where Mary Custis sat in her wheelchair, and Dr. Pendleton then said prayers for the dying. Custis was at his father's side. With dawn, the rain passed, and a bright sun shone through the bay window, heralding a crisp autumn day. It was October 11. At nine o'clock, Lee began struggling with his breathing. Then, around 9:30 a.m., the hero of the South, the southern apotheosis, the commander of the fabled Army of Northern Virginia, died. He was sixty-three years old.

The funeral was on October 15. Between Lee's death and the funeral, his body lay in state at the new chapel, whose construction he had only recently overseen. Cadets from Virginia Military Institute guarded his body in the period between his death and his funeral. A long procession of thousands marched in step to a muffled drum: townspeople, students, veterans and others who had simply come to see off their hero. A riderless Traveller followed the funeral procession.

The service was as somber as the procession: at Christ Episcopal Church there was "a simple reading of the beautiful Episcopal Order for the Burial of the Dead," followed by the placement of Lee's body in the crypt and then Lee's favorite hymn, "How Firm a Foundation Ye Saints of the Lord."[378] Lee's body, clad in the suit he had bought three years earlier for Rooney's wedding, was barely cold in its crypt when Mary Custis Lee deemed him a martyr whose blood had been shed for his country. She said that he was "the Hero of a lost cause," thus setting firmly in place a foundation for all that was to come: the "Lost Cause" catechism, the elevation of Lee to apotheosis and the use of religious imagery to describe his life and death.[379]

Throughout the South, a Lee cult sprang to life. Lee's life was now viewed as "spotless," "perfect" and free of original sin. He was Spartan, humble, bold and brilliant. No alcohol had ever passed his lips; he loved children, his wife, his family, his men, his country—*both* countries—and he was defeated only by overwhelming numbers and the incompetence of those below him in the chain of command. Others found him beyond description and bestowed on him the qualities of Christ, "the power of a 'divine example.'" They compared him to Napoleon, to Caesar and, in the North, even to Grant. "It all survived well until the late twentieth century, when a popular painting placed Lee at the right hand of Christ, in a triptych whose other secular saint is Elvis Presley."[380]

Douglas Southall Freeman perhaps carried this wave of adulation to its apex in his two massive treatments of Lee: *Lee's Lieutenants* and *R.E. Lee*, which generations of southern youth have read and accepted as gospel. But is this venerated, idealized Lee really the man? Is this how Robert E. Lee saw himself?

The answer to both questions is a simple "no." Lee refused to take himself or anyone else too seriously. He saw "the absurdity in the human condition" and had a "comic vision of life." He loved repartee with women, young women in particular, and although there is no evidence that he was ever unfaithful to Mary Custis, he engaged in "mock love affairs" with several women, including his distant cousin Markie Williams. His was not a happy marriage, and it was his marriage that pushed him toward other, younger women. During the war, staff officers said that Lee had a violent temper, although this characteristic of his personality is at odds with the prewar and postwar Lee. Moreover, he held on to his daughters to the extent that none ever married. What he thought of himself was perhaps best summed up on his 1870 trip through the South when he asked poignantly, "Why do they want to see me?"

Lee did see himself as a member of a "social elite" that he thought ought to govern. He was a career soldier who was deeply disappointed by his career in the Old Army. He was haunted by his military failures in West Virginia, at Malvern Hill, during the Maryland Campaign and, finally, at Gettysburg. He felt the shame of treason against his beloved United States, and he may or may not have been guilty of either ordering—or doing so himself—the whipping of runaway slaves. In short, Lee was a man, not a deity, and it was only through the work of others—Jubal A. Early principally—that he rose to the number one position in the southern pantheon of Civil War heroes, ahead of the martyred Stonewall Jackson and Jeb Stuart. Indeed, from 1863, when Jackson was killed, to 1870, when Lee died, it was Jackson who was "supreme military idol of the South." Thus, during that time, "Lee did not possess the aura of the invincible military chieftain."[381] Jackson did. Actually, early biographers criticized Lee for his military blunders, and they blamed Lee, not Longstreet, for losing at Gettysburg.

Between 1870 and 1885, the hero coin flipped. Lee came to surpass Jackson in the southern mind and memory, and he became the hero of the South, the "military idol…invincible on the battlefield." Then, between 1900 and World War I, he morphed into a *national* hero, "replete with religious overtones,"[382] surpassing even George Washington as a military genius and a historical colossus. Both Theodore Roosevelt—whose mother was a Georgian and a dyed-in-the-wool Southern sympathizer throughout the Civil War, even though she resided in New York City—and Woodrow Wilson extolled Lee as a military genius and for helping to save the Union by accepting defeat at and after Appomattox. President Calvin Coolidge authorized a fifty-cent coin with Lee's image to honor him. And finally, Congress passed, and President Gerald Ford signed, the bill posthumously restored Lee's citizenship in 1975.

Thus, for almost 150 years, Lee occupied a prominent place in America's usable past. That status ended when Dylann Roof killed nine African Americans at a church in Charleston, South Carolina, in 2017 and appeared online with a Confederate battle flag. Lee, Davis, Jackson—indeed, *all* Confederates—came under attack, and from one end of the country to the other, monuments to the Marble Man and other Confederates began coming down.

Lee the national hero no longer exists, nor is Lee the southern apotheosis that he was before 2017. His future historical significance is unclear, and it therefore remains to be seen what Lee's place in southern and national history will be. What is clear is that *only* the future can tell us the extent to which Lee will be written out of American history and relegated to historical obscurity. And what is also clear about Lee is that he was just a man—a great man, undoubtedly—who, as he told his soldiers at Appomattox when he returned from his surrender at the McLean house, did the best he could. And that was a lot.[383]

Chapter 10
TEN OTHERS

RICHARD STODDERT EWELL

"Dick," Baldy," "Old Bald Head"

Richard Stoddert Ewell was born in Georgetown in the District of Columbia on February 8, 1817. He was the grandson of Benjamin Stoddert, the first secretary of the navy, and he graduated thirteenth in his class of forty-two cadets at West Point. Ewell was five feet, eight inches in height and had gray eyes, a bushy brown beard and a bald head. He was irritable and profane but likeable, with a "wry sense of humor."[384]

Ewell, like so many other West Pointers, spent his formative military years at various assignments in the West and Southwest and then served in the Mexican-American War under General Winfield Scott. It was Ewell who, at the Battle of Contreras, accompanied Captain Robert E. Lee on his reconnaissance through the Pedregal, when together they found a way through the great lava field on Santa Anna's right flank. Scott cited Ewell for bravery at both Contreras and Churubusco. Between the Mexican-American War and the Civil War, Ewell again served at various posts in the West. At one point, he was wounded in a skirmish with Apaches led by Cochise.

In the years immediately prior to the Civil War, Ewell harbored pro-Union sentiments, but like Robert E. Lee, he chose his state, Virginia,

Richard Stoddert Ewell. *Library of Congress.*

over his country and followed it out of the Union when it seceded. Ewell began his Confederate career as a colonel in the cavalry but received a promotion to brigadier general and on to major general in command of a division, where he distinguished himself under Stonewall Jackson in the Valley Campaign of 1862. Again, in the Peninsula Campaign, he was a standout at the Battles of Gaines's Mill and Malvern Hill. Ewell followed this success with victories at Cedar Mountain and the Second Battle of Bull Run. At Groveton, Ewell took his second wound and lost his left leg below the knee.

After a long convalescence, Ewell returned to Lee's army after Chancellorsville and the death of Stonewall Jackson, and he took command of part of Jackson's Second Corps—A.P. Hill took command of Third Corps—and followed Lee into Pennsylvania. His performance at Gettysburg on the first and second days—when he failed to take Culp's and Cemetery Hills on Meade's right flank and thus enfilade Cemetery Ridge, rendering Meade's position untenable—began a long descent for his reputation.

Ewell participated in the three battles of the Wilderness Campaign, fighting well at the Wilderness, but Lee was forced to take personal command of Ewell's troops at the Mule Shoe of Spotsylvania because of Ewell's hesitation and inaction. His subsequent attack on the Union left flank at Spotsylvania was a failure, with high casualties. Lee then relieved him and sent him to Richmond. He remained there until Lee's retreat from Petersburg, when he rejoined the army and was subsequently captured at Sayler's Creek. Ewell remained in a Union prison until July 1865.

After the war, Ewell farmed successfully at his wife's farm near Spring Hill, Tennessee, and on a leased plantation in Mississippi. He was president of the Columbia Female Academy Board of Trustees and was president of the Maury County Agricultural Society. Ewell died on January 25, 1872, of pneumonia and is buried at Nashville's Old City Cemetery. In 1935, his book, *The Making of a Soldier*, was published posthumously. Civil War scholars praise him as a division commander, but the consensus among historians is that he was unqualified to command a corps, thus leading to his at least partial responsibility for the Confederate defeat at Gettysburg: "As an officer he showed great attention to detail, was a strict disciplinarian, and had excellent military instincts; however he lacked the self-confidence necessary to exercise independent command. Although the Confederacy produced officers of greater ability than Ewell, none fought more faithfully in its defense. As General James Longstreet commented, 'A truer and nobler spirit than Ewell never drew a sword.'"[385]

JOHN BROWN GORDON

John Brown Gordon was one of the most impressive generals of the Confederacy—indeed, of either side—but he remains vastly underrated and largely unknown. Gordon, sadly, is less famous than many Confederate generals who were far less capable and successful. Rising from captain to major general, his meteoric ascension is exceeded only by Bedford Forrest's rise from private to lieutenant general. Gordon was also one of the Confederacy's most successful generals *after* the Civil War.[386]

A native Georgian, Gordon was born in 1832 and grew up on a plantation in Walker County, which is in northwestern Georgia in the same area from which James Longstreet came. Gordon attended the University of Georgia and was a senior after only two years, with one of the highest grade point

John Brown Gordon.
Library of Congress.

averages in his class; then, without explanation, he withdrew and moved to Atlanta, where he studied law and passed the bar. Two years later, Gordon moved into his father's coal mining business and soon became a wealthy man with coal mining interests in three states. Next up for Gordon was politics, and he became a staunch proponent of southern rights.

At the outbreak of the war, Gordon, who had no military experience, formed a company of men from the mountains of northeastern Alabama who deemed themselves the "Raccoon Roughs." That unit became the Sixth Alabama Infantry, and Gordon commanded it. He received promotions subsequently to major and lieutenant colonel and became a full colonel by April 1862, although his regiment did not see action in the early battles of the war. The Peninsula Campaign followed, and Gordon took the wounded Robert Rodes's place as a brigade commander, serving with distinction during the Seven Days campaign, especially at Gaines's Mill and Malvern Hill. During the Seven Days, he established a record of outstanding leadership coupled with an equally outstanding grasp of tactics and aggressiveness that secured him both the loyalty of his troops and the praise of his superiors.

During the Maryland Campaign, Gordon again served with distinction—at South Mountain and Antietam—firmly establishing his reputation as one of the "rising stars" of the Confederate army. He led a defense at Antietam that resulted in him being wounded five times and a promotion to brigadier general with command of a brigade in Jubal A. Early's division. His brigade saw action at Chancellorsville and during the Pennsylvania Campaign, and his star continued its ascent.

Next came the three battles of the Overland Campaign, during which Gordon continued to distinguish himself. At the Wilderness, he led a savage attack on Grant's right, where he found Grant's flank "in the air," but Early would not let him attack it. Then, at the Mule Shoe six days later, he led a blistering counterattack that saved the day for Lee's army. For his performance in those battles, he received a promotion to major general and command of a division. Lee said that he was "characterized by splendid audacity."

Then there was service with Jubal A. Early in the Valley. He marched with Early to the northern outskirts of Washington and then back to the Valley for two defeats at Winchester and Fisher's Hill. But at Cedar Creek, he led one of the most successful flanking moves of the war. There, in what is known as the "fatal delay"—attributed either to Gordon's men pillaging Union supplies for food or to Early's failure to follow through the success of the initial attack on the battlefield—Philip Sheridan was able to rally his troops and, in another savage counterattack, rout Early's army. Early blamed Gordon for failure to control his troops during the morning's successful attack, and Gordon blamed Early for not taking Gordon's advice to continue the attack. The two men became bitter enemies, and their animosity continued into the postwar years.

After the Valley, Gordon returned to Lee's army at Richmond and assumed command of Lee's Second Corps, which had formerly belonged to Richard Ewell; however, he never received the concomitant promotion to lieutenant general that command of a corps dictated. Gordon again served with distinction at Petersburg, holding successfully the Southside Railroad and then leading the Confederate attack at Fort Stedman, where he was again wounded, this time in the leg. Finally, Lee selected Gordon to lead the final attack of the Army of Northern Virginia at Appomattox—a wild Rebel charge that succeeded before his numerically superior opponents recovered and drove his men back, and when that attack failed, Lee surrendered. Gordon led the final march of the Army of Northern Virginia at the surrender ceremony, when Hancock's troops rendered the famous salute to their defeated opponents in perhaps the most gracious gesture of the war.

Following the war, Gordon transferred his military success to success in life. He was elected three times to the U.S. Senate and served two and a half terms, as well as one term as governor of Georgia. He also developed a number of successful business ventures before retiring to the speaker's circuit and to be commander in chief of the United Confederate Veterans. In 1903, he published his *Reminiscences of the Civil War*. Like so many other memoirs, it was only partially accurate, and not unexpectedly, Gordon implicated his old enemy Early for the defeat at Cedar Creek and for his failure at the Wilderness to attack Grant's "in the air" right flank.

Although his leadership of the Klan has never been conclusively established, Gordon reputedly served as grand dragon of the Klan in Georgia. He testified before Congress, however, that he had never been involved with the Klan but did concede that he had been involved in a secret police organization whose goal was to preserve the peace.

Gordon died on January 9, 1904, in Miami and is buried at Oakland Cemetery in Atlanta. He was seventy-one years old at the time of his death. Fort Gordon, Georgia, is named for him.

WADE HAMPTON

Wade Hampton's name is synonymous with South Carolina and the South Carolina Legion, which he raised, organized and equipped with his own money. Hampton was the son of a wealthy planter whose family had a great military tradition: his grandfather Wade I fought in the Revolution, and his father, Wade II, fought in the War of 1812. Wade III graduated from South Carolina College—later the University of South Carolina—and inherited upon his father's death a large number of slaves working on two large plantations, one in South Carolina and one in Mississippi. He served in the South Carolina General Assembly but, like Gordon and Forrest, had no military experience at the outbreak of the Civil War.[387]

Although he had not supported secession, Hampton, age forty-two, went with his state and enlisted as a private in the South Carolina Militia.

Wade Hampton.
Library of Congress.

The governor of South Carolina, however, almost immediately appointed Hampton a colonel, and he then raised Hampton's Legion, consisting of six companies of infantry, one battery of artillery and four companies of cavalry. With Nathan Bedford Forrest and Richard Taylor, Hampton would be one of only three Confederate officers to attain the rank of lieutenant general.

Hampton and his legion saw action at First Manassas, where they fought with distinction and where Hampton was wounded. He then received a promotion to brigadier general in command of a brigade in Stonewall Jackson's division. In the Peninsula Campaign, he suffered a bad wound to the foot at Seven Pines, where he led a charge that earned him a commendation. Never dismounting, he received treatment in the saddle and continued to fight.

After the Peninsula, Lee assigned Hampton to take one of Jeb Stuart's brigades, with Fitz Lee taking the other, and during the Battle of Fredericksburg, Hampton led a number of successful attacks behind enemy lines that earned him a commendation from General Lee. His unit missed the Battle of Chancellorsville, but following the largest cavalry battle of the war at Brandy Station, when Union cavalry caught Stuart napping and embarrassed him, he went with Stuart on a wild ride around Meade's army that caused Stuart to lose contact with Lee. That move backfired badly, as it left Lee without information as to the size of Meade's force, its disposition, and the lay of the land at Gettysburg. Combined with the ineptitude of Ewell and Early on the left, the recalcitrance of Longstreet on the right and Lee's decision to mount Pickett's Charge in the center, Stuart's gambit was one of the great blunders that led to the Confederate defeat at Gettysburg. Nevertheless, Hampton saw action in the battle and was wounded three times. He returned to Virginia in the same ambulance as John Bell Hood.

Hampton and Stuart never got along. Hampton was a dyed-in-the-wool South Carolinian, and Stuart was a dyed-in-the-wool Virginian who tended to favor Virginians in his division. Hampton complained about Stuart's favoritism to Lee, which did nothing for his relationship with Stuart. As historian Jeffrey D. Wert pointed out, both men had "inordinate egos, which contributed to their relationship," or lack thereof.

Hampton received a promotion to major general and command of a cavalry division, which he commanded until Stuart died at Yellow Tavern; after three months without Lee naming a successor, a period during which Hampton performed brilliantly, Lee then appointed Hampton to take command of Stuart's corps until the end of the war, never losing a battle and, indeed, posting some significant triumphs. He was promoted to lieutenant general in February 1865, and Lee sent him and part of his cavalry to support Joseph Johnston in North Carolina. Hampton surrendered—very reluctantly—with Joseph Johnston in April 1865.

The war almost destroyed his fortune, and from 1865 to 1876, Hampton led the forces that fought—often violently—against Radical Reconstruction. In 1876, his election as governor signaled the end of Radical Reconstruction, and he was subsequently elected a U.S. senator for two terms, although he lost his right leg after being thrown from a mule while deer hunting just prior to his first term. President Grover Cleveland appointed the staunch Democrat United States railroad commissioner in 1893, and he served in that capacity until 1897.

Hampton, along with Jubal A. Early, was a leader of the Lost Cause movement that, among other goals, sought to blame James Longstreet for the defeat at Gettysburg and elevate Robert E. Lee to the position of a southern deity. Wade Hampton died in 1902 and is buried at Trinity Cathedral Churchyard in Columbia, South Carolina.

DANIEL HARVEY "D.H." HILL

Like Wade Hampton, D.H. Hill was a South Carolinian. He entered West Point in 1838 and graduated with the famous class of 1842, which produced seventeen general officers in the Civil War. Hill was about five feet, ten inches tall and stooped from a spine condition. He served in the artillery and saw action in Mexico, fighting under Winfield Scott in the successful campaign from Vera Cruz to Mexico City. Hill was brevetted to captain after Contreras and to major at Chapultepec; however, he left the army in 1849 to enter academia. Hill first served on the faculty at Washington College and then at Davidson College at Davidson, North Carolina, just north of Charlotte. While there, he authored a textbook on mathematics. In 1859, Hill accepted the presidency of the North Carolina Military Institute in Charlotte, where he served until the Civil War.[388]

When war broke out, Hill quickly aligned himself with the Confederacy and served as a colonel in the North Carolina Militia. He then commanded a North Carolina regiment in the Confederate regular army and soon accepted a promotion to brigadier general. A promotion to major general and command of a division quickly followed. Hill fought with distinction during the Peninsula Campaign, especially at Seven Pines, where Joseph Johnston was wounded and after which Robert E. Lee took command of the newly renamed Army of Northern Virginia.

Hill figured prominently in the Seven Days Campaign and once again fought hard and aggressively at Mechanicsville, Gaines's Mill and Malvern Hill. While Lee thought highly of Hill's fighting spirit and ability, he pointed out to Jefferson Davis that Hill lacked "administrative ability." After a tour in command of the North Carolina district, Hill rejoined Lee for the Maryland Campaign, in which he was blamed for the loss of Lee's orders, a subject about which historians still disagree. Hill denied the charge.

At South Mountain, Hill held several gaps, allowing Lee's army to reconstitute itself at Antietam, and at Antietam he held Lee's center against repeated attacks by a vastly superior Union force. His division missed most of

Daniel Harvey Hill. *State Archives of North Carolina.*

Lee's signal victory at Fredericksburg, and Hill then tendered his resignation from the army to Lee, citing health reasons. Lee expressed his regrets, but the likelihood is that Lee was glad to see the surly and carping officer leave field command. Hill had criticized everyone from Lee on down the chain of command for various alleged instances of nonfeasance, misfeasance and malfeasance. Hill had, therefore, justly earned a reputation as a "disputatious 'croaker.'"[389] Another official in the Confederate War Department said of Hill that he was "harsh, abrupt, often insulting in the effort to be sarcastic," and would "offend many and conciliate none." Lee did not accept Hill's resignation from the army, however, and instead sent him back to command the Department of North Carolina and then the defenses at Richmond. He sat out Chancellorsville and the Pennsylvania Campaign.

In July 1864, Jefferson Davis promoted him to lieutenant general, and he next returned to field command when he went to Tennessee to command a corps under Braxton Bragg. Hill fought at Chickamauga and then, as did so many other generals, became engaged in a "violent quarrel" with Bragg. Davis, of course, supported Bragg, and Hill was gone from Bragg's command immediately.

For Hill, that was about it. He returned to North Carolina, and his promotion to lieutenant general was never confirmed. He served as a volunteer aide to General Beauregard in the defense of Charleston, South Carolina, and then moved over to the Shenandoah Valley to fight David Hunter. After a stint as head of the military district of Georgia, he transferred to Joseph Johnston's army in North Carolina, where he took a division, fought at Bentonville and surrendered with Johnston to Sherman at Durham on April 26, 1865.

After the war, Hill became editor of *The Land We Love*, a monthly magazine that was a diatribe against the North and various Confederate general officers who had offended him during the war. Hill was also a major contributor to *Battles and Leaders of the Civil War* and later served as president of the precursor to the University of Arkansas. He left there to become president of the Middle Georgia Military and Agricultural College and, in 1889, died of cancer in Charlotte, North Carolina. He is buried at the Davidson College Cemetery. Stonewall Jackson was Hill's brother-in-law through his wife's sister.

FITZHUGH LEE

"Fitz"

Fitz Lee was the grandson of Light-Horse Harry Lee and the nephew of General Robert E. Lee by Robert's brother, the naval officer Smith Lee. Fitz Lee was also the great-grandson of George Mason, author of the Virginia Declaration of Rights, which served as the basis of the Bill of Rights to the U.S. Constitution. Fitz Lee was born in Alexandria, Virginia, and educated in private schools before his admission to West Point in 1852, where he failed miserably to distinguish himself. At the academy, he accumulated demerits at a meteoric rate, earning the ire of his uncle and West Point superintendent Robert, who threatened to expel him but at the last minute allowed Fitz to remain. Fitz finished forty-fifth out of forty-nine cadets who graduated in the class of 1856. He was about five feet, eight inches tall, sported a full beard and had bright-blue eyes and broad shoulders.[390]

Fitzhugh Lee, later in life. *Library of Congress.*

After graduation, Lee served in the cavalry on the Texas frontier, chasing and fighting Comanches, and he took an arrow through both lungs in one engagement in 1859. Surviving a near-death experience, he resigned from the army after Virginia left the Union and served first with General Richard S. Ewell. Fitz Lee missed First Manassas but was soon promoted to lieutenant colonel and then full colonel in command of the First Virginia cavalry regiment. With that storied regiment, he joined Jeb Stuart for his famous ride around McClellan's army on the Peninsula, earning, with Stuart's encouragement, a promotion to brigadier general and engendering for the first time—but not the last—the criticism of others who thought his promotion was because he was a Lee.

Fitz Lee was dilatory with his appearance at Second Manassas, earning the ire of Stuart; however, he redeemed himself subsequently at South Mountain and then again protecting the rear of the Army of Northern Virginia as it retreated from the Battle of Antietam. He played a significant reconnaissance role at Chancellorsville the next spring, where he found Hooker's right flank "in the air," and he accompanied Stuart on his deleterious lark at Gettysburg. There, after Stuart finally arrived, Fitz participated in an inconclusive cavalry fight. He had four horses shot from under him at Gettysburg. Following Gettysburg, he again received a controversial promotion, this time to major general. Uncle Robert wrote in his endorsement, "I do not know any other officer in the cavalry who has done better service."[391]

Fitz Lee gave commendable service at Spotsylvania Court House, and after Stuart was killed at Yellow Tavern, Lee took command on the battlefield of the cavalry corps. Robert Lee then gave command of Stuart's cavalry to Fitz Lee's senior, Wade Hampton, although he did not promote Hampton until February 1865.

Fitz then took his division to the Valley and became a part of Early's Army of the Shenandoah, a controversial part since Early hated his own cavalry. At the Third Battle of Winchester, a Confederate loss, Fitz took a shot through the thigh and was carried from the field. He took up a position in the line at Petersburg, and then, at a critical moment in the defense of the city, he and George Pickett abandoned their units to participate in the infamous "shad bake," which is where they were when Philip Sheridan launched his successful attack at Five Forks. His uncle Robert relieved Pickett but did nothing to Fitz, other than perhaps to issue a verbal reprimand.

Fitz Lee was with the Army of Northern Virginia when it surrendered, but he refused to surrender and slipped through Grant's lines before finally surrendering on April 22, 1865.

After the war, he farmed for the next twenty years and then was elected governor of Virginia in 1885. During these years, like his uncle Robert, he advocated acceptance of the outcome of the war and reconciliation of the South with the North. In April 1896, President Grover Cleveland rewarded him for his service in the Democratic Party with an appointment as consul general to Cuba. He resigned at the outset of the Spanish-American War and was commissioned as a major general of volunteers, ultimately commanding the Seventh Army Corps. He saw no combat, however, and in February

1901 received a brigadier general's commission in the regular army, from which he retired one year later.

In the meantime, he had become one of the principal proponents of the Lost Cause catechism, especially the veneration of his sainted uncle Robert. In 1894, he published his book, *General Lee*, "which offered a Christ-like portrayal of the Southern chieftain and not surprisingly, stinging criticism of James Longstreet."[392] Fitz Lee died on April 28, 1905, and is buried at Richmond's Hollywood Cemetery.

Stephen Dill Lee

Stephen Dill Lee was another South Carolinian. Born in Charleston in 1833, he attended and graduated from West Point in 1854, finishing seventeenth out of forty-six graduating cadets. Robert E. Lee was superintendent part of the time that Lee was at West Point, and future Union general George H. Thomas was one of his professors. Future Confederate general William Dorsey Pender was his best friend, and his other friends included future Union general Oliver Otis Howard and Confederate generals Custis Lee, John Pegram and Jeb Stuart.[393]

Prior to the Civil War, he served in the Third Seminole War in Florida and then in Kansas until February 1861, when he resigned from the United States Army to join the South Carolina Militia. One of his friends said that Lee regretted having to resign and that he was not optimistic with respect to the South's chances in its move to attain independence.

Subsequently, he received a commission in the regular Confederate army as a captain in the artillery, serving with Beauregard in Charleston. It was he who delivered the ultimatum to Union major Robert Anderson, who was in command of Fort Sumter, which Anderson refused, thus setting off the bombardment of Sumter that triggered the Civil War.

Later that year, Stephen Lee joined Hampton's Legion as a major and then received a promotion to lieutenant colonel in March 1862, serving as the artillery chief for McLaws's Division and, subsequently, for Magruder's Brigade. He participated in the Peninsula Campaign and the Seven Days before receiving a promotion to colonel of an artillery battalion in Longstreet's Corps. Then followed Second Manassas and Antietam, where he and his artillery had a major role in holding the line at Dunker's's Church against Union attacks through the infamous Cornfield. Later that

Stephen Dill Lee.
Library of Congress.

day, he moved to the Confederate right and helped repulse Burnside's attack at that point.

In November 1862, he was promoted to brigadier general and headed west, joining John Pemberton's ill-fated army fighting against Grant's ultimately successful Vicksburg Campaign. Lee fought at Champion Hill, the gateway to Vicksburg, and received a wound in the shoulder. Ultimately, he ended up in Vicksburg when Pemberton surrendered the city to Grant and became a prisoner. Paroled, he returned to the Confederate army, received a promotion to major general and, leaving field command, took command first of the Department of Mississippi and Eastern Louisiana and, next, the Department of Alabama and East Louisiana. Nathan Bedford Forrest and his corps were under Lee's command when Forrest routed a Union force at Brice's Crossroads. With Forrest, however, Lee suffered a defeat at the Battle of Tupelo. It is said that Lee was the only superior "to work well with that eccentric genius."[394]

In June 1864, Lee received a promotion to lieutenant general, which, at age thirty, made him the youngest lieutenant general in the Confederate army and the youngest officer to attain that rank in *either* army. Lee fought with John Bell Hood in the doomed Atlanta and Franklin-Nashville Campaigns—he was seriously wounded at Spring Hill—and after Hood's army disintegrated following the Battle of Nashville, Lee was able to hold what was left of his corps together and cover Hood's retreat. Lee took another wound during this retreat, and subsequently, he was assigned to Joseph Johnston's army in the Carolinas. Lee surrendered with Johnston in April and was paroled on May 1, 1865.

After the war, he settled in his wife's hometown, Columbus, Mississippi, where he farmed. He served as a state senator and was the first president of Mississippi A&M, later Mississippi State University. Lee was a delegate to the 1890 Mississippi Constitutional Convention, which authored the infamous Jim Crow constitution that effectively denied African Americans voting rights and relegated them to segregated facilities, from schools to trains. It also made a crime out of marriage between the races.

He was active in United Confederate Veterans functions and served as the organization's national commander in chief. He wrote two articles for *Battles and Leaders of the Civil War* and died in 1908, at age seventy-four, after giving a speech in Vicksburg to former soldiers of four Iowa and Wisconsin regiments. Lee is buried in Columbus, and there is a monument with a bust of him on the grounds of Mississippi State University.

GEORGE EDWARD PICKETT

George E. Pickett was a Virginian, born in Richmond on January 28, 1825. He entered West Point in 1842, following the graduation of that class of multiple Civil War generals. Pickett wore his hair in "flowing locks," and he wore ruffled shirts. He also loved fragrances, in which he bathed himself. These predilections engendered many demerits while at West Point, placing him a solid last in the class of 1846, an ignominious beginning to a somewhat checkered military career.[395]

Nevertheless, Pickett was not short on bravery. During the Mexican-American War, he seized the colors from a wounded James Longstreet and scaled a parapet at Chapultepec, which led to a brevet promotion to captain and the undying support of his future Civil War corps commander,

George Edward Pickett.
Library of Congress.

Longstreet. In the period between the Mexican-American War and the Civil War, Pickett served on the frontier in Texas and then in Washington State.

He did not resign his army commission until June 25, well after secession and Fort Sumter. Pickett received a major's commission in the artillery, and in February 1862, now a part of Longstreet's Division, he was promoted to brigadier general and given a brigade. Pickett proved competent at this level of command and fought well in both the Peninsula Campaign and the Seven Days. He was wounded at Seven Pines and missed Second Manassas and Antietam. Nevertheless, when he returned to the army that fall, he received a promotion to major general and took command of a division, which did not see significant action at Fredericksburg or during Longstreet's desultory Suffolk Campaign.

With Longstreet's corps, Pickett marched north with Robert E. Lee to Gettysburg, where he led the most famous charge of the war and one of the most famous in history. His division, however, was virtually destroyed, and he remained bitter about its use at Gettysburg for the rest of his life. Subsequently, Pickett proved that he could not command a division, and his reputation declined accordingly. Longstreet and his staff supervised him closely, and Longstreet always gave him detailed orders.

He took command of the Department of Virginia and North Carolina in September 1863, and after an unsuccessful attack on New Bern, North Carolina, he had twenty-three of his men hanged for desertion after they were found in Union uniforms, once again raising questions about his leadership and judgment. Pickett participated in the Battle of Cold Harbor, a Union debacle; then, during the Siege of Petersburg, he allowed his division to disintegrate while he spent time in Richmond with his wife, whom he had married the previous year when she was sixteen and he was thirty-eight. Next and most unfortunately, Robert Lee gave Pickett responsibility for defending Five Forks. The rest of Pickett's ignominious performance is well known: the shad bake, Sheridan's attack, the rout, Lee's retreat from Richmond to Appomattox and Lee's defeat and surrender. Lee relieved Pickett of command after the shad luncheon and told him to go find Jefferson Davis and report to him; however, Pickett remained with the Army of Northern Virginia until its surrender on April 9, 1865, prompting Lee when he saw Pickett to say, "I thought that man was no longer with the army." Lee relieved three generals during the war: Pickett after Five Forks, Richard Anderson after the debacle at Sayler's Creek and Jubal A. Early after his losses in the Valley during the last days before Appomattox.

Pickett headed for Canada after the surrender but returned to Norfolk in 1866 to work as an insurance agent. As did other Confederate generals who had resigned their commissions from the Old Army, Pickett had difficulty in attaining a pardon and did not receive one until 1874 by act of Congress. Although John Mosby said that Pickett blamed Lee for destroying his division, on another occasion, when asked why his charge at Gettysburg failed, he purportedly said, "I've always thought the Yankees had something to do with it." Pickett died in 1875 and is buried at Richmond's Hollywood Cemetery. His grave bears a large memorial.

Pickett's young wife, Sallie, lived long after his death and wrote three books that attempted to posit Pickett as a cavalier of the Old South and a gallant knight of the Lost Cause. Historians, however, consider her work largely fiction, and history now judges him as a good brigade commander who was promoted to a level of command beyond his competency. Fort Pickett in Virginia is named for him.

EDMUND KIRBY SMITH

"Seminole" (at West Point)

Edmund Kirby Smith was born to Connecticut parents at St. Augustine, Florida, on May 16, 1824. His father had been a career army officer stationed in St. Augustine when he received an appointment to a federal judgeship there. When he was twelve, Smith, who was called "Ned" or "Ted" by his family, went to Benjamin Hollowell's school in Alexandria, Virginia, which Robert E. Lee had attended, and then entered West Point in 1841, graduating in 1845, twenty-fifth in a class of forty-one.[396]

Upon graduation, Smith entered the U.S. Infantry, and with the outbreak of the Mexican-American War, he served first under Zachary Taylor for the Battles of Palo Alto and Resaca de la Palma and then under Winfield Scott on his successful campaign from Vera Cruz to Mexico City, distinguishing himself at Cerro Gordo, Contreras and Churubusco. His elder brother, Ephraim Kirby Smith, died at Molino del Rey during the war.

The end of the Mexican-American War saw Smith sent to the storied Second U.S. Cavalry in Texas, the outfit that was to produce seven Civil War generals: Albert Sidney Johnston, Robert E. Lee, Smith, John Bell Hood, Earl Van Dorn, George Thomas and William J. Hardee. Subsequently, Smith taught mathematics at West Point for three years and then returned to the Second Cavalry to fight Comanches along the Rio Grande, during which time, in 1859, he was wounded in the thigh. At this point, Smith was "five feet, ten inches tall with a dark complexion, brown hair, and hazel eyes."[397]

When Texas seceded from the Union, Smith, then a major, refused to surrender the Second Cavalry and Fort Colorado to the Texas Militia and threatened to fight. Nevertheless, he resigned his commission when Florida seceded and joined the Confederate army as a lieutenant colonel. Smith served in the Valley under Joseph E. Johnston and was promoted to brigadier general and given command of a brigade. At First Manassas, he received a serious wound in the neck and shoulder. After his return to the Army of Northern Virginia, he received a promotion to major general in command of a division.

In February 1862, Smith went west to command the Army of East Tennessee, and his army and Braxton Bragg's army invaded Kentucky, where Smith won a signal victory at Richmond. That win, however, was the highpoint of the Kentucky Campaign, which quickly unraveled, and Bragg

Edmund Kirby Smith.
Library of Congress.

and Smith retreated south to Tennessee after the Battle of Perryville. It was an ignominious end to a once promising campaign, but Smith nevertheless received a promotion to lieutenant general. With that, Smith was reassigned to take command of the Trans-Mississippi Department, which consisted of western Louisiana, Arkansas and Texas. He remained there until the end of the war, when he surrendered his forces to General E.R.S. Canby at Galveston and then, fearing arrest for treason, fled the country, first to Mexico and then on to Cuba.

Smith returned to the United States in the autumn of 1865 and took the amnesty oath in Lynchburg on November 14. He was president of the Accident Insurance Company for about a year and then, from 1866 to 1868, served for two years as president of the Pacific and Atlantic

Telegraph Company. Subsequently, he was president of the Western Military Academy and then served as chancellor of the University of Nashville. Now firmly entrenched in academia, he became a professor of mathematics at the University of the South at Sewanee, Tennessee, from 1875 until his death in 1893. He was the last living full general on either side and is buried at the Sewanee Cemetery. The State of Florida erected a statue of Smith in the U.S. Capitol. There is also a memorial to him at Sewanee, and a World War II Liberty Ship was named for him.

JOSEPH WHEELER

"Fighting Joe," "Little Joe"

Joseph Wheeler was born on September 10, 1836, near Augusta, Georgia. His parents were of New England ancestry, and Wheeler attended schools in Connecticut and New York as his parents moved about. He entered West Point in 1854—he barely met the height requirements—and graduated nineteenth in the class of 1859. Why it took him five years to graduate from West Point is unclear.[398]

Wheeler served in New Mexico, and with Georgia's secession, he resigned his commission and joined the Confederate army as a first lieutenant. That rank did not last long, and he quickly received a promotion to colonel and command of the Nineteenth Alabama Infantry regiment stationed first near Huntsville and then near Mobile. Wheeler and his regiment next moved to Corinth and participated in Albert Sidney Johnston's successful attack on the first day at Shiloh; however, with Beauregard now in command and Grant's savage counterattack on the second day, Wheeler covered Beauregard's ignominious retreat to Corinth and then on to Tupelo, before Beauregard, without authorization, claimed sickness and headed for Bladen Springs, Alabama, to "take the cure." Davis, of course, then relieved Beauregard with Braxton Bragg.

Bragg named Wheeler, still a colonel, head of his cavalry. Wheeler led several successful raids on the Union lines of supply and participated in the ill-fated Kentucky Campaign, which nevertheless led to his promotion to brigadier general. It was then that Bragg assigned Forrest's cavalry to Wheeler and told Forrest to go raise another cavalry, earning both Bragg and Wheeler Forrest's ire, which was considerable.

Joseph Wheeler. *Library of Congress.*

More successful raids followed, and Wheeler received a promotion to major general and command over Forrest's cavalry, as well as his own. They attacked the enemy at Fort Donelson but were repulsed, which led Forrest, who never gave up, to tell Wheeler, "There is one thing I want you to put in that report to General Bragg. Tell him that I will be in my coffin before I will fight again under your command."

Wheeler participated in the Tullahoma Campaign, the Battle at Chickamauga, various raids against the Union supply line out of Chattanooga and Longstreet's unsuccessful invasion of East Tennessee. He returned to Chattanooga in an effort to help Bragg against Grant, but Grant routed Bragg's army at Missionary Ridge and Bragg retreated into Georgia, with Wheeler covering his rear. Wheeler took a wound in the foot in one of several engagements during this retreat, and once at Dalton, Georgia, Joseph Johnston relieved Bragg. Sherman now commanded the Union army and began flanking Johnston to drive him back toward Atlanta. Nevertheless, Wheeler's cavalry screened Johnston's flanks during these retreats.

John Bell Hood relieved Johnston and sent Wheeler into Tennessee to raid Sherman's supply lines. Wheeler, however, did a Jeb Stuart and disappeared. He led his troops in a ride around Sherman's army with the same disastrous results: Hood was without his eyes and ears and, as a result of Sherman's brilliance and defeats in four battles, had to evacuate Atlanta.

Sherman began his March to the Sea, Hood invaded Tennessee and Wheeler stayed in Georgia to oppose Sherman, a thankless and futile task. Wheeler did, however, fight several successful engagements against Union cavalry led by Judson Kilpatrick, whom he knew from West Point, but the handwriting was on the wall and Beauregard replaced him as his head of cavalry with Wade Hampton, although Wheeler stayed on, reporting now to Hampton. Fighting all the way, Wheeler eventually ended up with a small command that tried to join up with fleeing Confederate president Davis but failed, and Union troops captured Wheeler on May 9, one month after Lee's surrender.

Wheeler initially was jailed with Davis at Fortress Monroe but soon was transferred to Delaware, where he was held in solitary confinement. On June 8, he was paroled and released, and he headed for New Orleans to work as a commission broker. In 1868, he and his family moved to northern Alabama, near a town that was eventually named Wheeler in his honor. There he farmed and became a member of the bar.

With the end of Reconstruction in 1876, Wheeler entered politics, and as a Democrat, he won in 1880 an election to Congress, to which he would be elected a total of eight times until 1900, when he resigned. In the meantime, the country went to war in 1898 against Spain, and Wheeler volunteered his services to President William McKinley. He was commissioned a major general of volunteers, which many saw as a positive development in reconciliation of the two sides in the Civil War.

Wheeler led his cavalry division through fights at Los Guasimas and, though ill, was present at San Juan Hill. He headed the commission that negotiated the Spanish surrender at Santiago. Wheeler next fought in the Philippines against the insurrection there and led a brigade in several battles. Upon his return, he was commissioned a brigadier general in the regular army, from which he retired in September 1900. He attended the 100th anniversary of the United States Military Academy in 1902, at which he wore the uniform of his most recent service and rank: a blue U.S. Army uniform with general's insignia. It was here that Longstreet made the famous statement, "Joe, I hope Almighty God takes me before he does you, for I want to be within the gates of hell to hear Jubal Early cuss you in the blue uniform."

After his retirement, Wheeler resided in Brooklyn, New York—a strange retirement choice for a Confederate general—until his death in 1906. He was buried at Arlington National Cemetery, one of the few Confederate officers to be buried there. Wheeler authored a number of books on both military and civilian subjects. In Wheeler's honor, the State of Alabama has placed a statue of him in the U.S. Capitol.

STAND WATIE

While not a major player in the Civil War, Stand Watie's story is certainly major in terms of appeal. Indeed, it is one of the most interesting and compelling stories of any general officer who served on either side.[399]

Watie was a three-quarter blood Cherokee Indian and a Georgian by birth. He was born at what is now Calhoun, Georgia, in 1806 and attended a Moravian mission school in Brainerd, Georgia, at the age of twelve. There, he learned English and converted to Christianity. He then attended an interdenominational school in Connecticut before returning to Georgia, where he became a slaveholding planter.

In 1835, Watie saw the handwriting on the Cherokee wall and decided that it was futile to resist further attempts by the federal or state governments

Stand Watie. *Oklahoma Historical Society.*

to take the Cherokees' land. Led by Watie, four tribal leaders signed a treaty to leave Georgia and head west to Oklahoma, which they did in 1836. Internecine tribal warfare ensued, however, and three of Watie's treaty cosigners were executed by tribal members who had opposed the treaty. Watie escaped, however, and became a slaveholding planter in Oklahoma.

When the war broke out, Watie had already headed an organization known as the Southern Rights Party, which sought to bring the Cherokee Nation into the Confederacy. Besides the slavery issue, Watie's group feared that the Union would make Oklahoma a state and thus jeopardize Cherokee lands. After secession, he organized a company of Cherokee cavalry that patrolled the northern border of the Indian Territory, where they took on raiding Jayhawkers from Kansas. On August 10, Watie's company fought at the Battle of Wilson Creek, where they "acquitted themselves well" by holding their ground under artillery fire that routed other Indians. Wilson's Creek was a victory for the Confederacy.

Subsequently, Watie's company and a larger one from the Cherokee Nation that had sought his life merged, and the Confederate government promoted Watie to full colonel in command of the combined group, which his superior assigned to guard the northern border of the Indian Territory. Watie's command fought bravely and successfully at Chustenahlah and again at Elkhorn Tavern, when his regiment attacked a full division and drove it back before a successful Union counterattack reclaimed the lost ground.

Watie then began to employ hit-and-run, guerrilla-type tactics in more than one hundred raids against Union troops and pro-Union Indians around the Indian Territory. He became the Bedford Forrest of the West with his unorthodox but highly successful tactics. His superior, Brigadier General William Steele, in what was likely a serious understatement, characterized him as "a gallant and daring officer." His regiment included not only Cherokee but also Seminole and Osage Indians.

One of his most spectacular attacks echoed Forrest's attacks on the federal gunboats on the Tennessee River in September 1864. On a raid, Watie encountered the USS *J.R. Williams* on the Arkansas River. His troops fired on the *Williams*, causing it to run aground; they killed four and captured five. Then, after taking much of its cargo, they set the vessel ablaze and disappeared. For this action, the Confederate government promoted him to brigadier general.

Watie's outfit fought also at one of the greatest and most famous battles in Indian Territory, the Second Battle of Cabin Creek on September 19, 1864. There, he participated in a raid that led to the capture of a Union wagon train worth roughly $1 million in supplies, wagons and mules. It is said that his unit participated in more battles than any other unit west of the Mississippi.

At the Canby-Smith Convention of May 26, 1865, Confederate general Edmund Kirby Smith surrendered Confederate forces west of the Mississippi. General Watie, however, did not participate in that meeting and did not surrender his regiment until June 23, when he surrendered the First Indian Brigade of the Army of the Trans-Mississippi. He was thus the last Confederate general to surrender.

After the war, Watie resumed his life as a planter and engaged in other business enterprises until his death in 1871. He died in present-day Delaware County, Oklahoma, where he is buried at Old Ridge Cemetery.

NOTES

Chapter 1

1. For prewar information, see generally Basso, *Beauregard*, 205–29; Davis and Hoffman, *Confederate General*, 1:85–90; Eicher and Eicher, *Civil War High Commands*, 124; Heidler and Heidler, *Encyclopedia of the American Civil War*, 197–242; Jones, *Historical Dictionary of American Civil War*, 171–83; Ritter and Wakelyn, *Leaders of the American Civil War*, 23–35; Williams, *P.G.T. Beauregard*, 2–250; Woodworth, *Jefferson Davis*, 72–103.
2. Davis and Hoffman, *Confederate General*, 1:85–90.
3. Ibid.
4. Basso, *Beauregard*, 173.
5. Williams, *P.G.T. Beauregard*, 257.
6. Basso, *Beauregard*, 297. See also Heidler and Heidler, *Encyclopedia of the American Civil War*, 200, and Williams, *P.G.T. Beauregard*, 263.
7. Basso, *Beauregard*, 295; Ritter and Wakelyn, *Leaders of the American Civil War*, 27; Williams, *P.G.T. Beauregard*, 275–81.
8. For postwar information, see generally Basso, *Beauregard*, 284–311; Davis and Hoffman, *Confederate General*, 1:90; Hathaway 28–20; Jones, *Historical Dictionary of American Civil War*, 72; Ritter and Wakelyn, *Leaders of the American Civil War*, 26–29; Williams, *P.G.T. Beauregard*, 251–330.
9. See John M. Barry, *Rising Tide: The Great Mississippi River Flood of 1927 and How It Changed America*, for a detailed discussion of Eads and his work on the Mississippi River.
10. Jones, *Historical Dictionary of American Civil War*, 172.
11. Williams, *P.G.T. Beauregard*, 292–93.
12. Ibid., 299–300.

13. Ibid., 303–6.
14. Ibid.
15. Basso, *Beauregard*, 308.
16. Ibid.; Williams, *P.G.T. Beauregard*, 307.
17. Ritter and Wakelyn, *Leaders of the American Civil War*, 1:26–29.
18. Basso, *Beauregard*, 304; Williams, *P.G.T. Beauregard*, 310.
19. Basso, *Beauregard*, 310; Ritter and Wakelyn, *Leaders of the American Civil War*, 1:28–29; Williams, *P.G.T. Beauregard*, 317–18.
20. Williams, *P.G.T. Beauregard*, 322–25.

Chapter 2

21. Basso, *Beauregard*, 310; Davis and Hoffman, *Confederate General*, 1:90; Hess, *Braxton Bragg*, 1–2, 53; Hewett, "Braxton Bragg," 5–7, 11; Martin, *General Braxton Bragg*, 3–7, 9–13; McWhiney, *Braxton Bragg*, 2–5; Ritter and Wakelyn, *Leaders of the American Civil War*, 1:28–29; Williams, *P.G.T. Beauregard*, 326–27; Woodworth, "Braxton Bragg," 54–55.
22. McWhiney, *Braxton Bragg*, 34.
23. Ibid., 35.
24. Ibid., 56.
25. Warner, *Generals in Gray*, 30; Woodworth, "Braxton Bragg," 55.
26. McWhiney, *Braxton Bragg*, 89–90.
27. Ibid., 100.
28. Hewett, "Braxton Bragg," 5–7, 11; McWhiney, *Braxton Bragg*, 83.
29. Hess, *Braxton Bragg*, 2–3.
30. Ibid.
31. For Bragg's service information, see generally Hess, *Braxton Bragg*, 11–263; Hewett, "Braxton Bragg," 113–15; Martin, *General Braxton Bragg*, 72–472; McWhiney, *Braxton Bragg*, 153–464; Seitz, *Braxton Bragg*, 543–45; Warner, *Generals in Gray*, 30–31; Woodworth, "Braxton Bragg," 54–65.
32. Hewett, "Braxton Bragg," 103; Martin, *General Braxton Bragg*, 4–20; McWhiney, *Braxton Bragg*, 26–43; Woodworth, "Braxton Bragg," 55.
33. McWhiney, *Braxton Bragg*, 179–80.
34. Ibid., 199–200.
35. Martin, *General Braxton Bragg*, 141.
36. Ibid., 159.
37. Hess, *Braxton Bragg*, 68–84; Hewett, "Braxton Bragg," 114; Martin, *General Braxton Bragg*, 182–208; McWhiney, *Braxton Bragg*, 312–24.
38. Chesnut, *Mary Chesnut's Civil War*, 469.
39. Henry, *Nathan Bedford Forrest*, 199.
40. Chesnut, *Mary Chesnut's Civil War*, 496.
41. Martin, *General Braxton Bragg*, 380.
42. Hess, *Braxton Bragg*, 68–84.
43. Ibid., 235–40.

44. Martin, *General Braxton Bragg*, 414.
45. Chesnut, *Mary Chesnut's Civil War*, 703.
46. Hess, *Braxton Bragg*, 256.
47. Hewett, "Braxton Bragg," 115; Seitz, *Braxton Bragg*, 543.
48. Martin, *General Braxton Bragg*, 467–68.
49. For postwar information, see generally Davis and Hoffman, *Confederate General*, 1:89; Hess, *Braxton Bragg*, 251–63; Hewett, "Braxton Bragg," 115; Seitz, *Braxton Bragg*, 543–44; Warner, *Generals in Gray*, 31; Woodworth, "Braxton Bragg," 60.
50. Hewett, "Braxton Bragg," 115.

Chapter 3

51. Cooling, *Jubal Early*, 1; Davis and Hoffman, *Confederate General*, 2:89; Early, *Lieutenant General Jubal Anderson Early*, 1; Osborne, *Life and Times of General Jubal A. Early*, 2–3.
52. Early, *Lieutenant General Jubal Anderson Early*, 1.
53. Ibid.
54. Cooling, *Jubal Early*, 3; Early, *Lieutenant General Jubal Anderson Early*, 1; Osborne, *Life and Times of General Jubal A. Early*, 9–18.
55. Cooling, *Jubal Early*, 4–5; Davis and Hoffman, *Confederate General*, 2:89; Early, *Lieutenant General Jubal Anderson Early*, 3; Osborne, *Life and Times of General Jubal A. Early*, 32–35.
56. Bushong, *Old Jube*, 23–24.
57. Davis and Hoffman, *Confederate General*, 2:89; Osborne, *Life and Times of General Jubal A. Early*, 35.
58. Early, *Lieutenant General Jubal Anderson Early*, 18–21; Osborne, *Life and Times of General Jubal A. Early*, 68–69.
59. Early, *Lieutenant General Jubal Anderson Early*, 18–21; Osborne, *Life and Times of General Jubal A. Early*, 68–69.
60. Freeman, *Lee's Lieutenants*, 3:469; Osborne, *Life and Times of General Jubal A. Early*, 4.
61. Osborne, *Life and Times of General Jubal A. Early*, 4–5.
62. Ibid., 55.
63. Early, *Lieutenant General Jubal Anderson Early*, 4.
64. Ibid., 77–78; see also Bushong, *Old Jube*, 104–14; Osborne, *Life and Times of General Jubal A. Early*, 130–36.
65. Osborne, *Life and Times of General Jubal A. Early*, 55.
66. Early, *Lieutenant General Jubal Anderson Early*, 123. See also Osborne, *Life and Times of General Jubal A. Early*, 187; Bushong, *Old Jube*, 147.
67. Osborne, *Life and Times of General Jubal A. Early*, 257.
68. Cooling, *Jubal Early*, 86.
69. For Civil War service information, see generally Bushong, *Old Jube*, 79–282; Cooling, *Jubal Early*, 130–31; Davis and Hoffman, *Confederate General*, 2:92; Freeman, *Lee's Lieutenants*, 3:68–78, 82, 83 fn 52, 188–91; Osborne, *Life and Times of General Jubal A. Early*, 14–399.
70. Bushong, *Old Jube*, 283; Osborne, *Life and Times of General Jubal A. Early*, 402.

71. Bushong, *Old Jube*, 286–87; Cooling, *Jubal Early*, 133; Osborne, *Life and Times of General Jubal A. Early*, 403–4.
72. Freeman, *Lee's Lieutenants*, 3:770; Osborne, *Life and Times of General Jubal A. Early*, 403.
73. Bushong, *Old Jube*, 289–90; Cooling, *Jubal Early*, 124–35.
74. Cooling, *Jubal Early*, 135.
75. Bushong, *Old Jube*, 296.
76. Early, *Lieutenant General Jubal Anderson Early*, 3–4.
77. Cooling, *Jubal Early*, 132–33.
78. Bushong, *Old Jube*, 297; Cooling, *Jubal Early*, 132; Osborne, *Life and Times of General Jubal A. Early*, 420–33.
79. Bushong, *Old Jube*, 297.
80. Ibid., 297–98; Cooling, *Jubal Early*, 141; Freeman, *Lee's Lieutenants*, 3:779.
81. Cooling, *Jubal Early*, 149; Osborne, *Life and Times of General Jubal A. Early*, 430–32.
82. Cooling, *Jubal Early*, 132–33; Osborne, *Life and Times of General Jubal A. Early*, 469.
83. Cooling, *Jubal Early*, 132–33; Osborne, *Life and Times of General Jubal A. Early*, 469.
84. Freeman, *Lee's Lieutenants*, 3:770; Osborne, *Life and Times of General Jubal A. Early*, 434–38.
85. Cooling, *Jubal Early*, 147.
86. Ibid.
87. Osborne, *Life and Times of General Jubal A. Early*, 472.
88. For postwar information, see generally Bushong, *Old Jube*, 283–306; Cooling, *Jubal Early*, 129–49; Davis and Hoffman, *Confederate General*, 2:90; Osborne, *Life and Times of General Jubal A. Early*, 402–33, 469–74.

Chapter 4

89. For childhood information, see generally Davis and Hoffman, *Confederate General*, 2:139; Davison and Foxx, *Nathan Bedford Forrest*, 18–47; Foote, *Civil War*, 1:171–72; Henry, *Nathan Bedford Forrest*, 13, 24–27; Hurst, *Nathan Bedford Forrest*, 19–23; Woodworth, *Jefferson Davis*, 131; Wyeth, *Life of General Nathan Bedford Forrest*, 5, 15–17.
90. Hurst, *Nathan Bedford Forrest*, 7; Woodworth, *Jefferson Davis*, 132.
91. Henry, *Nathan Bedford Forrest*, 15.
92. Ibid., 73.
93. Ibid., 32; Warner, *Generals in Gray*, 92.
94. Henry, *Nathan Bedford Forrest*, 32; Warner, *Generals in Gray*, 92.
95. Davison and Foxx, *Nathan Bedford Forrest*, 29; Hurst, *Nathan Bedford Forrest*, 91; Warner, *Generals in Gray*, 92.
96. Davison and Foxx, *Nathan Bedford Forrest*, 69; Hurst, *Nathan Bedford Forrest*, 91; Warner, *Generals in Gray*, 92.

97. Foote, *Civil War*, 1:349.
98. Ibid., 1:350; Hurst, *Nathan Bedford Forrest*, 92; Wyeth, *Life of General Nathan Bedford Forrest*, 78–79.
99. Foote, *Civil War*, 1:350; Hurst, *Nathan Bedford Forrest*, 92–93; Wyeth, *Life of General Nathan Bedford Forrest*, 78–79.
100. Woodworth, *Jefferson Davis*, 132.
101. Davison and Foxx, *Nathan Bedford Forrest*, 88–90; Hurst, *Nathan Bedford Forrest*, 105; Warner, *Generals in Gray*, 92.
102. Foote, *Civil War*, 2:65.
103. Ibid., 2:733.
104. Henry, *Nathan Bedford Forrest*, 199.
105. Foote, *Civil War*, 1:350; Hurst, *Nathan Bedford Forrest*, 92–93; Wyeth, *Life of General Nathan Bedford Forrest*, 78–79.
106. Davis, *Atlanta Will Fall*, 207; Foote, *Civil War*, 2:922; Hurst, *Nathan Bedford Forrest*, 153.
107. Hurst, *Nathan Bedford Forrest*, 155–56.
108. Davis and Hoffman, *Confederate General*, 2:142.
109. Davison and Foxx, *Nathan Bedford Forrest*, 229.
110. Warner, *Generals in Gray*, 92.
111. Davison and Foxx, *Nathan Bedford Forrest*, 343.
112. Ibid.
113. *Battles and Leaders of the Civil War*, 4:447.
114. For information on his Civil War service, see generally *Battles and Leaders of the Civil War*; Davis and Hoffman, *Confederate General*, 2:139; Davison and Foxx, *Nathan Bedford Forrest*; Foote, *Civil War*, vols. 1–3; Henry, *Nathan Bedford Forrest*; Hurst, *Nathan Bedford Forrest*; Warner, *Generals in Gray*; Woodworth, *Jefferson Davis*; Wyeth, *Life of General Nathan Bedford Forrest.*
115. Hurst, *Nathan Bedford Forrest*, 262; Davison and Foxx, *Nathan Bedford Forrest*, 408–9.
116. Davison and Foxx, *Nathan Bedford Forrest*, 410.
117. Hurst, *Nathan Bedford Forrest*, 230–31; Davison and Foxx, *Nathan Bedford Forrest*, 415–16; Wyeth, *Life of General Nathan Bedford Forrest*, 615–17.
118. Davison and Foxx, *Nathan Bedford Forrest*, 417, 418; Henry, *Nathan Bedford Forrest*, 441–42; Hurst, *Nathan Bedford Forrest*, 272–73.
119. Henry, *Nathan Bedford Forrest*, 440; Hurst, *Nathan Bedford Forrest*, 265–69; Davison and Foxx, *Nathan Bedford Forrest*, 413.
120. Hurst, *Nathan Bedford Forrest*, 297; Davison and Foxx, *Nathan Bedford Forrest*, 442.
121. Hurst, *Nathan Bedford Forrest*, 327–30.
122. Davison and Foxx, *Nathan Bedford Forrest*, 460–72; Hurst, *Nathan Bedford Forrest*, 338–45; Wyeth, *Life of General Nathan Bedford Forrest*, 618–18.
123. Hurst, *Nathan Bedford Forrest*, 346–47.
124. Davison and Foxx, *Nathan Bedford Forrest*, 474; Hurst, *Nathan Bedford Forrest*, 360.
125. Davison and Foxx, *Nathan Bedford Forrest*, 474; Hurst, *Nathan Bedford Forrest*, 368–69.
126. Hurst, *Nathan Bedford Forrest*, 375; Wyeth, *Life of General Nathan Bedford Forrest*, 622.

127. Davison and Foxx, *Nathan Bedford Forrest*, 479; Henry, *Nathan Bedford Forrest*, 460; Hurst, *Nathan Bedford Forrest*, 375–76; Wyeth, *Life of General Nathan Bedford Forrest*, 621–23.

128. Davison and Foxx, *Nathan Bedford Forrest*, 377–79; Henry, *Nathan Bedford Forrest*, 461; Hurst, *Nathan Bedford Forrest*, 377–79.

129. Hurst, *Nathan Bedford Forrest*, 381.

130. Henry, *Nathan Bedford Forrest*, 462; Hurst, *Nathan Bedford Forrest*, 382–83; Wyeth, *Life of General Nathan Bedford Forrest*, 635.

131. Woodworth, *Jefferson Davis*, 265.

132. Henry, *Nathan Bedford Forrest*, 463; Hurst, *Nathan Bedford Forrest*, 383.

133. Henry, *Nathan Bedford Forrest*, 463; Hurst, *Nathan Bedford Forrest*, 383.

134. Hurst, *Nathan Bedford Forrest*, 383–84.

135. For postwar information, see generally Davison and Foxx, *Nathan Bedford Forrest*; Henry, *Nathan Bedford Forrest*; Hurst, *Nathan Bedford Forrest*; Woodworth, *Jefferson Davis*, and Wyeth, *Life of General Nathan Bedford Forrest*. Quoted material is cited to specific sources.

136. Henry, *Nathan Bedford Forrest*, 464–65.

Chapter 5

137. McMurray, *John Bell Hood*, 1–3.

138. Ibid., 5.

139. Davis and Hoffman, *Confederate General*, 2:121; Hardin, *After the War*, 93–94; Hickman, "American Civil War: Lieutenant General John Bell Hood," 1; McMurray, *John Bell Hood*, 1–15.

140. Hickman, "American Civil War: Lieutenant General John Bell Hood," 1; McMurray, *John Bell Hood*, 7.

141. Davis and Hoffman, *Confederate General*, 2:121; Hardin, *After the War*, 94; Hickman, "American Civil War: Lieutenant General John Bell Hood," 1; McMurray, *John Bell Hood*, 7; Sword, *Confederacy's Last Hurrah*, 6.

142. Davis and Hoffman, *Confederate General*, 2:121; Hickman, "American Civil War: Lieutenant General John Bell Hood," 1; McMurray, *John Bell Hood*, 13–36; Woodworth, *Jefferson Davis*, 256–62.

143. Davis and Hoffman, *Confederate General*, 2:121; McMurray, *John Bell Hood*, 13–15.

144. Simpson, "Cry Comanche," 3–4; see also Woodworth, *Jefferson Davis*, 266.

145. Sword, *Confederacy's Last Hurrah*, 6; Davis and Hoffman, *Confederate General*, 2:121; Hardin, *After the War*, 94. Later, the famed diarist Mary Boykin Chesnut would later write of Hood, "The famous colonel of the Fourth Texas—by the name of John Bell Hood—him we called Sam because his classmates at West Point did so still—cause unknown." Chesnut, *Mary Chesnut's Civil War*, 441.

146. Freeman, *Lee's Lieutenants*, 1:xxviii, 198.

147. McMurray, *John Bell Hood*, 33.

148. Ibid., 34–36.

149. Hickman, "American Civil War: Lieutenant General John Bell Hood," 1; McMurray, *John Bell Hood*, 35; Woodworth, *Jefferson Davis*, 268.

150. Freeman, *Lee's Lieutenants*, 1:517–37.
151. Ibid., 2:138; Davis and Hoffman, *Confederate General*, 2:121; Hickman, "American Civil War: Lieutenant General John Bell Hood," 2.
152. Freeman, *Lee's Lieutenants*, 2:147; See also Hickman, "American Civil War: Lieutenant General John Bell Hood," 2.
153. Hickman, "American Civil War: Lieutenant General John Bell Hood," 2.
154. Commager, *Blue and the Gray*, 607; Hickman, "American Civil War: Lieutenant General John Bell Hood," 2.
155. Davis and Hoffman, *Confederate General*, 2:121; McMurray, *John Bell Hood*, 76; Woodworth, *Jefferson Davis*, 268. Mary Boykin Chesnut's diary contains extensive material on Hood's courtship of Buck, which ultimately, at her parents' insistence, came to naught. See, for example, 442–43, 502–3, 505, 509, 516 and 537–38. More material on Hood's courtship of Buck is found in Woodworth, *Jefferson Davis*, 212–16.
156. Woodworth, *Jefferson Davis*, 268.
157. McMurray, *John Bell Hood*, places the amount at $3,000; Woodworth, *Jefferson Davis*, at $3,100; and Hickman, "American Civil War: Lieutenant General John Bell Hood," at "nearly $5000.00." Davis and Hoffman, *Confederate General*, 2:121; Freeman, *Lee's Lieutenants*, 3:229–31; Woodworth, *Jefferson Davis*, 268–69; McMurray, *John Bell Hood*, 77.
158. Davis and Hoffman, *Confederate General*, 2:121; see also Hardin, *After the War*, 106; Hickman, "American Civil War: Lieutenant General John Bell Hood," 2; Symonds, *Joseph E. Johnston*, 32–34.
159. McMurray, *John Bell Hood*, 117.
160. Hardin, *After the War*, 107.
161. McMurray, *John Bell Hood*, 190–91.
162. Davis and Hoffman, *Confederate General*, 2:127.
163. For information on service from First Manassas through Gettysburg, see generally Anderson and Anderson, *The Generals*, 334–35; Davis and Hoffman, *Confederate General*, 2:121; Dyer, *Gallant Hood*, 127; Eicher and Eicher, *Civil War High Commands*, 303; Freeman, *Lee's Lieutenants*, 2:182–95, 204–9, 266; McMurray, *John Bell Hood*, 35–60; Sears 243; Warner, *Generals in Gray*, 143.
164. Chesnut, *Mary Chesnut's Civil War*, 710–11.
165. McMurray, *John Bell Hood*, 192.
166. Dyer, *Gallant Hood*, 304.
167. McMurray, *John Bell Hood*, 195.
168. Dyer, *Gallant Hood*, 315.
169. McMurray, *John Bell Hood*, 195; Wakelyn and Vandiver, *Biographical Dictionary of the Confederacy*, 239.
170. Hardin, *After the War*, 111.
171. McMurray, *John Bell Hood*, 199.
172. Ibid., 192–203.
173. Dyer, *Gallant Hood*, 319–20.
174. Ibid., 320.

175. Ibid.
176. For postwar information, see generally Chesnut, *Mary Chesnut's Civil War*, 710–11; Dyer, *Gallant Hood*, 304–19; Hardin, *After the War*, 103–13; McMurray, *John Bell Hood*, 192–203; Wakelyn and Vandiver, *Biographical Dictionary of the Confederacy*, 238–39.

Chapter 6

177. Govan and Livingood, *Different Valor*, 12–17; Johnston, *Narrative of Military Operations*, 193; Symonds, *Joseph E. Johnston*, 10–52; Vandiver, "Joseph Eggleston Johnston," 215; Wakelyn and Vandiver, *Biographical Dictionary of the Confederacy*, 259; Woodworth, *Jefferson Davis*, 173–74.
178. Symonds, *Joseph E. Johnston*, 40–71; Vandiver, "Joseph Eggleston Johnston," 215–16; Wakelyn and Vandiver, *Biographical Dictionary of the Confederacy*, 259–60; Warner, *Generals in Gray*, 161; Woodworth, *Jefferson Davis*, 174.
179. Govan and Livingood, *Different Valor*, 27–28; Woodworth, *Jefferson Davis*, 176.
180. Govan and Livingood, *Different Valor*, 42–71; Lash, *Destroyer of the Iron Horse*, 7–41; Symonds, *Joseph E. Johnston*, 116–24; Wakelyn and Vandiver, *Biographical Dictionary of the Confederacy*, 260; Woodworth, *Jefferson Davis*, 176.
181. Govan and Livingood, *Different Valor*, 72–80; Symonds, *Joseph E. Johnston*, 125–39.
182. Govan and Livingood, *Different Valor*, 98–128; Symonds, *Joseph E. Johnston*, 160–72; Vandiver, "Joseph Eggleston Johnston," 216; Warner, *Generals in Gray*, 162; Wakelyn and Vandiver, *Biographical Dictionary of the Confederacy*, 260; Woodworth, *Jefferson Davis*, 178. For a detailed discussion of the Peninsula Campaign, see Newton, *Joseph E. Johnston*.
183. Govan and Livingood, *Different Valor*, 166–284; Johnston, *Narrative of Military Operations*, 147; Lash, *Destroyer of the Iron Horse*, 7–41; McMurray, *John Bell Hood*, 193–94; Sifakis, *Who Was Who in the Civil War*, 347; Symonds, *Joseph E. Johnston*, 175–217; Vandiver, "Joseph Eggleston Johnston," 217; Woodworth, *Jefferson Davis*, 178.
184. For information on service from 1863 to 1865, see generally Govan and Livingood, *Different Valor*, 223–73, 327–57; Lash, *Destroyer of the Iron Horse*, 153–82; Sifakis, *Who Was Who in the Civil War*, 347; Symonds, *Joseph E. Johnston*, 249–382; Warner, *Generals in Gray*, 163.
185. Govan and Livingood, *Different Valor*, 380.
186. Symonds, *Joseph E. Johnston*, 375.
187. Ibid., 377.
188. Ibid., 378.
189. Govan and Livingood, *Different Valor*, 393–94.
190. Ibid., 394.
191. Ibid.
192. Govan and Livingood, *Different Valor*, 396–97; Sifakis, *Who Was Who in the Civil War*, 314; Symonds, *Joseph E. Johnston*, 380; Vandiver, "Joseph Eggleston Johnston," 218.

193. For postwar information, see generally Davis and Hoffman 196–97; Govan and Livingood, *Different Valor*, 377–97; McMurray, *John Bell Hood*, 194; Sifakis, *Who Was Who in the Civil War*, 314, 347, 360–72; Symonds, *Joseph E. Johnston*, 359–93; Vandiver, "Joseph Eggleston Johnston," 218–19; Wakelyn and Vandiver, *Biographical Dictionary of the Confederacy*, 260; Warner, *Generals in Gray*, 162.
194. Sifakis, *Who Was Who in the Civil War*, 347; Symonds, *Joseph E. Johnston*, 381.

Chapter 7

195. Davis and Hoffman, *Confederate General*, 4:191; Dinardo and Nofi, *James Longstreet*, 54; Longstreet, *From Manassas to Appomattox*, 1–2; Mendoza, *Confederate Struggle for Command*, 2; Piston, *Lee's Tarnished Lieutenant*, 2–3; Sawyer, *James Longstreet Before Manassas*, 7–15; Sifakis, *Who Was Who in the Civil War*, 347; Symonds, *Joseph E. Johnston*, 381; *Lee's Old Warhorse*, chapters 1–2; Wert, *General James Longstreet*, 17–25.
196. *Lee's Old Warhorse*, chapter 3; Sawyer, *James Longstreet Before Manassas*, 20.
197. For information on his time at West Point, see generally Davis and Hoffman, *Confederate General*, 4:191–95; Dinardo and Nofi, *James Longstreet*, 12, 54; Mendoza, *Confederate Struggle for Command*, 2–3; Sawyer, *James Longstreet Before Manassas*, 20–22; *Lee's Old Warhorse*, chapter 3; Wert, *General James Longstreet*, 26–41.
198. Dinardo and Nofi, *James Longstreet*, 12, 54; Eckenrode and Conrad, *James Longstreet*, 6; Mendoza, *Confederate Struggle for Command*, 2–3; Sawyer, *James Longstreet Before Manassas*, 20–22; *Lee's Old Warhorse*, chapter 3; Wert, *General James Longstreet*, 26–31.
199. Wert, *General James Longstreet*, 35.
200. Eckenrode and Conrad, *James Longstreet*, 6; Longstreet, *From Manassas to Appomattox*, 4; Sawyer, *James Longstreet Before Manassas*, 24–35; *Lee's Old Warhorse*, chapter 4; Wert, *General James Longstreet*, 34–56.
201. Davis and Hoffman, *Confederate General*, 4:191–95; Dinardo and Nofi, *James Longstreet*, 5–7; Eckenrode and Conrad, *James Longstreet*, 6; Mendoza, *Confederate Struggle for Command*, 5; Piston, *Lee's Tarnished Lieutenant*, 5–6; *Lee's Old Warhorse*, chapter 5; Wert, *General James Longstreet*, 42–46.
202. Longstreet, *From Manassas to Appomattox*, 6.
203. Davis and Hoffman, *Confederate General*, 4:191–95; Longstreet, *From Manassas to Appomattox*, 6; Mendoza, *Confederate Struggle for Command*, 3–6; Piston, *Lee's Tarnished Lieutenant*, 4, 11; Sawyer, *James Longstreet Before Manassas*, 24–25; *Lee's Old Warhorse*, chapter 4, 7; Wert, *General James Longstreet*, 33–36, 50–55.
204. Eckenrode and Conrad, *James Longstreet*, 88–112; Goree, *Longstreet's Aide*, 93–102; Wert, *General James Longstreet*, 153–79; Piston, *Lee's Tarnished Lieutenant*, 23–31; *Lee's Old Warhorse*, chapter 7.
205. For information on service from First Manassas to Gettysburg, see generally Davis and Hoffman, *Confederate General*, 4:191–95; Dinardo and Nofi, *James Longstreet*, 12–13; Eckenrode and Conrad, *James Longstreet*, 13–22, 40–51, 112, 131, 150; Goree, *Longstreet's Aide*, 19–31, 62–68, 93–102, 120; Mendoza, *Confederate Struggle for Command*, 12–19; Piston, *Lee's Tarnished Lieutenant*, 13–16, 19–20, 23–35;

Sawyer, *James Longstreet Before Manassas*, 4–6, 49–50; *Lee's Old Warhorse*, chapter 7; Wert, *General James Longstreet*, 64–67, 100–109, 126–52, 179–202, 221–83.

206. Chesnut, *Mary Chesnut's Civil War*, 469.

207. Ibid., 509.

208. Ibid., 495, 599, 509; Dinardo and Nofi, *James Longstreet*, 197–99; Mendoza, *Confederate Struggle for Command*, 104–40; Piston, *Lee's Tarnished Lieutenant*, 73–77; *Lee's Old Warhorse*, chapter 7.

209. For information on service from Gettysburg to Appomattox, see generally Bushong, *Old Jube*, 175; Davis and Hoffman, *Confederate General*, 4:91–94; Dinardo and Nofi, *James Longstreet*, 14–15, 88–153, 197–99; Eckenrode and Conrad, *James Longstreet*, 168–208, 215–35, 295–358; Goree, *Longstreet's Aide*, 59–183, 233–46, 261–74; Mendoza, *Confederate Struggle for Command*, 23–75, 104–40; Piston, *Lee's Tarnished Lieutenant*, 62–77, 87–92; Sawyer, *James Longstreet Before Manassas*, 51–53, 61–62, 64–65; *Lee's Old Warhorse*, chapter 7; Woodworth, *Jefferson Davis*, 231–48; Wert, *General James Longstreet*, 249–97, 306–25, 337, 392–97.

210. Wert, *General James Longstreet*, 408–9.

211. Sawyer, *James Longstreet Before Manassas*, 73–74; Wert, *General James Longstreet*, 409–10.

212. For information on service from 1865 to 1870, see generally Davis and Hoffman, *Confederate General*, 4:191–95; Desjardin, *These Honored Dead*, 114; Eckenrode and Conrad, *James Longstreet*, 373–74; Longstreet Chapter 44; Piston, *Lee's Tarnished Lieutenant*, 104–8; Sawyer, *James Longstreet Before Manassas*, 73–81; *Lee's Old Warhorse*, chapter 8; Wert, *General James Longstreet*, 400–17.

213. The white citizens of New Orleans erected a monument to the White Leaguers that was taken down when the city removed the Confederate monuments of Robert E. Lee, P.G.T. Beauregard and Jefferson Davis.

214. For information on service from 1870 to 1880, see generally Dinardo and Nofi, *James Longstreet*, 15; Piston, *Lee's Tarnished Lieutenant*, 119–41; Sawyer, *James Longstreet Before Manassas*, 81–95; *Lee's Old Warhorse*, chapter 8; Wert, *General James Longstreet*, 416–18.

215. Piston, *Lee's Tarnished Lieutenant*, 141; Wert, *General James Longstreet*, 419.

216. Wert, *General James Longstreet*, 421; *Lee's Old Warhorse*, chapter 8.

217. Piston, *Lee's Tarnished Lieutenant*, 144.

218. Ibid.

219. Ibid.

220. Ibid., 148.

221. Savage, *Last Years of Robert E. Lee*, 215.

222. Piston, *Lee's Tarnished Lieutenant*, 159; Sawyer, *James Longstreet Before Manassas*, 115.

223. *Lee's Old Warhorse*, chapter 8.

224. Ibid.

225. For information on service from 1880 to 1890, see generally Davis and Hoffman, *Confederate General*, 4:91–95; Piston, *Lee's Tarnished Lieutenant*, 137–60; Savage, *Last Years of Robert E. Lee*, 215; *Lee's Old Warhorse*, chapter 8; Wert, *General James Longstreet*, 419–25.

226. Connelly, *Marble Man*, 62.
227. Ibid., 63.
228. Sawyer, *James Longstreet Before Manassas*, 120–23; Piston, *Lee's Tarnished Lieutenant*, 152–53, 161.
229. Sawyer, *James Longstreet Before Manassas*, 126.
230. *Lee's Old Warhorse*, chapter 8; Wert, *General James Longstreet*, 425–26.
231. Eckenrode and Conrad, *James Longstreet*, 376; Piston, *Lee's Tarnished Lieutenant*, 167–269; Sawyer, *James Longstreet Before Manassas*, 126–27; *Lee's Old Warhorse*, chapter 8.
232. For information on service from 1890 to 1904, see generally Connelly, *Marble Man*, 62–63; Eckenrode and Conrad, *James Longstreet*, 316; Piston, *Lee's Tarnished Lieutenant*, 152–69; *Lee's Old Warhorse*, chapter 8; Wert, *General James Longstreet*, 422–26.

Chapter 8

233. Taylor, *Raphael Semmes of the Alabama*, 19.
234. Allardice, *More Generals in Gray*, 206; Davis and Hoffman, *Confederate General*, 5:141; Meriwether, *Raphael Semmes*, 15–31; Naval History and Heritage Command, *Captain Raphael Semmes*, 4; Taylor, *Raphael Semmes of the Alabama*, 12–23.
235. Allardice, *More Generals in Gray*, 208; Davis and Hoffman, *Confederate General*, 5:141; Delaney, "American Civil War: Rear Admiral Raphael Semmes," 1; Meriwether, *Raphael Semmes*, 15–44; Taylor, *Raphael Semmes of the Alabama*, 23–24.
236. Allardice, *More Generals in Gray*, 206; Foxx, *Wolf of the Deep*, 38; Taylor, *Raphael Semmes of the Alabama*, 33–34.
237. Dudley, "CSS *Alabama*," 2; Semmes, *Memoirs of Service Afloat*, 44; Taylor, *Raphael Semmes of the Alabama*, 48.
238. Semmes, *Memoirs of Service Afloat*, 68.
239. Taylor, *Raphael Semmes of the Alabama*, 73.
240. Boykin, *Ghost Ship of the Confederacy*, 44; Taylor, *Raphael Semmes of the Alabama*, 117, 172.
241. Taylor, *Raphael Semmes of the Alabama*, 75, 88.
242. Ibid., 92.
243. Semmes, *Memoirs of Service Afloat*, 248.
244. Boykin, *Ghost Ship of the Confederacy*, 23–24; Dudley, "CSS *Alabama*," 4; Semmes, *Memoirs of Service Afloat*, 248–53; Taylor, *Raphael Semmes of the Alabama*, 108.
245. For Civil War service information, see generally Allardice, *More Generals in Gray*, 202–9; Boykin, *Ghost Ship of the Confederacy*, 11, 19, 23–35, 44, 158; Chesnut, *Mary Chesnut's Civil War*, 623; Davis and Hoffman, *Confederate General*, 5:141; Delaney, "American Civil War: Rear Admiral Raphael Semmes," 2; Dudley, "CSS *Alabama*," 3–7; Luraghi, *History of the Confederate Navy*, 228; Meriwether, *Raphael Semmes*, 92, 148–79, 184; Naval History and Heritage Command, *Captain Raphael Semmes*, 3–15; Semmes, *Memoirs of Service Afloat*, 41–46, 49, 108, 214–15, 247–73, 462–91, 500–512, Taylor, *Raphael Semmes of the Alabama*, 48–233.

246. Taylor, *Raphael Semmes of the Alabama*, 236.
247. Ibid., 245.
248. Delaney, "American Civil War: Rear Admiral Raphael Semmes," 3; Roberts, *Semmes of the Alabama*, 252; Taylor, *Raphael Semmes of the Alabama*, 247–51.
249. Taylor, *Raphael Semmes of the Alabama*, 251–52.
250. Ibid., 257.
251. Ibid., 259–63.
252. Ibid., 267–68.
253. For postwar information, see generally Delaney, "American Civil War: Rear Admiral Raphael Semmes," 3; Foxx, *Wolf of the Deep*, 247–49; Meriwether, *Raphael Semmes*, 184–86, 196–98; Roberts, *Semmes of the Alabama*, 240–63; Semmes, *Memoirs of Service Afloat*, 514–23; Taylor, *Raphael Semmes of the Alabama*, 222–73.
254. Taylor, *Raphael Semmes of the Alabama*, 272–73.

Chapter 9

255. For childhood information, see generally Connelly, *Marble Man*, 5–6; Cooke, *Life of General Robert E. Lee*, 1, 3–6; Korda, *Clouds of Glory*, 1–26; Pryor, *Reading the Man*, 2–14; Thomas, *Robert E. Lee*, 21–43.
256. Cooke, *Life of General Robert E. Lee*, 6; Freeman, *Robert E. Lee*, 1:82–83; Korda, *Clouds of Glory*, 27–58; Pryor, *Reading the Man*, 55–69; Thomas, *Robert E. Lee*, 38–55.
257. Thomas, *Robert E. Lee*, 72.
258. Pryor, *Reading the Man*, 204; Thomas, *Robert E. Lee*, 148–49.
259. Pryor, *Reading the Man*, 201.
260. Thomas, *Robert E. Lee*, 106.
261. Ibid., 107.
262. Ibid., 102.
263. Pryor, *Reading the Man*, 201; Thomas, *Robert E. Lee*, 107.
264. Pryor, *Reading the Man*, 95.
265. For information on this army career from 1829 to 1846, see generally Connelly, *Marble Man*, 6; Cooke, *Life of General Robert E. Lee*, 6; Korda, *Clouds of Glory*, 59–102; Pryor, *Reading the Man*, 95, 107; Thomas, *Robert E. Lee*, 56–112.
266. Thomas, *Robert E. Lee*, 145.
267. Connelly, *Marble Man*, 8; Cooke, *Life of General Robert E. Lee*, 6–7; Korda, *Clouds of Glory*, 103–55; Thomas, *Robert E. Lee*, 111–42.
268. Thomas, *Robert E. Lee*, 140.
269. Ibid., 140–41.
270. For information about Lee's "peaceful interlude," see generally Korda, *Clouds of Glory*, 157–210.
271. Korda, *Clouds of Glory*, 206–8; Thomas, *Robert E. Lee*, 178.
272. Thomas, *Robert E. Lee*, 184.
273. For information about the early travails of Lee's Civil War service, see generally Cooke, *Life of General Robert E. Lee*, 12–15; Thomas, *Robert E. Lee*, 191–217; Korda, *Clouds of Glory*, 209–89.

274. Connelly, *Marble Man*, 16–17; Thomas, *Robert E. Lee*, 209–10.
275. Connelly, *Marble Man*, 17; Cooke, *Life of General Robert E. Lee*, 15; Korda, *Clouds of Glory*, 273–318; Thomas, *Robert E. Lee*, 211–17.
276. Connelly, *Marble Man*, 17; Korda, *Clouds of Glory*, 291–318; Thomas, *Robert E. Lee*, 226.
277. Cooke, *Life of General Robert E. Lee*, 19–32; Korda, *Clouds of Glory*, 331–95; Thomas, *Robert E. Lee*, 230–45.
278. Korda, *Clouds of Glory*, 458.
279. For Second Manassas/Second Bull Run information, see generally Cooke, *Life of General Robert E. Lee*, 39–40; Korda, *Clouds of Glory*, 424–55; Thomas, *Robert E. Lee*, 245–54.
280. Thomas, *Robert E. Lee*, 259.
281. For Maryland Campaign information, see generally Cooke, *Life of General Robert E. Lee*, 40–51; Korda, *Clouds of Glory*, 467–86; Thomas, *Robert E. Lee*, 256–73.
282. Korda, *Clouds of Glory*, 37.
283. For Fredericksburg information, see generally Cooke, *Life of General Robert E. Lee*, 55–60; Korda, *Clouds of Glory*, 487–504; Thomas, *Robert E. Lee*, 265–74.
284. Thomas, *Robert E. Lee*, 278–79.
285. Ibid., 282.
286. For Chancellorsville information, see generally Cooke, *Life of General Robert E. Lee*, 67–85; Korda, *Clouds of Glory*, 509–21; Thomas, *Robert E. Lee*, 275–87.
287. For Pennsylvania Campaign information, see generally Cooke, *Life of General Robert E. Lee*, 85–104; Connelly, *Marble Man*, 53–58, 83–90; Korda, *Clouds of Glory*, 523–601; Pryor, *Reading the Man*, 349–60; Thomas, *Robert E. Lee*, 287–303.
288. Freeman, *Robert E. Lee*, 4:39–40. Pickett and Fitz Lee left their troops to attend a shad bake some two miles from their unit. Hosted by General Thomas Rosser on the afternoon of April 1—he had caught the shad ealier when they were running in the Nottoway River—the feast unfortunately took place at the precise moment when Sheridan launched an attack on their troops at Five Forks. Whether their presence would have changed the outcome will never be known, but Sheridan's attack against the leaderless (at the top) Confederate troops caused a rout. As a result, Grant broke Lee's lines, Lee had to abandon Petersburg, Lee's retreat west was ensured and the retreat ultimately led to Lee's surrender at Appomattox. The shad bake thus became embedded in southern collective memory as the cause of Lee's surrender at Appomattox.
289. For information on Gettysburg to Petersburg, see generally Cooke, *Life of General Robert E. Lee*, 122–29; Korda, *Clouds of Glory*, 617–49; Savage, *Last Years of Robert E. Lee*, 9–93; Thomas, *Robert E. Lee*, 310–55.
290. Savage, *Last Years of Robert E. Lee*, 157.
291. Ibid.
292. Flood, *Last Years*, 20.
293. Winik, *Month that Saved America*, 191.
294. Ibid., 197.
295. Savage, *Last Years of Robert E. Lee*, 161.
296. Ibid., 152.

297. Flood, *Last Years*, 27.
298. For Appomattox information, see generally Cooke, *Life of General Robert E. Lee*, 141–47; Flood, *Last Years*, 1–29; Korda, *Clouds of Glory*, 649–70; Savage, *Last Years of Robert E. Lee*, 133–57; Thomas, *Robert E. Lee*, 356–67; Winik, *Month that Saved America*, 124–97.
299. Flood, *Last Years*, 41.
300. Ibid., 56.
301. Ibid., 49–51.
302. Korda, *Clouds of Glory*, 687; Savage, *Last Years of Robert E. Lee*, 180.
303. Flood, *Last Years*, 70.
304. Ibid., 72.
305. Ibid., 73.
306. Ibid., 84; Korda, *Clouds of Glory*, 682.
307. Flood, *Last Years*, 97.
308. Thomas, *Robert E. Lee*, 376.
309. Savage, *Last Years of Robert E. Lee*, 188.
310. Flood, *Last Years*, 102.
311. Ibid.
312. Ibid., 103.
313. Thomas, *Robert E. Lee*, 377.
314. Flood, *Last Years*, 109.
315. Korda, *Clouds of Glory*, 685.
316. Flood, *Last Years*, 127.
317. Ibid., 130.
318. For information on the period from April 12 to December 31, 1865, see generally Flood, *Last Years*, 28–132; Korda, *Clouds of Glory*, 671–85; Pryor, *Reading the Man*, 428–29; Savage, *Last Years of Robert E. Lee*, 163–88; Thomas, *Robert E. Lee*, 368–81.
319. Flood, *Last Years*, 130.
320. Savage, *Last Years of Robert E. Lee*, 190.
321. Thomas, *Robert E. Lee*, 381.
322. Ibid.
323. Savage, *Last Years of Robert E. Lee*, 191.
324. Korda, *Clouds of Glory*, 686.
325. Thomas, *Robert E. Lee*, 383.
326. Flood, *Last Years*, 132.
327. Ibid., 139–40.
328. Pryor, *Reading the Man*, 197.
329. Flood, *Last Years*, 144.
330. Ibid.
331. Thomas, *Robert E. Lee*, 384.
332. For information on the year 1866, see generally Flood, *Last Years*, 131–46; Korda, *Clouds of Glory*, 685; Savage, *Last Years of Robert E. Lee*, 189–93; Thomas, *Robert E. Lee*, 364–65.
333. Flood, *Last Years*, 146.

334. Ibid., 148–49.
335. Ibid., 150.
336. Thomas, *Robert E. Lee*, 391.
337. Flood, *Last Years*, 167.
338. Thomas, *Robert E. Lee*, 386.
339. Flood, *Last Years*, 153–54.
340. Ibid., 156.
341. Thomas, *Robert E. Lee*, 387.
342. For information on the year 1867, see generally Flood, *Last Years*, 148–73; Pryor, *Reading the Man*, 434–35; Savage, *Last Years of Robert E. Lee*, 194–95; Thomas, *Robert E. Lee*, 385–93.
343. Thomas, *Robert E. Lee*, 387.
344. Savage, *Last Years of Robert E. Lee*, 196. Compare with his admonition to the Confederate veteran about the veteran's "lost" years in the war.
345. Flood, *Last Years*, 175.
346. Ibid.
347. Ibid., 187.
348. Thomas, *Robert E. Lee*, 390.
349. Ibid., 391.
350. Flood, *Last Years*, 191.
351. Thomas, *Robert E. Lee*, 392.
352. Ibid., 397.
353. Savage, *Last Years of Robert E. Lee*, 198–99.
354. For information on the year 1868, see generally Flood, *Last Years*, 174–99; Korda, *Clouds of Glory*, 686; Savage, *Last Years of Robert E. Lee*, 196–99; Thomas, *Robert E. Lee*, 387–99.
355. Flood, *Last Years*, 213–14.
356. Ibid., 215.
357. Ibid., 216.
358. Ibid., 224.
359. For information on the year 1869, see generally Flood, *Last Years*, 201–24; Korda, *Clouds of Glory*, 691–92; Pryor, *Reading the Man*, 460–65; Savage, *Last Years of Robert E. Lee*, 199–202; Thomas, *Robert E. Lee*, 391–414.
360. Thomas, *Robert E. Lee*, 405.
361. Flood, *Last Years*, 229.
362. Ibid., 230.
363. Thomas, *Robert E. Lee*, 407.
364. Flood, *Last Years*, 233.
365. Thomas, *Robert E. Lee*, 406.
366. Ibid., 407.
367. Flood, *Last Years*, 242.
368. Ibid., 243.
369. Ibid., 244.
370. Thomas, *Robert E. Lee*, 409.
371. Ibid.

372. Ibid.
373. Ibid., 409–10.
374. Flood, *Last Years*, 250.
375. Thomas, *Robert E. Lee*, 411.
376. Ibid.
377. Flood, *Last Years*, 259.
378. Pryor, *Reading the Man*, 464–65.
379. Ibid.
380. Ibid., 466–67.
381. Connelly, *Marble Man*, 4.
382. Ibid.
383. For information on the year 1870, see generally Flood, *Last Years*, 226–61; Korda, *Clouds of Glory*, 689–92; Pryor, *Reading the Man*, 460–65; Savage, *Last Years of Robert E. Lee*, 202–10; Thomas, *Robert E. Lee*, 145, 406–14; Winik, *Month that Saved America*, 84–89.

Chapter 10

384. For information on Ewell, see generally Davis and Hoffman, *Confederate General*, 2:110–11; Eicher and Eicher, *Civil War High Commands*, 229; Freeman, *Lee's Lieutenants*, 1:769; Warner, *Generals in Gray*, 84–85.
385. Davis and Hoffman, *Confederate General*, 3:111.
386. For information on Gordon, see generally Davis and Hoffman, *Confederate General*, 3:8–12; Eicher and Eicher, *Civil War High Commands*, 260; Gordon bio page at http:///www.civilwarhome.com; Warner, *Generals in Gray*, 111–12.
387. For information on Hampton, see generally Davis and Hoffman, *Confederate General*, 2:50–51; Warner, *Generals in Gray*, 122.
388. For information on Hill, see generally Davis and Hoffman, *Confederate General*, 2:102–4; Freeman, *Lee's Lieutenants*, 3:769, 778; Warner, *Generals in Gray*, 136–37.
389. Davis and Hoffman, *Confederate General*, 2:104.
390. For information on Fitzhugh Lee, see generally Davis and Hoffman, *Confederate General*, 4:36–39; Warner, *Generals in Gray*, 184–85.
391. Davis and Hoffman, *Confederate General*, 4:38.
392. Ibid., 4:39.
393. For information on Stephen Dill Lee, see generally Davis and Hoffman, *Confederate General*, 4:59–63; Eicher and Eicher, *Civil War High Commands*, 345; Wakelyn and Vandiver, *Biographical Dictionary of the Confederacy*, 282; Warner, *Generals in Gray*, 183–84.
394. Davis and Hoffman, *Confederate General*, 4:63.
395. For information on Pickett, see generally Davis and Hoffman, *Confederate General*, 5:29–34; Eicher and Eicher, *Civil War High Commands*, 428; Pickett Society, researched online at http://www.picketsociety.com; Warner, *Generals in Gray*, 239–40.

396. For information on Smith, see generally Davis and Hoffman, *Confederate General*, 5:153–67; Eicher and Eicher, *Civil War High Commands*, 493–94; Simpson, *Second U.S. Cavalry*, 1; Warner, *Generals in Gray*, 279–80.
397. Davis and Hoffman, *Confederate General*, 5:163.
398. For information on Wheeler, see generally Davis and Hoffman, *Confederate General*, 6:128; Eicher and Eicher, *Civil War High Commands*, 563; Warner, *Generals in Gray*, 332–33.
399. For information on Watie, see generally Davis and Hoffman, *Confederate General*, 6:110–11; Warner, *Generals in Gray*, 327–28; Stand Watie biography, American Civil War, https://civilwarhome.com/watiebio.html.

BIBLIOGRAPHY

Allardice, Bruce S. *More Generals in Gray.* Baton Rouge: Louisiana State University Press, 1995.

Anderson, Nancy Scott, and Dwight Anderson. *The Generals: Ulysses S. Grant and Robert E. Lee.* New York: Alfred Knopf, 1988.

Baldwyn, John, and Ron Powers. *Last Flag Down: The Epic Journey of the Last Confederate Warship.* New York: Crown Publishers, 2007.

Basso, Hamilton. *Beauregard: The Great Creole.* New York: Charles Scribner's Sons, 1933.

Battles and Leaders of the Civil War. 4 vols. New York: Thomas Yoseloff Inc., 1956. First published as a series of articles in *Century Magazine* from November 1884 to November 1887 and subsequently as a four-volume set in November 1887.

Boykin, Edward. *Ghost Ship of the Confederacy.* New York: Funk and Wagnalls Company, 1957.

Brackin, Dennis M. "Controversy Between Jefferson Davis and Joseph E. Johnston." Master's thesis, Mississippi State University, August 1979.

Bradford, Gamaliel, and J. Mitchell, illustrator. *Confederate Portraits.* Boston: Houghton Mifflin Company, 1914.

Burnette, O. Lawrence. *Historical Lawrence County: A Bicentennial History.* N.p., GoogleBooks, 2007. Available at https://books.google.com.

Bushong, Millard K. *Old Jube.* Shippensburg, PA: White Mane Publishing Company Inc., 1955.

Campbell, R. Thomas, ed. *Voices of the Confederate Navy.* Jefferson, NC: McFarland and Company, 2007.

Canon, Jill. *Civil War Heroes.* Santa Barbara, CA: Bellerophon Books, 2002.

Castel, Albert. *Decision in the West: The Atlanta Campaign of 1864.* Lawrence: University Press of Kansas, 1992.

Chesnut, Mary Boykin. *Mary Chesnut's Civil War.* Edited by C. Vann Woodward. New Haven, CT: Yale University Press, 1981.

Civil War Trust. *Raphael Semmes.* Accessed online at https://www.civilwar.org.

Coffee, David. *John Bell Hood and the Struggle for Atlanta.* Abilene, TX: McWhinney Foundation Press, 1998.

Commager, Henry Steele. *The Blue and the Gray.* Indianapolis, IN: Bobbs Merrill Company, 1950.

Connelly, Thomas L. *The Marble Man: Robert E. Lee and His Image in American Society.* Baton Rouge: Louisiana State University Press, 1977.

Cooke, John Esten. *A Life of General Robert E. Lee.* New York: D. Appleton & Company, 1871. Reprint, Library of Alexandria, Virginia, 2012.

Cooling, Benjamin Franklin, III. *Jubal Early, Robert E. Lee's "Bad Old Man."* Lanham, MD: Rowman and Littlefield, 2014.

Davis, Steven. *Atlanta Will Fall: Sherman, Joe Johnston and the Heavy Battalions.* Wilmington, DE: Scholarly Resources Inc., 2001.

Davis, William C., and Julie Hoffman, eds. *The Confederate General.* 6 vols. Harrisburg, PA: National Historical Society, 1991.

Davison, Eddy W., and Daniel Foxx. *Nathan Bedford Forrest: In Search of the Enigma.* Gretna, LA: Pelican Publishing Company, 2007.

Delaney, Norman C. "American Civil War: Rear Admiral Raphael Semmes." Encyclopedia of Alabama. Auburn University Outreach, Alabama Humanities Foundation. www.encyclopediaofalabama.org.

Desjardin, Thomas A. *These Honored Dead.* New York: De Capo Press, 2003.

Dinardo, R.L., and Albert A. Nofi, eds. *James Longstreet: The Man, the Soldier, the Controversy.* Boston: Da Capo Press, 1998.

Dudley, Wade C. *Confederate Raider Raphael Semmes: Catch Me If You Can!* N.p., n.d. Accessed online at http://historynet.com.

Dudley, William S. "CSS *Alabama*: Lost and Found." Naval History and Heritage Command, May 13, 2014. https://www.history.navy.mil/research/underwater-archeology/sites.

Dyer, John P. *The Gallant Hood.* New York: Bobbs-Merrill Company, 1950. Reprint, with permission, New York: Konecky and Konecky, 1995.

Early, Jubal A. *Lieutenant General Jubal Anderson Early, CSA, Autobiographical Sketch and Narrative of the War Between the States.* Philadelphia, PA: J.B. Lippincott Company, 1912.

Eckenrode, H.J., and Bryan Conrad. *James Longstreet: Lee's War Horse.* Chapel Hill: University of North Carolina Press, 1936.

Eicher, John M., and David J. Eicher. *Civil War High Commands.* Palo Alto, CA: Stanford University Press, 2001.

Flood, Charles Bracelen. *Lee: The Last Years.* Boston: Houghton Mifflin Company, 1998.

Foote, Shelby. *The Civil War: A Narrative.* 3 vols. New York: Random House, 1974.

Foxx, Stephen. *Wolf of the Deep: Raphael Semmes and the Notorious Confederate Raider CSS Alabama.* New York: Knopf, 2007.

Freeman, Douglas Southall. *Lee's Lieutenants: A Study in Command.* 3 vols. New York: Charles Scribner's Sons, 1942.

———. *R.E. Lee.* 4 vols. New York: Charles Scriber's Sons, 1943.

Gallagher, Gary W., ed. *Lee the Soldier.* Lincoln: University of Nebraska Press, 1966.
Govan, Gilbert K., and James W. Livingood. *A Different Valor.* Indianapolis, IN: Bobbs-Merrill Company Inc., 1956.
Goree, Thomas J. *Longstreet's Aide: The Civil War Letters of Major Thomas J. Goree*. Edited by Thomas W. Cutter. Charlottesville: University of Virginia Press, 1995.
Hardin, David. *After the War.* Chicago: Ivan R. Dee, 2010.
Heidler, David S., and Jeanne T. Heidler, eds. *Encyclopedia of the American Civil War.* Santa Barbara, CA: ABC-CLIO Inc., 2000.
Henry, Robert Self. *Nathan Bedford Forrest: First with the Most.* New York: Mallard Press, 1991.
Hess, Earl J. *Braxton Bragg: The Most Hated Man of the Confederacy.* Chapel Hill: University of North Carolina Press, 2016.
Hewett, Lawrence L. "Braxton Bragg." In *The Confederate General.* 6 vols. Edited by William C. Davis and Julie Hoffman. Harrisburg, PA: National Historical Society, 1991.
Hickman, Kennedy. "American Civil War: Lieutenant General John Bell Hood." Accessed at militaryhistory.about.com.
Holloway, Don. "High Seas Duel." *Civil War Quarterly* (Fall 2014).
Hurst, Jack. *Nathan Bedford Forrest: A Biography.* New York: Vintage Books, 1994.
Johnston, Joseph Eggleston. *Narrative of Military Operations during the Civil War.* Boston: Da Capo Press Inc., 1959. Originally published by D. Appleton, New York, 1874.
Jones, Terry L. *Historical Dictionary of American Civil War.* Lanham, MD: Scarecrow Press Inc., 2002.
Korda, Michael. *Clouds of Glory: The Life and Legend of Robert E. Lee.* New York: HarperCollins, 2014.
Lash, Jeffrey N. *Destroyer of the Iron Horse.* Kent, OH: Kent State University Press, 1991.
Lee's Old Warhorse: The Life and Career of General James Longstreet. N.p., Charles River Publishing, n.d. Note that the pages in this source are not numbered, so all references are to chapter.
Longstreet, James. *From Manassas to Appomattox: Memoirs of the Civil War in America.* Philadelphia, PA: J.B. Lippincott, 1896. Reprint, First Rate Publishers.
Luraghi, Ramondo. *A History of the Confederate Navy*. Translated by Paolo E. Coletta. Annapolis, MD: Naval Institute Press, 1996.
Martin, Samuel J. *General Braxton Bragg, C.S.A*. Jefferson, NC: McFarland and Company Inc., 2011.
McMurray, Richard M. *John Bell Hood and the War for Southern Independence.* Lincoln: University of Nebraska Press, 1992.
McWhiney, Grady. *Braxton Bragg and the Confederate Defeat.* Vol. 1. New York: Columbia University Press, 1969.
Mendoza, Alexander. *Confederate Struggle for Command: General James Longstreet and the First Corps in the West.* College Station: Texas A&M University Press, 2008.
Meriwether, Colyer. *Raphael Semmes*. Cranbury, NJ: Scholar's Bookshelf, 2007. First published in 1913.

Naval History and Heritage Command. *Captain Raphael Semmes and the C.S.S. Alabama.* Washington, D.C.: Naval Historical Foundation Publication, 1968. Accessed online at https://www.history.navy.mil/research/library/online-reading-room.

Newton, Steven H. *Joseph E. Johnston and the Defense of Richmond.* Lawrence: University of Kansas Press, 1998.

Osborne, Charles C. *The Life and Times of General Jubal A. Early.* Chapel Hill, NC: Algonquin Books, 1992.

Pfanz, Harry W. *Gettysburg: The Second Day*. Chapel Hill: University of North Carolina Press, 1987.

Piston, William Garrett. *Lee's Tarnished Lieutenant: James Longstreet and His Place in Southern History.* Athens: University of Georgia Press, 1987.

Pryor, Elizabeth Brown. *Reading the Man: A Portrait of Robert E. Lee through His Private Letters.* New York: Penguin Group, 2007.

Ritter, Charles F., and Jon L. Wakelyn, eds. *Leaders of the American Civil War: A Biographical and Historiographical Dictionary.* Westport, CT: Greenwood Press, 1998.

Roberts, W. Adophe. *Semmes of the Alabama.* New York: Bobbs-Merrill Company, 1938.

Robertson, James. "After the Civil War." *National Geographic*, 2015.

Robinson, Charles M., III. *Shark of the Confederacy.* Annapolis, MD: Naval Institute Press, 1995.

Savage, Douglas. *The Last Years of Robert E. Lee.* New York: Taylor Trade Publishing, 2016.

Sawyer, Gordon. *James Longstreet Before Manassas & After Appomattox*. Gainesville, GA: Sawyer Press, 2005.

Seitz, Don Carlos. *Braxton Bragg, General of the Confederacy.* Columbia, SC: State Company, 1924.

Semmes, Raphael. *Memoirs of Service Afloat, During the War Between the States.* N.p.: Civil War Classic Library, 1869. Originally published in 1868.

Sifakis, Stephen. *Who Was Who in the Civil War.* New York: Facts on File Publications, 1980.

Simpson, Harold B. "Cry Comanche: The Second United States Cavalry in Texas." *Handbook of Texas Online*. Hillsboro, TX: Hill Junior College Press, 1979.

Simpson, Harold B. *The Second U.S. Cavalry.* Texas State Historical Association.

Sinclair, Arthur. *Two Years on the Alabama.* New York: Konecky and Konecky, n.d.

Sorrel, General G. Moxley. *At the Right Hand of Longstreet: Recollections of a Confederate Staff Officer.* Lincoln: University of Nebraska Press, 1905.

Spencer, James. *Civil War Generals.* Westport, CT: Greenwood Press, 1937.

Sword, Wiley. *The Confederacy's Last Hurrah: Spring Hill, Franklin and Nashville*. Lawrence: University Press of Kansas, 1993.

Symonds, Craig L. *Joseph E. Johnston: A Civil War Biography.* New York: W.W. Norton, 1992.

Taylor, John M. *Raphael Semmes of the Alabama.* McLean, VA: Brassey's Inc., 1994.

Thomas, Emory M. *Robert E. Lee: A Biography.* New York: W.W. Norton & Company, 1995.

Tucker, Spencer C. *Raphael Semmes and the Alabama.* Abilene, TX: McWhinney Foundation Press, 1998.

Vandiver, Frank Everson. "Joseph Eggleston Johnston." In *Leaders of the American Civil War: A Biographical and Historiographical Dictionary.* Edited by Charles F. Ritter and Jon L. Wakelyn. Westport, CT: Greenwood Press Westport, 1998.

Wakelyn, Jon L. "John Bell Hood." In *Leaders of the American Civil War: A Biographical and Historiographical Dictionary.* Edited by Charles F. Ritter and Jon L. Wakelyn. Westport, CT: Greenwood Press Westport, 1998.

———. "Raphael Semmes." In *Leaders of the American Civil War: A Biographical and Historiographical Dictionary.* Edited by Charles F. Ritter and Jon L. Wakelyn. Westport, CT: Greenwood Press Westport, 1998.

Wakelyn, Jon L., and Frank E. Vandiver, advisory ed. *Biographical Dictionary of the Confederacy.* Westport, CT: Greenwood Press, 1977.

Warner, Ezra J. *Generals in Gray: Lives of the Confederate Commanders.* Baton Rouge: Louisiana State University Press, 1987.

Welsh, Jack D. *Medical Histories of Confederate Generals.* Kent, OH: Kent State University Press, 1979.

Wert, Jeffrey D. *From Winchester to Cedar Hill: The Shenandoah Campaign of 1864.* New York: Simon & Schuster, New York, 1987.

———. *General James Longstreet: The Confederacy's Most Controversial Soldier.* New York: Simon & Schuster, 1993.

Williams, T. Harry. *P.G.T. Beauregard: Napoleon in Gray.* Baton Rouge: Louisiana State University Press, 1965.

Winik, Jay. *April 1865: The Month that Saved America.* New York: Harper Perennial, 2001.

Woodworth, Steven E. "Braxton Bragg." In *Leaders of the American Civil War: A Biographical and Historiographical Dictionary.* Edited by Charles F. Ritter and Jon L. Wakelyn. Westport, CT: Greenwood Press Westport, 1998.

———. *Jefferson Davis and His Generals.* Lawrence; University of Kansas Press, 1990.

Wyeth, John Allan, MD. *Life of General Nathan Bedford Forrest.* Reprint, Edison, NJ: Blue and Gray Press, 1996. Originally published in New York, 1899.

ABOUT THE AUTHOR

A native of Lexington, Mississippi, Allie Povall grew up there during the halcyon 1950s. After graduation from Ole Miss, Povall served as a naval officer during the Vietnam War and then earned a law degree from Ole Miss and an LLM from the Yale Law School. He practiced law in multiple locations representing BellSouth Corporation before his retirement in 1998. Povall is the author of three other books, one of which, *The Time of Eddie Noel*, was a finalist for the Mississippi Institute of Arts and Letters Best Nonfiction Award in 2010, as well as *Foreward Magazine*'s Best True Crime Award, also in 2010. *The Time of Eddie Noel* will soon become a motion picture. Povall and his wife, Janet, live in Oxford, Mississippi. They are the parents of three grown children and the grandparents of four girls.